FEMINIST
PRAXIS
REVISITED

FEMINIST PRAXIS REVISITED

CRITICAL REFLECTIONS ON UNIVERSITY– COMMUNITY ENGAGEMENT

AMBER DEAN, JENNIFER L. JOHNSON, AND SUSANNE LUHMANN, EDITORS

WILFRID LAURIER UNIVERSITY PRESS

LAURIER
Inspiring Lives.

This book has been published with the help of a grant from the Canadian Federation for the Humanities and Social Sciences, through the Awards to Scholarly Publications Program, using funds provided by the Social Sciences and Humanities Research Council of Canada. Wilfrid Laurier University Press acknowledges the support of the Canada Council for the Arts for our publishing program. We acknowledge the financial support of the Government of Canada through the Canada Book Fund for its publishing activities. This work was supported by the Research Support Fund.

Canadä

Canada Council   Conseil des arts
for the Arts   du Canada

ONTARIO ARTS COUNCIL
CONSEIL DES ARTS DE L'ONTARIO
an Ontario government agency
un organisme du gouvernement de l'Ontario

Library and Archives Canada Cataloguing in Publication

Feminist praxis revisited : critical reflections on university–community engagement / Amber Dean, Jennifer L. Johnson, and Susanne Luhmann, editors.

Includes bibliographical references and index.
Issued in print and electronic formats.
ISBN 978-1-77112-377-8 (softcover).—ISBN 978-1-77112-378-5 (EPUB).—
ISBN 978-1-77112-379-2 (PDF)

1. Women's studies—Canada. 2. Community education—Canada. 3. Feminism—Canada.
I. Dean, Amber Richelle, 1975–, editor II. Johnson, Jennifer L. (Jennifer Lesley), 1976–, editor
III. Luhmann, Susanne, 1963–, editor

HQ1180.F46 2018   305.40971   C2018-903163-8
                                                          C2018-903164-4

Cover and text design by Daiva Villa / Chris Rowat Design. Front-cover image from Qweek/iStock.

This book is printed on FSC° certified paper and is certified Ecologo. It contains post-consumer fibre, is processed chlorine free, and is manufactured using biogas energy.

Printed in Canada

RECYCLED
Paper made from
recycled material
FSC
www.fsc.org   **FSC® C103567**

CONTENTS

CRITICAL APPROACHES TO PRAXIS /
IN AND OUT OF THE CLASSROOM

LEARNING ELSEWHERE? CRITICAL REFLECTIONS ON UNIVERSITY–COMMUNITY ENGAGEMENT AS FEMINIST PRAXIS

SUSANNE LUHMANN, JENNIFER L. JOHNSON, AND AMBER DEAN

Teaching not just about, but for, social change has been a core value in Women's and Gender Studies (WGS) since the inception of the field. Many WGS practitioners would agree that their aim, to invoke a popular Marxist axiom, is "to not only interpret the world, but change it." Accordingly, many WGS degree programs have adopted some kind of praxis component. "Praxis" as a term and a program refers to applying and enacting ideas. Besides tracing its roots to the Marxist injunction invoked above, we note the influence of a central theorist of pedagogical praxis, the liberation pedagogue Paulo Freire (1970). Freire called for a pedagogy of "reflection and action upon the world in order to transform it" (1970/2000, 51). In this book, we use the term praxis to speak about the various ways in which WGS has sought to integrate a variety of different opportunities for experiential, community-based learning into degree programs. In a recent survey of Canadian WGS program descriptions available online, Johnson and Luhmann (2016) found that nearly half of the programs have some form of practicum, internship, community placement, or co-operative education component advertised on their websites, either as a compulsory or optional part of the undergraduate—and increasingly the graduate—degree. WGS's long-standing dual orientation toward knowledge production and action-oriented community engagement in both teaching and research has, at times, been used by critics to try to present the field as insufficiently "academic." That said, Canadian universities are undergoing a significant shift in institutional priorities in the early twenty-first century, and one of those involves an increased emphasis on providing students with opportunities for community engagement (see Dean's and Johnson's chapters in this book for overviews of these shifting commitments at Canadian universities). While co-op, practicum, and internship placements have long been part of the disciplines in professional schools (including such varied fields as social work, law, education, medicine, and engineering), increasingly liberal arts faculties are also promoting community engagement across research and teaching. The reasons for this vary: they include a growing emphasis on universities' responsibilities toward their surrounding communities, an increased demand for labour market-ready students, and a desire to more proactively market a liberal arts education to employers, students, and their parents. In any of these scenarios, this shift toward integrating community-engaged learning into post-secondary education creates both challenges and possibilities for WGS and other liberal arts programs.

Increasingly, all liberal arts programs are being encouraged (or directed) to transform pedagogical and curricular approaches to ensure that at least some portion of student learning happens *elsewhere,* outside the traditional classroom and preferably also outside the university itself, within local or international community-based settings. While there are potential benefits for faculty, students, and communities arising from these transformations, there are also risks, including devaluing classroom learning that focuses on, for example, the close analysis and discussion of texts, or on learning theory that might not have (at first glance, anyway) an immediate application to a "real-world" context. In this book, we raise critical questions about this new emphasis on the value of *learning elsewhere,* while also staying open to the possibility that a robust approach to feminist praxis can include carefully designed and implemented approaches to community-based learning. But feminist praxis, our contributors insist, also happens *in* the classroom (see Francis' and Johnson's chapters in particular), and at times the classroom may, in fact, be better suited to providing opportunities for praxis than community-based placements that can be time-consuming and unnecessarily burdensome for everyone involved. (For more on the potential burdens of community-based learning for students, see Johnson's chapter. For the potential burdens on community organizations, see Dean's, Parkins', and Hurst's chapters in particular.) Thus we pose "learning elsewhere?" as a question not because we are opposed to the opportunities this new emphasis on community engagement makes possible for learning outside of traditional classroom contexts, but because we remain curious about how the new emphasis on community-based learning might draw attention away from praxis happening *in* as well as outside of the classroom, which may put undue pressure on WGS and other liberal arts programs to transform ourselves into something along the lines of the professional school models.

Collectively, WGS programs have much experience with developing and implementing community-based learning, and this should position them well within Canadian post-secondary institutions' turn toward increased community engagement. One might anticipate that WGS programs both benefit from and receive recognition as leaders in the provision of community-based research and teaching. But the fact is that WGS' expertise in praxis is rarely recognized when post-secondary institutions develop community-based service-learning programs or practicum components. And the new emphasis within post-secondary institutions on producing "workplace-ready" students puts WGS in, at times, an ambivalent position of having to "capitalize" on teaching feminist praxis. It appears as though we are at a crossroads, where WGS and other liberal arts programs will have to decide to what degree our approaches to praxis can coexist with—or indeed, survive within—the market-driven neoliberal university.

One of the challenges that this shift in emphasis in post-secondary education raises is the question of how (and whether) WGS approaches to praxis distinguish themselves from the approaches to "community service," "civic engagement," "volunteering," or "charity" that universities might seek to foster. How do WGS programs negotiate institutional and community expectations (and modes of institutionalization) to maintain the activist-oriented social justice frameworks we tend to be committed to (Orr 2011; Forbes et al. 1999; Bubriski and Semaan 2009)? How do WGS programs continue prioritizing the critiques of inequality, power, privilege, and identity so central to the intellectual work of the field in the face of a post-secondary push toward community engagement as resumé-building, skill acquisition, and the bridging of town-and-gown differences? How do we in WGS respond to this new emphasis on community-based learning at universities across the country, and how do we assess the degree to which this new institutional priority may potentially serve, rather than challenge, the ongoing corporatization of the university and large-scale cuts to government spending on social welfare and public services that are so central to neoliberal economic and ideological agendas? How does an increasing demand by governments, corporations, students, and parents alike for post-secondary institutions to offer workplace-relevant education and workplace-ready graduates shape and change how WGS programs institutionalize feminist praxis in our curricula? In short, how does this shift toward community engagement in the university create opportunities for WGS—or does it pose too great a threat to the field's integrity?

We are also curious about how the emphasis on "doing good" through the approaches to community-based service-learning currently being embraced by our institutions risks mobilizing a colonial and imperialist logic that downplays (or disavows altogether) the ways that academic institutions and knowledge-making have historically been, and continue to be, deeply implicated in the furtherance of colonialist and imperialist projects (for further discussion, see the chapters by Dean, Francis, and Srivastava in this book). Though race is seldom, if ever, raised as an issue when universities pronounce community engagement or community service to be a new priority, the figure of the benevolent white saviour of colonialist logics haunts these renewed emphases on "doing good" in local and global communities, and because of the gendered nature of concepts like "service," it is a white woman who is most often imagined as the subject of this benevolent and charitable orientation to the world. This re-centring of whiteness and the figure of the white woman as saviour has a particular resonance in WGS because of long-standing debates in the field about the centrality of what Amy Brandzel calls the "whitenormative citizen-subject" (2011, 503). Critics have often raised concerns about the centrality of whiteness and the insufficient attention given to race and racism in both feminist theory and WGS programs (e.g., Moraga and Anzaldua 1981; hooks 1981, 1984; Lorde 1984; Davis 1981; Moreton-Robinson 2000; Najmabadi 2008; Mahmood 2008; Guy-Sheftall and Hammonds 2008; Maparyan 2012; and Rowe 2008, 2012), and as such, WGS practitioners are concerned about how an uncritical embrace of the post-secondary turn to community engagement might risk re-centring whiteness—and white women in particular—in the field yet again. (For further discussion of whiteness in relation to praxis in WGS, see chapters by Dean, Francis, Gotell, Johnson, Srivastava, and Parkins in this book, as well as Orr's afterword.) Thus it has become clear that the dominant rhetoric and practices of community engagement currently emerging at universities across the country might both shape and delimit the possibilities for developing, supporting, or retaining more critical approaches to feminist praxis in WGS.

These and other questions and concerns are addressed in the chapters that make up this edited collection, which brings together the work of WGS practitioners from across Canada to explore whether and how distinctions between WGS approaches to praxis and more typical service- or community-based learning approaches hold up under scrutiny. Are WGS approaches really so different? What tensions arise from the different agendas of post-secondary institutions and WGS's social justice orientation? Do WGS programs subvert or adjust to this orientation toward community engagement currently being advanced by our universities and colleges? And what creative alternatives to more traditional service learning and the practicum do WGS practitioners develop in response?

In this way we understand the praxis component as a productive site for studying how WGS and other liberal arts programs negotiate the changing landscape of post-secondary education in Canada, and how our programs position themselves vis-à-vis the demands that these changes make on all academic units. Elsewhere, Johnson and Luhmann (2016) argue that in the self-descriptions of WGS programs online, the goal of feminist teaching for social change sits side by side with the claim they are preparing students for the labour market. Here we draw from and elaborate on some of this previous work, but further research is needed to more fully understand the extent to which the WGS praxis component becomes a site of collision between feminist activist aspirations and the new managerialism and goals of workplace readiness so evident in the neoliberal university. In this collection, we offer some examples of how programs and individual instructors adapt creatively to changing post-secondary agendas without submitting fully to the neoliberal, entrepreneurial agenda of the contemporary university. But contributors also query the tensions arising from efforts to distinguish and maintain WGS' commitments to a feminist praxis directed toward social justice within the context of these changing post-secondary priorities, as well as an increasingly depoliticized non-profit sector (on the latter point, see Gotell's and Muzak's chapters in particular). Together, the chapters in this collection explore how (and whether), in the context of an ongoing struggle for survival and relevance, WGS programs are changed as universities change and appear to be moving away from the historically broad liberal arts education at the undergraduate level toward an increasing emphasis on workplace readiness and the employability of graduates.

The Neoliberal University as Context

Neoliberal policy approaches affect post-secondary education in Canada as the culture of post-secondary education has been shifting under the broader influence of neoliberalism (Newson and Polster 2010, 2015). Neoliberalism affects both the organization and funding of university education at federal and provincial levels as well as the strategic research and teaching goals of individual university administrations. Prominent among these shifts is governmental underfunding of education and a corresponding increase in tuition rates (CAUT 2012a); the devolution of full-time faculty positions into part-time casual labour (CAUT 2012b); and the overall devaluation of any degree program that cannot be said to lead directly to a specific job in the paid labour force upon graduation and, more specifically, that is not located in academic fields thought to lead to the development of new products and services, such as the sciences, engineering, and health (Newson and Polster 2010). Less prominent, but equally problematic, is the way in which education-related services, including everything from food and cleaning services to the private medical insurance on psychological counselling services, have been steadily parceled out on a contract basis to private corporations over the last twenty-odd years (Reimer and Ste. Marie 2010, 139, 149). Furthermore, the trend toward handing upper-level administrative positions over to those whose credentials are no longer Ph.D. but rather M.B.A. marks a significant shift in the academic culture of Canadian post-secondary institutions toward managerialism (Newson and Polster 2010).

In a global context, especially in contrast to those countries considered to be "developing," Canada is rather fortunate to have enjoyed the protection and support of post-secondary education by the state for so long following the Second World War. Intergovernmental organizations such as the World Bank, the Organization for Economic Co-operation and Development (OECD), and the Asia-Pacific Economic Co-operation (APEC), among others, have increasingly become "major sites for the organization of knowledge about education, and have created a cajoling discourse of 'imperatives of the global economy' for education" (Rizvi and Lingard 2010, 79). This discourse has supported policies on financial austerity for education in the world's poorest countries, where the World Bank has frequently required states to download the full fee for the delivery of post-secondary education to the student in order to receive loans that support the functioning of the rest of the state apparatus. Globally, states have largely been absent from the responsibility of subsidizing all levels of education (whether primary, secondary, and tertiary), and in many countries education is traded as a service that can be commodified at any number of levels (Tomasevski 2006; Rizvi and Lingard 2010). The Canadian Association of University Teachers (CAUT) documents that "[b]etween 1981 and 2011, the proportion of university operating revenue provided by government sources has declined from 84% to 55% while the proportion funded by student tuition fees has increased from 13% to 37%" (2013–14, 1). Canadian provincial governments continued to fund, on average, about 65 percent of the cost of university education in 2009; though that has decreased from 90 percent in 1979, Canadian students might even consider themselves fortunate in comparison (CAUT 2012a).

Provincially, the funding relationships between governments and universities is complex, and subject to political whim. For better or worse, it is worth considering the rapprochement of provincial government policy and the everyday activities of universities suggested in some recent election platforms. For example, in Ontario the Progressive Conservative Ford government has promised to expand the role of the Higher Education Quality Council of Ontario (HECQO), a policy and research organization at arm's length from provincial government, to include a complaint and investigation process related to free speech in Ontario universities (Ontario Progressive Conservatives, 2018). In the platform, the Conservative government promises to tie provincial funding to universities' ability to maintain an as-of-yet undefined concept of free speech. The few details available suggest that the results of individual high-profile complaints about pro-life advocacy and pushback on the use of gender-neutral pronouns by students and employees have been the basis for this promise, and could be used to discipline other aspects of university functioning.[1]

Universities in other parts of the world have long since learned to operate as private enterprises in terms of the policy structure, goals, and values attached to their degrees, and now Canadian universities are in the process of having to do so as well. The impacts of these shifts are most evident in the critiques of the university advanced by both student and faculty organizations. Organizations like the Canadian Association of University Teachers, numerous part- and full-time faculty unions across the country, and student general assemblies have been the most vocal in making clear the impacts of increased tuition and decreased essential resources, such as fewer full-time faculty, as demonstrated in Quebec in 2012 (Marshall 2012).

Predictably, the question of post-secondary education's applicability to the knowledge-based job market has captured the attention of administrators, students, and university marketers alike. This preoccupation is itself indicative of the encroaching managerialism of the institution. There is no shortage of interest in university education. One large UNESCO study says there has been "a 53% increase in the global demand for university in the last 10 years" (cited in Miller 2010, 200). But what exactly is this demand for? Despite some evidence from the UK that employers outside the professions and trades prefer to train their own employees (Parker 2003, 533), many universities are trying strenuously to demonstrate that a university degree is a direct job-entry qualification. Indeed, it already is. Statistical evidence shows that humanities graduates have comparable rates of employment to graduates of other types of college and university education (Walters and Frank 2010). Nevertheless, university administrations and policy experts have developed the notion that every student must arrive on the job market with directly transferrable skills and that certain fields, such as the liberal arts, cannot possibly hope to address this need without major adjustments. The conclusions of the Commission on the Reform of Ontario's Public Services, known simply as the "Drummond Report" for its author, suggest that the transformation of universities can partly be accomplished through the institutionalization of work placements and internships prior to graduation (Drummond 2012). And this is one of the strategic directions that, for example, the Faculty of Arts at the University of Alberta is taking, having created in recent years both a co-op and an Arts-specific work experience (AWE) program. The latter aims at "connect[ing] students, employers, and community as a first step in achieving individual, educational and organizational success." AWE aims to be a launch site for Arts students to explore both "engaged citizenship" and "career opportunities" in "a supportive environment which builds student confidence in their abilities to achieve academic and career success," while "demonstrat[ing] the value of an Arts degree on and off campus."[2]

In Ontario, the recommendations of the Drummond report have come about in the context of proposed major restructuring in the public sector economy to reduce the provincial deficit, and in the process require universities to streamline their offerings. For example, in their survey of "the new baccalaureate programs in Ontario universities that have been approved over the past six years, about 90 percent have titles that suggest a *career orientation*" (Clark et al. 2009). The liberal arts have come under scrutiny in this context for not producing students as proto-professionals with a specific job title awaiting them. Public criticism is heaped upon the liberal arts for creating a failed middle class, as suggested below in an editorial response to the students' general strike in Quebec in 2012 (the strike protested the threatened gradual retraction of provincial funding from post-secondary education):

> The protesters do not include accounting, science and engineering students, who have better things to do than hurl projectiles at police. They're the sociology, anthropology, philosophy, arts, and *victim-studies* students, whose *degrees are increasingly worthless* in a world that increasingly demands *hard skills*. The world will not be kind to them. They're the baristas of tomorrow and they don't even know it, because the adults in their lives have sheltered them and encouraged their mass flight from reality. (Wente 2012, emphasis added)

It has been suggested that students increasingly think of themselves as consumers and expect their education to be a made-to-order product (Brulé 2004). Some have even developed typologies of commodification to describe the neoliberal university environment. For example, Brian Miller (2010) lists several modes of commodification that include: universities as a point of sale for credentials or a skill set, and a university education as a step toward ever more voracious consumption through increasing one's future earning power.

Administrators and faculty of WGS programs are sympathetic to the reality that students face a pared-down learning environment rich in private-sector-sponsored technology but short on full-time faculty, as well as increasingly tremendous debt post-graduation. Those who run WGS programs also feel the pressure to address more directly the context of fear and anxiety about future youth unemployment. Youth unemployment in Canada stands at 14.7 percent for those in the fifteen-to-twenty-four-year age range, double that of Canada's total jobless rate; in 2012, 27,000 fewer youth were currently employed than in the year prior (Penhorwood 2012). Though these rates are holding or even slightly improved—at least for students planning on returning to school in the fall semester—they are still very high (Statistics Canada 2017). This is the context in which students make decisions about which courses to take and what program of study to commit to. And this is the context in which WGS programs undergo curricular reform.

WGS Praxis Between Service and Activism

Given the wealth and diversity of institutionalized praxis and community-based learning opportunities in Canadian WGS programs, surprisingly little critical literature exists that reflects upon this curriculum component in the specific contexts of these programs either from a feminist or gender perspective or in the context of current trends in Canadian post-secondary education more broadly.[3] The same cannot be said for the American context, where an extensive body of literature analyzes the university-organized WGS praxis component. An even larger body of American literature is concerned with the role of what is called "service-learning" in the wider university. In part, the lack of Canada-specific critical literature can be explained by the fact that the broader term "community service-learning" (CSL), meaning the integration of work in and with the community into university learning, is still a relatively new concept for Canadian post-secondary institutions, while it has been around in US post-secondary education for at least two decades, during which it has received presidential support, first by the Clinton administration, and later from the Obama administration.[4] However, just like their US counterparts, Canadian WGS programs have been early practitioners of institutionalizing community-based learning initiatives (Naples 2002c).

Given the wealth of the (overwhelmingly) American body of literature addressing community service learning broadly and WGS community-based learning specifically, a complete literature survey is impossible. In the following, we draw out some of the more problematic assumptions underlying the literature and bring into view the more helpful reflective critical engagements with community-based learning initiatives. The wider US literature on community service-learning asserts a whole range of associated benefits of such approaches to learning, many also embraced by feminist literature. For students, community involvement is thought to make theoretical material more relevant—by providing "real world contexts" (Dugger 2008, 1; also Evans et al. 2006)—enhancing variously their academic skills and social character; communities are presumed to have their needs met; and universities can improve their community relations (Bubriski and Semaan 2009). Seemingly, it's a "win-win" situation for all. Needless to say, much of the literature is rather enthusiastic about the benefits of community-based learning, with critical responses and approaches few and far between.

Common to the feminist literature is the assumption of a quasi-natural affinity of WGS and community-based learning, probably due to the widely circulated origin story of academic WGS as having emerged as the "arm" or "academic wing" of the second-wave women's (liberation) movement (Dugger 2008; Washington 2000). From this, many WGS practitioners continue to take for granted a specific activist WGS mandate and make activism the raison d'être of the field. Accordingly, merely teaching *about* feminism or "raising feminist consciousness" is considered insufficient by many. Some, like Nancy Naples, even charge the institutionalization of Women's Studies in the academy with "constrain[ing] the development of collective political action" (2002c, 387). More widely shared, however, is the self-understanding that in WGS, "we teach not only to educate our students, but also to enable them to use this knowledge to work for social justice" (Williams and Ferber 2008, 47). To do so requires us "to teach students to merge feminist theory with social action in order to transform systemic gender, class, and race inequalities" (Bubriski and Semaan 2009, 91). Within this view, the WGS community practicum, internship, placement, action project, university-based community service learning, and co-op program becomes invested not only with promoting, but actually accomplishing transformative learning that targets (structural) change—a rather grand expectation, to say the least.

One issue with the field's deep attachment to activism, as Catherine Orr has pointed out, is that activism is "an ill-defined, endlessly-elastic term." Another is that this activist orientation is often "used in punitive ways to chastise WGS practitioners whose scholarly projects or theoretical orientations stray too far from the practical—and thereby political ... application that activism is said to represent" (Orr 2012, 90). The elasticity of the term means that nearly anything can qualify as "activism," and a distinction between charity, volunteerism, and social justice work is often missing. At the same time, certain forms of community engagement—such as the daily struggles that marginalized people must engage in to survive—are rarely recognized in these terms, as forms of activism in their own right (Orr 2012, 87–89). Orr suggests that the less obviously or immediately political is frequently lost or devalued in this insistence on the field's activist roots as its founding principle (97). Building on Orr's analysis, we suggest that when WGS practitioners devalue the less immediately or obviously political this risks a collusion with the neoliberal reduction of university learning to its "use value." The emphasis on the greater "use value" of certain forms of learning over others is central to the technocratic and corporate evaluation strategies employed in the neoliberal university, and thus is something we might want to resist rather than embrace. Margot Francis in this collection offers one example of doing so, when she fundamentally refuses to turn to learning *elsewhere*, now so popular in post-secondary education, in order to incorporate praxis as an element of students' learning. Instead, Francis makes the case for recognizing "feminist praxis *inside* the classroom" (131). Rather than engaging students in street activism or placing them with community organizations to learn "about 'others' who are presumably not in the university," she engages in a feminist praxis that challenges settler colonization within her teaching and among her students, right in the classroom.

Francis' arguments add to an interesting and ongoing dialogue about (political) urgency in WGS, which for some practitioners drives the need for the curricular institutionalization of praxis components *outside* of the WGS classroom. The shifting political climate of the last thirty years, marked simultaneously by the neoliberal attack on the welfare state, increased privatization, and larger global/local interdependence, makes community service learning within WGS a political necessity today, some argue (see, e.g., Barber 2012). For others, institutionalizing community engagement has a compensatory function: to make up for the loss of what once were vibrant larger social movements and the (presumably) decreased involvement of WGS students (and faculty) in community activism today (Forbes et al. 1999; Bubriski and Semaan 2009). However, whether WGS students today are truly less engaged in "activism" than previous generations is certainly debateable. Judith Taylor's essay in this collection focuses her critical lens on students, many of whom turn away—prematurely, in her view—from feminist non-profit organizations because they fail to recognize the constraints they operate under, dismissing them too quickly as insufficiently "political." Encountering the limits of social change in non-profit contexts is also explored in Joanne Muzak's chapter, but here the challenges faced by these organizations are framed within the wider neoliberal agenda that limits the political or activist work of frontline organizations, especially when they rely on corporate and government funding dedicated to increasing women's "employability" and market participation, something that should not be foreign for students themselves who are increasingly asked to see university education primarily as a means to a job. But Muzak's students also begin to see the many complex forms that activism can take, and although these varied forms are not always as politically "pure" as Taylor's students might desire, they represent change nevertheless. Read together, Taylor's and Muzak's students seem to support quite different notions of what constitutes social change. In Muzak's introductory class, for example, students appear to be less rigid than Taylor's upper-level students who are more deeply "trained" or "disciplined" in/by WGS, and their more advanced critical analysis, something we pride ourselves on in our field, might not have prepared them sufficiently for bearing the dilemmas that community organizations face when muzzled by neoliberal politics. Reading Muzak's and Taylor's chapters together also allows us to think about the kinds of suggestions and critiques students bring back to community organizations, and how organizations may or may not be (able to be) interested in the kinds of insights students can offer—just as students sometimes might be too hasty and harsh in their assessments of the limits of the organizations.

Taylor also alerts us to how the low status of frontline feminist community work might hold little appeal to students who have embraced the promise of upward social mobility that a post-secondary degree is presumed to provide. Sarita Srivastava's chapter in this collection offers an interesting counterpoint on students' commitment to community and activist engagement. She describes an impressive range of activist projects that her students organize as part of their WGS degree. Srivastava's insistence on having students organize their own projects, as opposed to having them organized for them by an internship or CSL office, raises interesting questions about how developing their own praxis projects might produce a different sense of ownership over what students do. In any case, taken together, all of the essays in this collection make more complex any simple lament that today's students are "less engaged." Instead, these essays provide insight into the conditions which structure students' attachments or detachments from community engagement and activism. In the Canadian context, as Muzak (2012 and in this volume) reminds us, the conservative government under former Prime Minister Harper, after coming into office in 2006, systematically defunded women's (and any other) advocacy organizations that opposed the government's socially and fiscally conservative agenda. Subsequently, Canadian non-profit organizations struggled with strict regulations about the use of federal funds for research, advocacy, or lobbying, which in turn shaped the kinds of work organizations could and could not do over the past decade. While the Trudeau Liberals have been reviewing and changing some of these funding regulations, more research is required to assess the long-term effects of the defunding of advocacy under the Harper Conservatives. As a consequence of the long-standing ban on advocacy or political participation, feminist non-profit organizations necessarily became more depoliticized and were increasingly called upon to provide social services instead of political advocacy or activism. Further, as Lise Gotell points out, neoliberal policies often compel non-profits "to adopt an individualized and depoliticized lens" (2009, 2) for social problems, gendered or otherwise. This, together with insufficient numbers of available placements in feminist non-profits, even in many large urban centres, means fewer opportunities for students to observe actual activist or advocacy work during community placements. Instead, community placements may lead to students mistaking social service work, as important as it may be, with work that targets the very social structures that perpetuate social inequalities and injustices.

Lise Gotell's chapter in this collection offers a smart approach to using community service learning and placements within community organizations as an educational tool to help students recognize and experience the impact that neoliberal policies and political constraints have had on the work of feminist community organizations. Gotell's endorsement of the pedagogical potential of learning about neoliberalism's effects through community placements is productively in tension with early American Women's Studies scholar

Bonnie Zimmerman's caution that an emphasis within WGS on placements and volunteer activities "may actually reinforce current power structures and relations by taking on some of the work that used to be considered the responsibility of the state" (2002, 188). Canadian educator Don Dippo (2005) similarly asks us to consider whether community placements—by feeding our and our students' illusions of doing "something"—inadvertently advance, rather than challenge, the "neo-conservative fantasy" that volunteer work can replace the welfare state. In her chapter in this collection, Amber Dean raises similar questions about whether students released into communities en masse to "do good" might actually risk doing harm to the very communities they are foisted upon to help.

While anxieties over the present state of politics mixed with a nostalgic longing for a lost activist feminist past might animate much of the WGS praxis literature, the critical voices cited above should remind us that community-based learning should not always be equated with activism. Assuming that a WGS praxis component is "activist" simply because it requires students to learn from/with communities or engage in activities outside of the traditional classroom seems faulty—as is assuming that broadly practised community service learning is incapable of spawning activist commitments among students. Whether WGS praxis constitutes activism or charity might, in fact, depend upon the audience and student preferences.[5] Indeed, WGS' exemplary "community involvement" is also strategically employed to demonstrate the field's continued (now civic) relevance to university administrators looking at WGS programs with the budget axe already in hand. Case in point here is one of the editors' universities, where a new graduate WGS program received public approval from the provost precisely for its mandatory community *service* component, an approval that certainly did not laud this component for its feminist activist agenda. Rather, the community service component received the provost's support because students' community engagement is perceived as enhancing the university's claim to work for the "public good" while also making our graduates more intelligible as "workforce-ready," thus seemingly increasing the value of the program to the public.

WGS and the Community

In the US literature on community service learning and WGS, some practitioners worry whether students' work assignments sufficiently correspond with community needs, or whether they risk draining further resources from already overburdened organizations (Forbes et al. 1999); others rightly wonder how to distinguish short-term charitable, status-quo-preserving work from sustainable interventions into larger structural inequality. Certainly, the amount of time spent in the community setting and the kind and extent of reflection taught in university courses that accompany the praxis component matter greatly. In our experience, the praxis components of WGS programs most often follow the tendency in the wider practice of community service-learning to create partnerships with formal non-governmental or charitable organizations, rather than with more grassroots or activist-oriented groups or networks. The reasons for this are myriad, including at times a reliance on a university's CSL office to establish the placement options to begin with. But community-based learning in WGS need not always rely on partnerships with established organizations (see the Francis, Johnson, and Srivasta chapters in this volume for examples of alternative assignments not reliant on such formal partnerships; see also Dean 2007; Naples 2002b, 2002c). However, most contributors to the book focus on the more common scenario of partnerships with feminist non-profits, reflecting on their benefits and potential challenges.

WGS programs with a deep theoretical commitment to challenging hierarchy and transforming unequal relations of power may be well suited to initiate meaningful relationships with community partners where, even if the individual students are somewhat transitory from year to year, the institutional commitments of the program to the host organization buoy up a substantial relationship of trust. Two chapters in this collection, by Rachel Alpha Johnston Hurst and Ilya Parkins, take up the question of whether and how community-based learning actually benefits the community. The two articles do so from quite different perspectives and in significantly different contexts. Parkins' students created a memorial project for the families of women who had been murdered in their community, while Hurst's students translated theoretical concepts central to the work of a specific community organization into digital media form, for the organization to utilize in their work. Read together, these two chapters open up the question of whether communities benefit from the placements, training, and projects they provide to students in productive ways, while still leaving open the question of whether praxis components in WGS build sustainable relationships with community groups, especially in contexts in which programs are pressured to deliver experiential learning outside the classroom with limited resources and under serious time constraints.

Another concern arising in the literature is the question of whether a short-term excursion into marginalized communities and populations can effectively rework students' grasp of the roots of marginalization, or whether the practicum becomes a trip to "the other side of the tracks" with the risk of reinforcing the racist and classist presumptions it seeks to challenge. Recalling the role of community service in the criminal justice system as a "punishing pedagogy," Forbes et al., for example, are skeptical of compulsory service learning because "forced volunteerism...is at best an exercise in observing otherness and at worst a missionary expedition" (1999, 162). In these authors' minds, the promise that community service provides students with experiences of the "real world," of "different people...presents volunteerism as a way to experience and uplift the unknowing underprivileged" (162). A less scathing view considers that even successfully changed consciousness does not necessarily amount to larger structural change. And, encountering differences and inequality in the community, not unlike learning about it in the classroom, does not guarantee attitudes of identification, empathy, or solidarity with those who suffer. It may just as well lead students to a refusal of those "too saturated with injury," as Judith Butler reminds us (1993, 100). Such a refusal might well be at stake for the students Taylor observes in her chapter in this collection.

Is Praxis Learning in WGS Really So Different?

The mostly short-term community involvement proffered in praxis courses and assignments may promise meaningful learning experiences and the acquisition of new skills (or at least a line on the CV) to university students, serve the self-understanding of the instituting program, and raise universities' public image. But the question remains: what, if anything, makes feminist praxis different from other internships or traditional service learning? Sheila Hassal Hughes' suggestion that only the latter "tend[s] to signal professionalization and self-advancement" is not really persuasive (2008, 37), since Johnson and Luhmann's (2016) research on the web-based self-representation of WGS programs suggests an emphasis on these potential benefits of praxis components as well. Indeed, the very desire to neatly distinguish "problematic" mainstream service learning from "critical" feminist praxis is neither borne out in the literature nor in the content analysis Johnson and Luhmann undertook of the web descriptions of praxis components in Canadian WGS programs.[6] While we might want to claim that feminist praxis institutionalized in the WGS program has a distinctly different genealogy that squarely places it within intersectional and structural analyses of power and engages in dissident citizenship, the contributions to this collection paint a much more complex picture. As Johnson and Luhmann (2016) discovered, some WGS praxis-based course descriptions certainly emphasize activism, but others underline the professionalization and career advancement that internships and service learning offer to students. While these might be strategic representations that reflect an effort to prove the field's ongoing relevance in the contemporary neoliberal university, the question remains: how do programs negotiate their activist aspirations, assuming they have them, with the demands for job preparation and workplace readiness so central to current neoliberal post-secondary education agendas?

WGS program pages utilize a wide spectrum of different terms to name and promote the specific qualities of the praxis components they offer: some speak of "volunteer opportunities," others of "on-the-job training," "practical experience," "working in the community," and/or "activism." Certainly, these different terms connote significantly different values, with "volunteering" being evocative of charity work, and "activism" of social change. Other seemingly neutral terms such as "practical experience" and "working in the community," nevertheless are energized by a hegemonic valuing of the practical over the theoretical, where "community" is often equated with the "real" world and "university" with the illusive "ivory tower." Thus, even apparently neutral terms risk widening the very gap between theory and praxis, between university and community learning, that the praxis component seeks to overcome. However filtered the complexity of the relationship between theory and praxis may be at times on WGS program pages, Johnson and Luhmann (2016) distinguish three distinct approaches to the relationship of theory and praxis in program descriptions: The first, *the exposure to praxis approach,* imagines that students will learn from organizations through observation; for example, they will learn "how to do activism." In the exposure model, the organization is presumed to know and the student in need of knowledge. The second, *the application approach,* reverses the relationship between students and organizations. Students are assumed to bring feminist theory and knowledge, acquired in their university education, to the organization. A third approach, more humbly and perhaps more usefully, emphasizes that the practicum is a site of *integration and synthesis,* meaning that in the practicum or placement course, students are supposed to integrate knowledge acquired in course work with what they learn at the organization. Alternatively, the purpose of the practicum course is described as a process of reflecting upon the experience of field-based learning in the community. Some program descriptions do not link theory and praxis in any discernible way. Maybe the "practical (work) experience in Women's Studies" seems so self-evidently valuable and intrinsic to the field that it requires no further elaboration. Besides the three different approaches to the relationship of theory to praxis (exposure, application, and integration/synthesis), WGS program web pages also suggest different approaches to skills training. These definitions offer some insight into how WGS programs imagine themselves responding strategically to neoliberalism. Training is broadly imagined as the practice of knowledge acquired in WGS alongside other skills gained in a liberal arts education (such as questioning, writing, communication, and research skills) with a strong emphasis on refining these skills in a "real-life" workplace. Thus skill descriptions are emphasized differently: *job skills training, research skills training*, and *training in feminist activism.* An emphasis on WGS praxis components providing training in job skills promises that the WGS practicum will yield a "high quality resumé," "contacts" and a set of other seemingly marketable skills. A second approach to skills training in WGS praxis components emphasizes research skills or knowledge production, while a third approach sees praxis components as skills training for feminist action/activism. However, even WGS praxis components and community engagements that are explicitly "activist" can become another line on the CV, or another marketable skill, thereby illustrating once more the "elasticity" of the term, as noted by Orr (2012).

Johnson and Luhmann's (2016) preliminary analysis of the web-based descriptions of praxis components in WGS seems to support the concern that the character of community engagement in WGS might be changing from outright activist aspirations that initiated the first wave of integrating practicums and community engagement in WGS programs, to a rhetoric of promoting WGS praxis and community engagement in terms more reminiscent of the neoliberal agenda that drives universities to become centres for job preparation. Under the current pressure to make all liberal arts education intelligible to both communities and government, the rhetoric of praxis threatens to make skills training for the so-called real world the primary goal of *all* community engagement, whether in WGS or the wider university. However, we have to keep in mind that Johnson and Luhmann's (2016) research focused on analyzing the program descriptions on the web, which offer only the "public"—and often strategic, but also somewhat generic—face of WGS programs. This collection of chapters by WGS practitioners reflecting upon what they do and what happens when they teach or supervise praxis components offers a range of much more complex perspectives on the state of feminist praxis in Canadian WGS programs, perhaps even more so because we have asked practitioners to do something quite difficult; namely, not just provide us with the "heroic tales" and feminist success stories about the transformative work we do in the field. Instead, we asked contributors to think critically about their community-engaged or experiential teaching, and about the challenges involved in integrating "learning elsewhere" in WGS programs. This is not an easy task. A public, reflexive analysis of what we do in WGS continues to be challenging because of the defensive position many of our programs consistently find themselves in. But also, more personally, to openly analyze the shortcoming of one's approach to community-engaged learning, institutionally or in the classroom, feels risky. Thus, we applaud our contributors and their willingness to take these risks.

Throughout this collection, we intentionally work with a capacious understanding of what constitutes praxis. Accordingly, the chapters collected here represent a wide range of contexts and formats of praxis and community engagement within WGS programs. These range from community-based learning as an option within introductory WGS courses, to the mandatory inclusion of a praxis component in an upper-year undergraduate course. Increasingly, a praxis component can also be found in graduate courses. Some authors reflect upon teaching WGS courses in partnership with their institutions' well-established community service-learning centres or practicum placement services, which match students directly with non-profit community organizations (see the Gotell, Muzak, Taylor, and Hurst chapters); others analyze student-initiated and run activist projects (see the Srivastava and Dean chapters) or praxis learning *in* the classroom (see the Francis and Johnson chapters) while still others risk reflecting seriously on the limitations—and sometimes the outright failures—of their approaches to praxis (see the Parkins and Hurst chapters).

All of the contributors challenge the far too common binaries of praxis/theory and community/university, which WGS practitioners have simultaneously challenged and reinstituted in fiercely fought disputes within the field (Orr 2012). One concern is with how these binaries construct both praxis and the university in the process. By contrasting an alleged "real-world" community always imagined outside of the university to the fantasy of the university as a rarefied "ivory tower," the university risks being imagined as a supposedly safe, gated community rather than as a site of complex social and power relationships and deeply entrenched inequities, injustices, and exclusions (see the Hurst and Dean chapters in this book). At the same time, "community" and "praxis" become imagined as the only "real" that matters. What is lost in these constructions are the complex ways that all of us are positioned differently across a diverse range of communities, within and outside of the university, and how these communities are all sites of co-education, dialogue, and relationality, as well as tension and inequity. In her chapter, Jennifer L. Johnson further questions the new emphasis on instituting praxis through learning elsewhere, which passes over the daily praxis of students' everyday lives and seemingly fails to understand that all of us are always already "elsewhere" as citizens, parents, employees, and so on.

Providing further evidence of the ways *elsewhere* is difficult to pin down, we note the complex intersections of learner experiences in WGS programs where the learner can simultaneously be a member of the "community" and also the "university" expert. There are likely many examples across Canada, but one instance of this played out during the writing of this chapter, where students from a Women's and Gender Studies distance education program at Laurentian University collaborated with students from Wilfrid Laurier University's Faculty of Social Work. The students met through the Walls 2 Bridges program, which brings university and incarcerated learners together as peers under the guidance of a university instructor and the government-employed educators at a women's penitentiary (http://wallstobridges.ca/). In this program, social work students and inmates at a penitentiary take a class together onsite in the educational facilities at a prison for university credit, challenging the common binaries of praxis/theory and community/university through its philosophical goals and praxis (Pollack 2016). In this case, several of the learners were WGS students who had been studying for a Bachelor of Arts degree by distance education. Given their subject position as student inmates, they were unlikely to have had the opportunity for experiential learning *elsewhere*, and were more likely positioned as the people social work students would ultimately come to "help" on placement. Who *should* be considered the expert in such a setting: the students who have been incarcerated but are already adept at discussing feminist theories of power and de-colonization? Or the students of social work whose growing critical knowledge of social work theory is greatly enhanced by these interactions? On the one hand, the WGS students had been taking core WGS arts-based courses on gender and violence, feminist theory, and colonialism, so they could simultaneously be positioned as knowledgeable about their own experiences as incarcerated women and about these theories. The social work students, on the other hand, could be understood as both learners in their own field and the subjects of the incarcerated WGS students' experiential learning. When Jennifer L. Johnson was invited to attend a meeting of the class and meet the WGS students for the first time, it was evident that this vibrant learning group consisted of many "experts," something made possible by the political awareness and analytic concerns inherent in the pedagogy of Walls 2 Bridges.

Taken together, the chapters in this collection also put those of us doing or thinking about instituting community-based learning in WGS *elsewhere* on notice. The authors offer us much to work with in order to deepen our understanding that the novelty and excitement of community-based learning must not preclude us from doing the difficult, reflexive, and critical work that feminist knowledge production demands. And while this collection works with case studies from within WGS programs, the issues authors discuss also apply to critical approaches to community engagement in numerous other disciplines. All of the authors speak to how important the classroom remains as a site of critical reflection, of thinking carefully and critically about the kind of doing that *learning elsewhere* entails. One concern in instituting community-based learning is certainly that the urgency of the "real" issues students experience in their placements, internships, and co-op settings will come to dominate the more careful, less certain, more critically reflective work that feminist theorizing requires. All of the chapters in this collection highlight the importance of the conceptual, theoretical, and reflective work we do in the classroom, suggesting that community-based learning never happens only, or even primarily, *elsewhere*. While the question of whether feminist praxis in WGS is really so different remains up for debate, what all the chapters in this volume make clear is that the critical, reflexive, intellectual work of our field must be applied with equal measure to its praxis components, or we risk too much capitulation to and collusion with the neoliberal university. But they also make clear that feminist praxis in WGS, whether occurring in the classroom or elsewhere, can be strengthened only by analyses that employ the critical tools of feminist knowledge production so well honed in our field. And perhaps it is this openness to subjecting our own praxis to feminist critique that truly establishes WGS as in the vanguard of developing critical approaches to community-based learning within and beyond the post-secondary classroom.

Notes

Portions of this introduction were previously published in Jennifer L. Johnson and Susanne Luhmann, "Social Justice for (University) Credit? The Women's and Gender Studies Practicum in the Neoliberal University," *Resources for Feminist Research* 34, no. 3/4 (2016): 40–59. Reprinted with permission from the authors.

1 The Progressive Conservative Party promises to expand the role of HECQO to include a complaints and investigation process about free speech. This platform promise appears to be based on the following two cases: https://www .theglobeandmail.com/canada/article-documents-reveal-new-details-in -lindsay-shepherd-wilfrid-laurier/, and https://thevarsity.ca/2018/02/28/court -rules-in-favour-of-utmsu-in-lawsuit-with-anti-abortion-student-group/.

2 See https://www.ualberta.ca/arts/student-services/arts-work-experience/ prospective-awe-students.

3 Exceptions here are Muzak (2012) and Parkins (2014). The latter is reprinted in a revised version in this collection. For an extensive bibliography of the existing community service-learning (CSL) literature, go to https:// cloudfront.ualberta.ca/-/media/arts/departments-institutes-and-centres/ community-service learning/documents/reports/2015-03-24-canadian-csl -studies-resource-base.pdf.

4 For details of the history of service-learning in Canada, see the web page of the Canadian Alliance for Community Service learning: http://www .communityservicelearning.ca/en/welcome_what_is.htm. For the US history, see the National Service learning Clearing House: http://www.servicelearning .org/what_is_service learning/history.

5 On student preferences for charity over activist work, see Bickford and Reynolds (2002).

6 Certainly, some authors draw a distinction between charity and social change work; however, feminists are not the only ones to do so (see, e.g., Marullo and Edwards, 2000).

FEMINIST PRAXIS /
FOR CREDIT /
UNDER NEOLIBERALISM

CHAPTER TWO

COLONIALISM, NEOLIBERALISM, AND UNIVERSITY–COMMUNITY ENGAGEMENT: WHAT SORTS OF ENCOUNTERS WITH DIFFERENCE ARE OUR INSTITUTIONS PRIORITIZING?

AMBER DEAN

In 2011, the president of McMaster University (where I currently work as an Associate Professor of Cultural Studies and Gender Studies) declared Community Engagement (CE) one of our institution's top new priorities (Deane 2011). Similar declarations are occurring at post-secondary institutions across Canada, demarcating a noticeable turn to community-engaged research, teaching, and learning that has intensified over the past decade or so.[1] For many of us at McMaster, President Patrick Deane's emphasis on improving undergraduate education and on our "obligation to serve the greater good of our community—locally, nationally, and globally" was met with optimism, even enthusiasm, about what these changed priorities might make possible for scholars committed to collective struggles for greater justice (2011, 5). My own enthusiasm has since been somewhat dampened, however; in fact, the similar rhetoric used to support this new emphasis on CE at universities across the country has led me to reflect on the degree to which this turn to CE as an institutional priority might serve, rather than challenge, the ongoing transformations of the university and large-scale cuts to government spending on social welfare and public services so central to neoliberal economic and ideological agendas. Further, the emphasis on "doing good" through CE mobilizes a colonial and imperialist logic of benevolence that risks downplaying (or forgetting altogether) the ways that academic institutions have historically been, and continue to be, deeply implicated in the furtherance of colonialist and imperialist projects. I argue, then, that the dominant rhetoric of CE currently emerging at universities across the country might both shape and delimit the possibilities for more ethical encounters across difference through community-engaged research, teaching, and learning conducted in Women's and Gender Studies (WGS) and other related (inter) disciplines in the liberal arts. By questioning some of the assumptions about "The University" and "The Community" that seem to underpin this dominant rhetoric, its reliance on colonial logics becomes clearer and the insidiousness of neoliberal governmentality in this recent turn to CE is also exposed. But lest it seem as though I am advocating a total abandonment of CE, I conclude by exploring how engagement with feminist, post-colonial, and Indigenous theorizing might provoke CE practices that are critically reflexive about the sorts of encounters with difference they are likely to produce—practices that invite faculty and students to recognize ourselves as implicated participants in *collective* struggles for greater justice.

As Wendy Brown reminds us, neoliberalism is not just a "bundle of economic policies" (2005, 38), but is also a form of "governmentality—a mode of governance encompassing but not limited to the state, and one that produces subjects, forms of citizenship and behaviour, and a new organization of the social" (37). Brown is concerned with the *political* implications of a neoliberal governmentality that *"extends and disseminates market values to all institutions and social action"* (40, emphasis in original). For my purposes, it is neoliberal governmentality's effects on popular understandings of individual responsibility and agency that holds the most significant implications for how teachers and students may come to understand our*selves* differently through practices of CE. For example, Brown insists that "[t]he model neoliberal citizen is one who strategizes for her- or himself among various social, political or economic options, not one who strives with others to alter or organize these options" (43). While shifting understandings of post-secondary education as primarily for the acquisition of marketable skills, and of students as consumers in this education "marketplace" are much discussed of late, at first glance it appears that a commitment to "doing good" through practices of CE might work *against* some of these changing understandings of what a university education represents. But I suspect, in fact, that the opposite may be true: that the widespread turn to CE on university campuses may instead facilitate the production of the sort of "model neoliberal citizen" that Brown describes above, a citizen-student who views CE primarily as an opportunity to increase the value of one's degree than as an invitation to engage in a collective struggle with others (often from quite different social and cultural locations) to alter forms of injustice in which we are all—albeit differently—implicated.

Part of my initial optimism about this turn to CE as an institutional priority arose from how I imagined it might be strategically mobilized to lend added support and legitimacy to my own efforts to bridge community-based organizing and activist work with my academic responsibilities of research, teaching, and service.[2] As discussed in the introduction to this book, projects and initiatives now launching under the auspices of CE have a long history in WGS, where a commitment to bridging theory/practice and university/community divides can be traced back to the field's founding (Orr 2011; Zimmerman 2002). However, as Catherine Orr notes, WGS approaches to CE typically involve "social justice frameworks that distinguish engagement from 'service' or 'volunteering,' where too often issues of power and privilege go unquestioned" (2011, 10). As a result, the terminology and dominant rhetorics of CE are often eschewed in WGS in favour of "the language of social justice and activism," and one might be optimistic that institutional commitments to community or civic engagement can be harnessed to further the activist-oriented research, teaching, and service often associated with WGS (Orr 2011, 22). However, my own efforts to engage undergraduate and graduate students in collective struggles for greater justice through activist-oriented assignments have led me to question the degree to which the oft-assumed more politicized and social justice–focused approaches of WGS can be disentangled from the dominant rhetorics and frameworks of CE that are emerging—or indeed, whether they were ever so different in the first place.[3]

At certain times, students' projects in response to a range of activist-oriented assignments have left me hopeful about the possibilities of integrating forms of collective struggle with academic agendas. However, at other times they have been a source of anxiety, frustration, even sheer terror. My students most often approach such assignments by positioning themselves as "experts" (or, at least, as privileged knowers) about a particular issue or problem, charging themselves with raising awareness about the suffering or struggles of people they tend to view and often represent as less fortunate "others" in dire need of their benevolence, charity, or philanthropy. It seems to me that this is entirely consistent with models for social responsibility that cohere with neoliberal governmentality, for students view themselves as deploying their superior (entrepreneurial) skills to "develop" or "improve" others who are largely imagined as the authors of their own suffering. Wendy Brown suggests that those who "fail to navigate impediments to prosperity" are understood, under neoliberal governmentality, as living "a mismanaged life": widespread social injustices that privilege some and disadvantage others become signs of individual failure (2005, 42). This understanding of injustice as caused by individual failings and alleviated by individualized solutions seems to underpin several projects my students have undertaken. For example, one group of undergraduate students aimed to raise awareness among the student population about women living in poverty. They proceeded to set up displays on campus that primarily highlighted statistics about women's poverty levels in Canada and encouraged other students to make donations to a local women's shelter. At least two assumptions seemed to underpin their project: one, that women living in poverty are not among the ranks of post-secondary students; and two, that the poverty of these (non-student) "other" women could best be alleviated through charitable donations rather than structural change, representing an individualized and highly entrepreneurial response.

A lack of awareness about collective forms of struggle for greater justice also shapes the sorts of projects my students propose. Another group of white undergraduate students, for example, planned to raise awareness about rape in Democratic Republic of Congo by dressing up in "African costumes" and participating in a local charitable fashion show—and they thought their performance might be enhanced by painting their skin black (readers will no doubt be relieved to know this project was modified, at the proposal stage, thanks to intensive intervention by a very skilled graduate teaching assistant). This act of sympathetic benevolence rooted in racial privilege is but the starkest of numerous examples of such "othering" practices that have arisen in student projects. In her book *Regarding the Pain of Others*, Susan Sontag eloquently summarizes my concerns with such projects when she writes:

> So far as we feel sympathy, we feel we are not accomplices to what caused the suffering. Our sympathy proclaims our innocence as well as our impotence. [Let's] set aside the sympathy we extend to others...for a reflection on how our privileges are located on the same map as their suffering, and may—in ways we might prefer not to imagine—be linked to their suffering, as the wealth of some may imply the destitution of others. (2003, 102–3)

David Jefferess similarly argues that through such benevolent approaches to social change, "[c]onflict and poverty are dehistoricized; our relation to the suffering of Others is defined in terms of benevolence—our compassion and decency—rather than in terms of material interconnections" (2011, 80). In other words, sympathetic or benevolent approaches to social change are not innocent. In fact, Jefferess argues that these approaches frequently "do more harm than good" (80) in that they perhaps make it even more difficult to identify how the privileges of some connect to the suffering of others.

Given that the dominant rhetoric of CE encourages students to frame their projects through benevolent, sympathetic impulses, it is not surprising that these are the sorts of projects they most commonly propose. But I find myself repeatedly surprised that, despite my best efforts to design courses and assignments that seek to problematize benevolent, charitable approaches to addressing social injustices—aiming to historicize such impulses and situate them in relation to histories of colonialism, imperialism, and the racial logics they rely upon—*my students frequently continue to embrace and advocate such approaches, even at the end of the course.* I suspect this speaks to how powerfully the dominant rhetoric of CE itself supports and advocates such approaches, but also to how this dominant rhetoric both draws on and supports the pervasive and insidious discourses of self-interested entrepreneurship characteristic of neoliberal governmentality, as well as the discourse of benevolence that so often props up colonialist and imperialist projects (see Razack 2004; Jefferess 2011). My undergraduate students in particular often have little or no previous learning about histories of collective struggle, such as slavery abolition, civil rights, decolonization and Indigenous sovereignty movements, feminist or queer struggles, or other forms of anti-racist struggle. Although simply being made aware of these histories of collective struggle and complex solidarities is obviously not a guarantee that students will come to question their benevolent and frequently othering approaches to engagement, their utter lack of such awareness does likely make these sorts of proposals more common.

Despite my struggles with benevolence in students' approaches to their projects, I do believe that CE *can* be transformative, in the sense that at its best it might facilitate the "face-to-face encounters with others" that Gayatri Spivak insists are necessary for any sort of collective struggle (in Ahmed 2000, 178). But attention to the *sorts* of encounters brought about by these forms of engagement is necessary for the development of CE practices that attempt to avoid reinforcing the "strangeness" of others, particularly those "others" who are the least privileged and most marginalized (and thus often sought to be on the receiving end of CE practices). As Sara Ahmed observes, "[t]he assumption that we can tell the difference between strangers and neighbours…functions to conceal forms of social difference" (2000, 3). In other words, some bodies are more likely to be recognized as "strangers" than others. Whether we associate strangers with danger or welcome them for their unique differences, we "turn the stranger into something that simply *is*," which "*cuts 'the stranger' off from the histories of its determination*" (5, emphasis in original). Such "stranger fetishism," for Ahmed, risks producing encounters through which "[t]he journey towards the stranger becomes a form of self-discovery, in which the stranger functions yet again to establish and define the 'I'" (6). This is, of course, a version of the same sort of logic that underpins colonialism; as Ahmed goes on to insist, "the colonial project was not *external* to the constitution of the modernity of European nations: rather, the identity of these nations *became predicated on their relationship to the colonised others*" (10, emphasis added; see also Razack 2004 on this point).

Margaret Himley, drawing on Ahmed, explains that service learning (as a practice of CE) involves "figuring and approaching the stranger," and it "emerge[s] within colonizing impulses and practices":

> Service has roots in the volunteerism of white middle- and upper-class women... where these hopeful and idealistic (and perhaps naïve) volunteers went out into poor and working class neighbourhoods to improve the material and moral lot of the less fortunate they found living there. (2004, 419)

Himley is optimistic that the embodied encounters made possible through service learning might productively "agitate us, teachers and students alike" by inciting "a recognition not just of the stranger *but also of the social and historical conditions that produce that recognition*" (434, emphasis added). I am curious, however, about how some of the key assumptions about "The University" and "The Community" that underpin this recent turn to CE might hamper any potential it holds for assisting us in identifying the social and historical conditions that cause us to recognize ourselves and others in particular ways.

"The University" and "The Community"

While acknowledging that communities can be based on geography, interest, affiliation, or identity, the McMaster Community Engagement Task Force recommended that "McMaster focus primarily on its neighbouring communities," while also recognizing our connection to "the global community" (2012, 4–5). This attention to what we mean when we talk about "the community" seems important, given that much of the literature on service learning and community engagement has, as the task force acknowledges, neglected to consider or consult communities about the desirability or benefits of community engagement practices, focusing instead on the benefits of CE for students and universities (2012, 4). Yet, questions about how to define "the university" or why universities must be prompted to engage in CE are seldom asked, other than the occasional vague gesture to the university's reputation for ivory tower elitism. Most of the rhetoric about CE embedded in official documents and strategic plans suggests that universities have civic responsibilities for serving less fortunate "others" or for "doing good," while communities are primarily framed as having unmet needs.[4] While there is much discussion about how CE practices must value reciprocity and be mutually beneficial to the university and the community, there is very little discussion of why these values need to be explicitly stated: namely, the university's long history of exploiting various communities, in particular communities of colour and Indigenous communities, in the interests of controlling the production and reproduction of knowledge for its own benefit (and too frequently, in the interests of white supremacy). Let me unpack some of the assumptions about "The University" and "The Community" that seem to me to underpin this new turn to CE:

1. The Homogeneity of "The University"

The turn to CE as a strategic priority rests on the assumption that the university is first and foremost an entity separate from the community. I suspect this assumption continues to inform the dominant rhetoric of CE because of the very real physical and structural barriers that often do separate universities from their surrounding communities; yet, while I understand and even sympathize with why this assumption is made, it remains a source of frustration for many of us who have never viewed our lives in the university as existing somehow outside of, or separate from, the rest of our everyday existence. This assumption reproduces, rather than challenges, the elitism universities are often accused of, and sometimes produces outcomes that are comical (such as when a non-profit organization I worked with agreed to take on some students for a CE project recently and I found myself positioned as a representative of "the community" whom a student seemed to presume was in dire need of her superior research skills). Indeed, the dominant rhetoric frames the university as the site of privilege when it comes to CE, while the community is framed as the site of underprivilege and "otherness." These assumptions can cause serious dissonance for students and faculty who do not always seamlessly occupy or come from backgrounds of privilege, adding to our "imposter syndrome" or sense of non-belonging within the university. Here, I am reminded of a student who recently resisted a CE assignment that required students to participate in a walking tour of our inner city aimed at familiarizing students with the extent of the neighbourhood's poverty (I presume in the interests of conveying to them the importance of requiring university students to go out and "do good" in the community). This particular student had relied upon many of the social services the tour was drawing attention to, and understandably did not relish the thought of having to revisit these sites with a group of gawking (albeit likely sympathetic in the most benevolent sense) classmates.

I think that this assumption about the university as a homogenous site of privilege has quite a lot to do with how approaches to CE are increasingly framed through the emerging dominant rhetoric as opportunities for students and faculty to demonstrate compassion, benevolence, philanthropy, and good citizenship by giving back to a community *that we are simultaneously framed as both separate from and superior to.* Even when discussions of CE locate universities within their geographical communities (as the McMaster CE task force does), there still remains a sense that the university is a separate entity from the community and must now become a "better neighbour," in a sense, by giving back. Perhaps Margaret Himley puts it best when she writes, "regardless of a student's actual economic status or social identity, the dominant version of the rhetoric of community service may position each and every community service student in a privileged way" (2004, 430). In this version of CE, students and faculty have resources, and communities have unmet needs; students and faculty are knowers, and their community counterparts can benefit from their wisdom; students and faculty are accomplished, and people in communities need improvement. Given this framing, it will continue to be extremely challenging to "disrupt the binary relationship that has been falsely created between the 'University' and the 'Community,'" as the task force at McMaster proposes, because the dominant rhetoric of CE *relies* on this binary in order to rationalize its importance and its value (2012, 11).[5]

The university is also imagined in the dominant rhetoric as a site where CE could become equally valued and practised widely across campus as a result of being declared a strategic priority, without any acknowledgement of the vast differences—ideological, methodological, and epistemological—that persist across, and even within, various faculties and disciplines. This assumption fails to acknowledge widely differing commitments to (or even interest in) collective struggles for greater social justice across the university, and denies the investments of the institution itself in maintaining the status quo. Unless the dominant rhetoric of CE shifts—so that critical questions about what makes this turn to it necessary in the first place become central to its discussion, framing, and practice—I am increasingly doubtful that much about the "regimes of the normal" at the university is likely to be shaken by this new priority (Warner 1993, xxvii).

2. The Homogeneity of "The Community"

While I appreciate the definition of community at my university, and also tend to agree that there are good reasons to focus on a geographic community with proximity to the university in question, not enough work has been done to acknowledge the differences and disparities *within* "The Community" as it is framed by the dominant rhetoric of CE. And although efforts are being made to imagine the community as including governments, other professionals, and (with relish) the "business community" (a point I will return to shortly), I argue that the community in the CE paradigm is imagined primarily as poor, disenfranchised, marginalized, and too frequently racialized as "other." These are the groups most often viewed as the logical beneficiaries of service from privileged members of the university. Curiously, though, it is only very rarely acknowledged that the members of the community to whom the university reaches out in order to design and implement its CE projects are *not* actually these intended beneficiaries, but the helping professionals who *serve them* (Rosenberger 2000, 40–41). I have noticed a strong tendency to collapse the distinction between community-based service providers and the people that they serve in discussions of CE, as though we imagine that these service providers can, and should, speak for (and will necessarily represent the best interests of) the communities they themselves serve. In a world where, increasingly, accessing any form of social assistance means submitting to various forms of social surveillance and control, this seems like a significant ethical concern that is currently under-addressed in discussions about CE.

Similarly, although there is apparently little to no research to support the assumption that CE inherently provides something of value to the community, this does indeed seem to remain a key assumption underpinning the dominant CE rhetoric. For instance, few advocates of CE seem to imagine that there might be significant risks of harm to the community on the receiving end of CE. Those implementing CE projects could here take counsel from some of the evaluative work that has been done in humanitarian and global development contexts, which highlights several harms, or risks of harm, to the communities receiving services or support. According to David Jefferess, for example, the impulse to "do good" (via "voluntourism," for example) "constitutes a new form of colonial paternalism and often harms the host communities" (2012, 22). Jefferess summarizes these harms (documented in the work of several critical development scholars) as follows: "Volunteers are frequently untrained and often not competent in the labour they perform," such that houses, wells, or other physical structures intended to benefit a community fall apart, quickly need repair, or become unsafe; "projects can fuel conflict among and within communities"—by partnering with certain organizations or agencies over others, for example, universities might further entrench local animosities or competitions for scarce resources; "projects focus on the symptoms of poverty rather than its causes," primarily through approaches to charity and aid that fail to attend to the structural conditions through which poverty in some places or for some people becomes naturalized; "volunteers often take the place of local labour" (see also Zimmerman 2002 on this point); and "projects often reinforce neoliberal policies that weaken governments and allow foreign donors to determine social policy" (2012, 22). Similar harms are undoubtedly also a risk of CE, even when practised in communities local to our universities. Thus, the neoliberal and colonial/imperialist impulses underpinning this widespread turn to CE should, at the very least, make us cautious about the development and implementation of such projects, as well as about how we talk about and represent the importance and value of CE as an institutional priority.

The Insidiousness of Neoliberal Governmentality

At a 2012 panel on the turn to CE (one of the "Big Thinking" events at the Congress of the Humanities and Social Sciences, sponsored by the Canadian Foundation for Innovation and composed of various deans and VPs advocating for CE), one panellist seemed quite excited to pronounce that of course community can mean many things, including "the business community." While he did not elaborate, I would interpret his comment as suggesting that CE practices that contribute to the everyday advancement of global capitalism and further the facilitation of market-driven values into all aspects of social life can and should be considered as valuable a form of CE as practices that focus on challenging the myriad injustices produced and reinforced by our current economic system. At my most cynical, I imagine that this will result in CE projects the university "serves" the business community with by providing free labour and/or the free development of products of monetary value, while the business community in turn comes to further appreciate the value of making financial donations to its new partner. Indeed, in a 2012 issue of *Academic Matters*, an article that ostensibly had nothing to do with CE mentioned a recent case in the US in which a university designed a course that had, as its central goal, the creation of a website and advertising campaign for a consortium of companies, where the CEO was an alumnus and major university donor (Ginsberg 2012, 25).

It concerns me that there seems to be very little discussion about the ethical quandaries involved in practising CE with the for-profit business "community." Even in the more traditional model of CE as serving a community's needs, we need to be asking about the ethics of providing such services via university students at a moment when vast government cuts are decimating the public sector. Non-profit and charitable organizations, as well as public services in the health, education, and justice sectors, are increasingly unable to meet the needs of the communities they are intended to serve, and could easily become reliant on universities that compel their students to attempt to fill the roles of laid-off workers if we are not paying attention. In other words, the university might contribute to advancing neoliberal transformations of the public sector by offering students private credentialing for undertaking work formerly done by public sector workers. Both through the increasing interest in developing partnerships with for-profit businesses and industry, and by stepping in to fill the void created by a massive reduction in public and social services, the turn to CE furthers neoliberal ideologies and economic reforms. But really, one has to wonder if furthering neoliberal agendas is perhaps what governments have in mind by encouraging this turn to CE in the first place. It is no coincidence that there was such an upsurge in the development of service-learning programs in the economically strapped early 1990s in the US, while we witnessed the same sort of transformation in Canada at the exact same moment as the ideologically driven neoliberal restructuring of the public sector under former Prime Minister Stephen Harper's Conservative government.

Engaging with Feminist, Post-colonial, and Indigenous Theorizing: Possibilities for (More) Ethical Encounters

An advertisement for the same "Big Thinking" panel on "Research, Education, and Service to the Community" held at the Congress of the Humanities and Social Sciences in 2012 conveys a clear sense of what haunts the university's recent turn to CE. For Avery Gordon, "haunting describes how that which appears to be not there is often a seething presence, acting on and often meddling with taken-for-granted realities" (1997, 8). Gordon is interested in projects tracking "that which makes its mark by being there and not there at the same time," and in forces that "cajol[e] us to reconsider ... the very distinctions between there and not there, past and present" (6). Although this panel ostensibly had nothing to do with Indigeneity, an advertisement for the panel featured a photograph of Haida artist Bill Reid's well-known sculpture *The Raven and the First Men* overlaid by text that proclaims: "Research preserves our culture, and research builds communities." This claim and image mark the absent-but-still-seething presence of colonial imaginaries in the dominant rhetorics of CE. The affirming claims of the advertisement are haunted by the absent presence of a history (and present) in which Indigenous communities are not only "preserved" and "built" but also appropriated, exploited, and decimated in the name of research. While certainly some Indigenous communities benefit from particular approaches to research, many communities have also been forced to reclaim control of their languages, cultural products, knowledges, and stories from anthropologists, scientists, historians, and literary scholars (it is telling, for example, that the text of the "Big Thinking" panel advertisement that overlays Reid's sculpture is printed in English and French, but *not* in Haida or any other Indigenous language). It is the tendency to idealize the "preserving" and "building" functions of CE while conveniently remaining silent about the exploitative and harmful, even violent ones, that concerns me. As Linda Tuhiwai Smith insists,

> From the vantage point of the colonized ... the term "research" is inextricably linked to European imperialism and colonialism. ... The ways in which scientific research is implicated in the worst excesses of colonialism remains a powerful remembered history for many of the world's colonized people. It is a history that still offends the deepest sense of our humanity. (1999, 1)

This history of the exploitation and harm that can arise from universities' "engagement" with marginalized and colonized communities is precisely what haunts the dominant rhetoric that frames CE as a practice of purportedly harmless benevolence: these histories are always *present*, even in the face of efforts to vanquish and/or depoliticize them.

What might the scholarship and practice of CE gain by engaging with feminist, post-colonial, and Indigenous theorizing? If we concede that the university has a long (and ongoing) history of doing various communities harm, then perhaps it might be beneficial to examine the current move to CE in relation to theorizing and activism arising from transnational feminist organizing, politicized approaches to reconciliation, and decolonizing struggles. What we might gain from grappling with insights from these approaches is recognition of the futility of trying to define a community in advance of a shared struggle, and an acknowledgement that the "we" of any community *is the very thing that needs to be worked toward*. Many transnational feminist theorists have long acknowledged, for example, that "full ethical engagement" with others is actually not a possibility at present because any alliance across differences is necessarily shaped by deeply entrenched injustices and inequalities (Spivak in Ahmed 2000, 178). Instead, Ahmed emphasizes "the intimacy of the political and the ethical as ways of achieving 'better' relationship[s] to others" (2000, 179), and for her, "the 'we' in such a collective politics is what must be worked for, rather than being the foundation of our collective work" (180). Thus, the work of transnational feminist alliances necessarily involves "remaking *what it is that we may yet have in common*" (181, emphasis in original). By refusing either to collapse or essentialize differences, Ahmed emphasizes the difficult work of building communities premised on greater justice. Such alliances require "a proximity that does not allow merger, benevolence or knowledge" (178)—in other words, we cannot assume to be, become, or know the "others" with whom we might build such alliances, nor can we assume that our actions will necessarily "do good." Similarly, Andrew Schaap, a political theorist of post-colonial reconciliation, argues that there is a problem with "representing community as the given end of politics rather than a contingent historical possibility that conditions the possibility of politics in the present" (2007, 26). As he elaborates, "the conflicts of the past can only be 'resolved' and community thereby 'restored' by a reductive representation that silences political objections that question how such a 'we' is possible in the first place. Yet it is precisely the possibility of such questioning that is the enabling condition of a reconciliatory politics" (26). Indigenous theorists Marie Battiste and James [Sákéj] Youngblood Henderson advocate an engagement with Indigenous epistemologies that both acknowledges the risks of "cognitive imperialism" but also recognizes the important contributions of Indigenous knowledge

(2000, 17). These theorists insist that, "[i]n the Indigenous worldview... [l]ife is to be lived not according to universal, abstract theories... but as *an interactive relationship in a particular time and place*" (2000, 27, emphasis added). In many Indigenous languages and knowledges, these authors affirm, *relationality* is paramount. What engaging with these fields can offer CE, then, is a clear sense that the "we" of a community *should be the project* of CE, rather than some benevolent, abstract notion of "serving the greater good."

If the "we" of a community is the aim that we must work toward, then faculty, students, and community members engaged in CE must grapple collectively with the many ethical dilemmas arising from its practice. In other words, we need to question the politics of knowledge and knowledge production across the university; the politics of representation in the university community and other diverse communities we engage with; and the troubling ethical questions arising from the function CE might be playing in the ongoing neoliberal restructuring of the university and the public sector. We must also open up the university to the communities it desires to engage, not just in the fairly straightforward way of making the university a site for cultural and athletic events, but also by asking the harder questions of who has access to a post-secondary education and who does not. An important and connected point here is to interrogate assumptions about whose knowledge counts and is widely recognized as knowledge, and whose is not. Faculty and students need to engage in critical self-reflection about the social and political structures and histories of conflict, violence, and injustice that make this "we" so difficult to achieve and so fragile, yet at the same time, ethically necessary to pursue. We ought to critically interrogate our motivations for these impulses to "do good" by asking some key questions of any proposed practice of CE. Such questions have been explored at length in the fields of feminist, post-colonial, and Indigenous studies, namely: (1) Who benefits? (2) Who can/should speak for whom? and (3) How are authority and resources distributed, and what are the consequences (for community members and students, in particular) of choosing *not* to engage?

I feel conflicted about raising these concerns with CE because I am aware that the struggle to transform what we do at the university, to make us better at engaging the communities we are already very much a part of, is facing backlash from those who fail to recognize that the elite knowledge-producing and knowledge-affirming practices of the university *stand directly in the way* of a more just world. Those who are admirably pushing forth the CE agenda do so, I recognize, in an environment where many seem to believe that faculty and students at a university need only engage with the community of scholars who share their discipline, or with the "community" of business and industry that is increasingly relied upon to fund research. In such an environment, it seems risky to dwell on the problems arising from doing CE poorly, lest these problems become a justification for not doing it at all. Yet, for me, the hopeful future of the transformed university-to-come can be achieved only when we begin to link what "we" do "here" with the broader collective struggles for social justice taking place all around us. When it comes to CE, then, if we are not committed to letting those collective struggles inform and shape our pedagogy, then we are most certainly missing something. More specifically, we need to better historicize and directly address the myriad problems with this dominant rhetoric of CE with our students in the classroom, and to think carefully about how we talk about and frame our commitments to community-based research, teaching, and learning at all levels, so that we can at minimum disrupt how these practices collude with the interests of neoliberal governmentality and interrupt the myriad ways that they reproduce colonial logics.

Notes

This chapter was previously published in *Unravelling Encounters: Ethics, Knowledge and Resistance Under Neoliberalism*, ed. Caitlin Janzen, Donna Jeffery, and Kristin Smith (Waterloo, ON: Wilfrid Laurier University Press, 2015), 175–194. Reprinted with permission from WLUP.

1   See, for example, Simon Fraser University's 2012 rebranding as "The Engaged University"; UBC's commitment to the advancement of community-service learning and community-based research as part of its 2010 strategic plan; the University of Victoria's commitments to CE in its 2002, 2007, and 2012 strategic plans; the University of Alberta's 2011 launch of a Centre for Public Involvement which aims to help the university "pursue its strategic goal of enhancing its leadership capacities in the scholarship of community engagement"; the development of a "Community Engagement Hub" at the University of Saskatchewan; an "emphasis on engagement" in the University of Manitoba's 2011 strategic plan update; York University's 2010 President's Task Force report on community engagement, "Towards an Engaged University," and the launch of the York University–TD Community Engagement Centre; the University of Toronto's commitment to building community partnerships in their "Toward 2030" strategic planning process; and McGill University's 2011 report of the Principal's Task Force on Diversity, Excellence, and Community Engagement. No doubt a more thorough search could produce many more recent examples of this new prioritization of CE at Canadian universities. At one of the "Big Thinking" events during the 2012 Congress of the Humanities and Social Sciences sponsored by the Canadian Foundation for Innovation, composed of various deans and VPs advocating for CE, Jeff Keshen, Dean of Arts at Mount Royal University, said that in 2000 there were only two service-learning programs of note in the country: one at UBC and another at St. Francis Xavier University. Quite a change, then, between 2000 and 2012. While

there were likely many other CE-related programs or courses on Canadian campuses that pre-date 2000, perhaps most notably in Women's and Gender Studies, what I want to draw attention to here is the shift to making CE an *institutional* priority and the corresponding growth in centres, hubs, and programs in the first decade or so of the twenty-first century.

2 These commitments are primarily to feminist movements to end rape and other forms of violence against women, to prison abolition struggles, to LGBTQ community organizing, to sex worker organizing and the movement to decriminalize sex work, and, more recently, to solidarity work with Indigenous sovereignty struggles.

3 I have used a Feminist Activism Assignment in several different Introductory Women's Studies courses (see Dean 2007), and I have used a Culture Jamming Assignment in Introductory Cultural Studies. I have also been involved in developing a core course called Knowledge in Action for master's students in the Gender Studies and Feminist Research program at McMaster, a course that involves partnering students with local feminist and other social justice organizations. I have attempted throughout my career to integrate my activist commitments with my research, but for the purposes of this paper I will focus primarily on teaching and learning.

4 The community's needs are mentioned four times in the seventeen-page McMaster Community Engagement Task Force position paper, for example, and this association of the community with needs is commonplace in discussions about the importance or value of CE.

5 Sherene Razack (2004) makes a similar argument about how the popular understanding of Canada and "Canadianness" as representing a middle-power, peacekeeping, benevolent nation *relies* on the construction of nations like Somalia as representative of savagery and "evil," while Margot Francis (2011) points out numerous associations between "Canadianness" and "doing good," arguing that "the very 'Canadian' idea of a normally benign and compassionate nation" (ix) manages to co-exist with "a continuing apathy towards...Indigenous people" (xi). Both authors thus link benevolence, compassion, and a desire to be recognized for "doing good" with distinctly Canadian imperialist and colonial projects.

CHAPTER THREE

FEMINIST PRAXIS AND COMMUNITY SERVICE-LEARNING IN CANADA'S CHANGING NON-PROFIT SECTOR

JOANNE MUZAK

This chapter is concerned with the pedagogical implications of government-mandated and socio-economic changes that have shifted the work of social justice–oriented non-profit organizations, including women-centred organizations, away from advocacy and institutional change toward individualized social service provision and the management of social welfare based on corporate culture. Although these changes reflect broad trends in the non-profit sector, experienced across the West since at least the 1980s with the entrenchment of neoliberalism (Wolsh 1989; Baines 2010), I am interested specifically in the more recent Canadian context: when the Harper government took office in 2006, for example, it systematically sought to silence and dismantle equality-seeking (a term I use interchangeably with *social justice-oriented*) non-profit organizations, starting with particularly aggressive funding cuts to women's groups and programs, including the Status of Women Canada (SWC). Federal funding cuts to high-profile national voluntary organizations that criticized government policies during the Harper era produced what policy studies scholars such as Rachel Laforest called a "profound advocacy chill" (2012, 190–91). With the implementation of the Canada Revenue Agency's political activity audit program, which as of October 2014 targeted fifty-two charities (mostly environmental, human rights, anti-poverty, and international aid organizations) to determine whether they were violating a rule that limits their spending on political activities to 10 percent of resources (Broadbent Institute 2014), the advocacy chill deepened.[1] Although the Trudeau Liberals, elected in 2015, suspended the remaining political activity audits in May 2017, there are long-term implications from the cuts and advocacy chill under Harper's conservative government that remain important for both faculty and students engaged in praxis learning in Canadian Women's and Gender Studies (WGS) programs.

The landscape of Canada's non-profit sector, long characterized as "a criti-cal space for democratic public participation and resistance" (Drevland 2007, 153), has been dramatically changed (Gergin 2011).[2] As of April 2012, the Gov-ernment of Canada had cut or ended funding to forty-one women's organi-zations and programs (CFUW 2012). This list almost doubles when we add broader social justice–oriented community organizations, agencies, research bodies, and programs (Gergin 2011). As I sat down to write this chapter, news of another closure of a women's organization made a tiny wave in my Face-book feed. On November 21, 2014, the Canadian Women's Health Network (CWHN), an influential voluntary national research and activist organiza-tion dedicated to improving women's health and equality, quietly announced a "suspension of activities due to lack of funds," after operating since 1993 (CWHN 2014). As the CWHN press release explained, the network "has not been able to secure sustainable funds to replace the federal funding that was withdrawn in 2013. . . . The CWHN was not alone in losing its funding: the end of Health Canada's Women's Health Contribution Program meant that all Centres of Excellence for Women's Health and other partner organizations lost their funding in 2013. Some of these centres have already made the dif-ficult decision to close their doors."

Given that women-centred non-profit organizations have historically been upheld as sites of feminist research, knowledge, and activism—organizations to which we, as WGS instructors and experiential learning practitioners, often send students in the hopes that they will witness and/or enact feminist praxis and activism—I am curious about how the changed landscape of Canada's non-profit sector is playing out in our classrooms when students engage with it as part of the course curriculum. Has the regime of government regulation that has significantly prohibited advocacy, policy research, and lobbying nec-essarily meant that students have fewer opportunities to experience feminist praxis and activism in their service-learning placements? How do students experience feminist activism in the context of neoliberalism and the marketi-zation of the non-profit sector? Does service-learning in WGS curricula rep-resent a possible intervention in Canada's anti-feminist political climate? Can service-learning help students re-politicize the work of social justice–oriented and women-centred non-profit organizations? Or, as Lise Gotell argues in this volume, is it instead the case that students can learn more about the many bar-riers to feminist activism facing non-profits than they can about engaging in activism through service-learning? What do these learning experiences look like inside and outside of the classroom?

This chapter begins with a review of the Harper government's stance on women's advocacy followed by a broader outline of the neoliberal restructur-ing of the non-profit sector. I do not mean to imply that changes in Canada's non-profit sector, specifically a shift from advocacy to social services provision, started with the Harper government or even decades earlier with neoliberalism. I use this context simply as a way to think about how specific political climates and ideologies are reflected in WGS curricula when service-learning is used. When I began to send my students into women-centred non-profit organizations as part of the Introduction to Women's Studies course curriculum in 2007, I was unwittingly placing them in a political climate characterized by a government that silenced dissenting voices with increasing rigour and systematically dismantled organizations that advocate for women's equality and rights protection (Gergin 2011); a non-profit sector that was overworked, underfunded, muzzled, and notably, run largely by women (HR Council 2008; Mailloux, Horak, and Godin 2002); and an increasingly global political economic practice that "recasts the role of the welfare state by shifting responsibility from state to market and from the collective to the individual" (Garrow and Hasenfeld 2014, 301).[3] What are the implications of these circumstances when they become part of the WGS classroom? I then turn to my Introduction to Women's Studies courses and explore three examples of students' experiences of feminist praxis or activism in their service-learning placements with women-centred non-profit organizations to attempt to answer that overarching question.

The Harper Government's Stance on Women's Advocacy

The Harper government's systematic dismantling of women- and social justice–oriented non-profit organizations is not news to most Canadian feminists, but I provide a quick recap of its well-defined stance toward state support of women's advocacy here. In 2006, the newly elected minority government cut funding to the Status of Women Canada (SWC) by 37 percent, which necessitated the closure of twelve of the sixteen offices across the country (Gergin 2011; Voices-Voix 2012). Concurrently, the government "took all mention of 'equality' out of the Terms and Conditions of the Women's Program" (CRIAW 2006, 2), the SWC's grants and contributions program that "provides both funding and technical assistance to women's groups and other equality-seeking organizations" (SWC 2006, 1). The terms *advocacy*, *action*, and *access to justice* were also removed from the SWC's mandate and various documents, including their website (O'Grady 2006/07; Voices-Voix 2012). "Previous objectives such as helping women's organizations participate in the public policy process and increasing the public's understanding of women's equality issues ... [were] eliminated from government literature" (Canadian Press 2006). Feminist critic Kathleen O'Grady (2006/07) characterized these changes as "a chilling process of erasure that attempts to change history." These changes amounted to a fundamental transformation to the SWC's mandate.

As most readers will know, the SWC's Women's Program "funded a number of non-profit organizations working on women's issues, such as violence against women, pay inequality, and democratic participation"—issues that require systemic approaches, research, and public interest work (Voices-Voix 2012). Changes to the SWC's mandate made it impossible for the SWC to fund organizations that advocate and lobby for or research women's rights issues. At the same time, the government made for-profit organizations eligible to receive SWC funding (O'Grady 2006/07; Voices-Voix 2012).

The House of Commons Standing Committee on the Status of Women held hearings on the budget cuts and reforms to the SWC. The committee asserted that the cuts "will make it harder for women across the country to participate in the economic, social, cultural and political aspects of society" (Standing Committee on Status of Women 2007). It characterized the changes to the Terms and Conditions of the SWC as "draconian," and argued that they "undermine the very basis of our democracy—the ability to advocate on behalf of vulnerable groups" (Standing Committee on Status of Women 2007). The committee asked the government to reverse the $5-million cut to the SWC's operating budget and reinstate the original Terms and Conditions of the Women's Program. In March 2007, the federal government re-funded $5 million to the Women's Program (calling it a 40 percent increase in the SWC's budget [Government of Canada n.d.]), but refused to restore the SWC's original mandate or change the funding criteria (Voices-Voix 2012). In a strictly symbolic gesture in 2008, the government quietly re-added the word *equality* to the SWC's documentation (Reaume 2008; see also SWC's webpage, "Who We Are"), but the general ban on advocacy, policy research, and lobbying remains (CFUW 2012).

As Voices-Voix (2012)—a non-partisan Canadian coalition that documents the federal government's silencing of dissenting organizations and individuals—explains, these changes to the SWC funding criteria resulted in the elimination or significantly reduced capacity of many previously influential women's organizations, including the National Association of Women and the Law, the Canadian Research Institute for the Advancement of Women, and the Feminist Alliance For International Action. The SWC's Women's Program is now largely focused on training-oriented projects, with the goal of "increasing women's economic security and prosperity" (SWC 2018). As Gergin (2011) puts it, "at best, the safeguarding of women's equality has been subjected to market efficiency considerations."

Another series of cuts in the 2012 federal budget hit women's non-profit health organizations particularly hard, as the Canadian Women's Health Network (2014) also reminded us in their closure announcement. Health Canada cut the Women's Health Contribution Program, which provided funding to six research programs, including the Native Women's Association of Canada and Le Réseau québécois d'action pour la santé des femmes (CFUW 2012). Again, these budget cuts have either forced the organizations to close their doors or significantly curtailed their operations and activities. For organizations that are still functioning on inadequate budgets, the pursuit of funding has become a preoccupation, or as some critics say, a distraction from the organizations' goals (Drevland 2007).

While it is easy to see the Harper government's cuts to women's organizations as attempts "to muzzle women's voices across the country" (O'Grady 2006/07), the government's stance on advocacy in the non-profit sector must also be considered in the broader context of the restructuring of the non-profit sector in the West to conform to a neoliberal market model of social service provision and citizenship. The changes that the federal government imposed on the non-profit sector under Harper are the materialization of neoliberalism and the restructuring of the social welfare state (Fyfe and Milligan 2003; Wolsh 1989), with governments increasingly downloading responsibility for social services to the non-profit sector while, paradoxically, decreasing funding to it. The changes to the sector brought about by these cuts also represent a restructuring of the non-profit sector as a "new growth industry," shaped by "market fundamentalism" (Drevland 2007). The next section provides an overview of this restructuring and its consequences. When we use service-learning and community placements as part of a feminist pedagogy, the neoliberal characteristics and values of the non-profit sector that are emerging in this process also resonate in our classrooms.

Neoliberal Restructuring and the Non-profit Sector
Budget cuts to the non-profit sector and declining governmental responsibility for the provision of social services are nothing new in Western societies (see Wolsh 1989), but we have seen an acceleration of what Donna Baines (2010) calls the "neoliberal drift" since the 1980s (see also Kirkby 2014a). As Baines explains,

> Neoliberalism is a set of political beliefs, values, and practices that valorize the private market, economic rationalism, and individual rather than collective, responsibility for social and individual ills.... Neoliberal values and processes are played out at the macro level in the shrinking of the welfare state; the adoption of trade, financial, environmental, and labor market policies advancing the interests of corporations and international capital; and the curtailment of the power of social movements and their supports. (2010, 11–12)

In the non-profit sector, neoliberalism has meant that "business-like" and private-sector strategies[4] have supplanted "discourses of collective care, economic equality, and social solidarity" (Baines 2010, 12). In the neoliberal welfare regime, the "availability and allocation of welfare resources are subject to market forces.... Proponents of neoliberalism argue that privatizing government services will save money and improve the quality of services" (Garrow and Hasenfeld 2014, 1479).

Neoliberalism in the non-profit workplace, as Baines argues, "saturates managerial models" so that employees are coached in "best practices" and "increasing professional competencies" via standardized work practices and an increased pace and volume of work (2010, 12). One of the most fundamental changes to the non-profit sector brought about by neoliberalism has been the move from core funding to project funding (Baines 2010; see also Kirkby 2014a). As many scholars have argued—and as community partners have repeatedly explained to me—new funding formulas do not cover overhead costs, which has increased dependence on private fundraising and generated competition among organizations (Baines 2010). Moreover, "juggling fundraising, grant applications, and reporting requirements from multiple sources has caused an explosion in the volume of paperwork required of managers and frontline staff, taking them away from direct service, most notably client care" (Baines 2010, 12). In her article "Women's Activism and the Marketing of the Non-Profit Community," Randi Drevland succinctly summarizes the implications of neoliberal restructuring:

> As government recedes from its social obligations—retooling state-societal relations on a set of principles touted as private-public partnership—international capital and market fundamentalism is stepping in.... The voluntary sector is, then, recreated as a site of production, consumption and entrepreneurialism; and competitiveness in the delivery of public services becomes the new maxim while people become clients and consumers as social services become commoditized. (2007, 156)

Furthermore, under neoliberalism, social problems such as sexual violence and the feminization of poverty become individual problems, and social services become a tool for assigning individual responsibility (Collins et al. 2011; see also Lise Gotell in this volume).

Yet the non-profit sector is also commonly identified in "policy and academic discourses as a 'panacea' to many of the problems faced by neoliberal states. Not only are [non-profit organizations] crucial to strategies of welfare pluralism, but they are also viewed as 'places where politics can be democratized, active citizenship strengthened, [and] the public sphere reinvigorated'" (Brown et al. 2000, 57 in Fyfe and Milligan 2003, 398). The non-profit sector has long been considered essential to a healthy and participatory democracy.

"The 'participatory spirit' of the non-profit sector is understood as that which occurs when democratic actors come together to provide service, advocacy, and empowerment for themselves and others ... [in] ways that emphasize participation and inclusion" (Baines 2010, 13). It is worth noting here that these sentiments closely parallel the original American discourse on service-learning, which also upholds it as a means to reinvigorate participatory democracy (Rocheleau 2004) and teach students how to be "active citizens."

Despite these challenges, feminist scholars often work to prove that women's organizations are still sites of resistance to neoliberalism. In their 2011 study of women's groups in Ontario and British Columbia, for example, Stephanie Baker Collins and her co-authors write, "[w]hat we have seen are signs of how these organizations try to keep alive, albeit under difficult circumstances and in vitiated form, a vital social space that serves as a catalyst for resisting an individualized citizenship" (298). Lise Gotell recounts that WGS students in service-learning placements in her courses have observed that women's organizations "adopt an outwardly depoliticized stance" but "committed women workers and volunteers ... engage in daily acts of resistance" (2009, n.p.; see also her chapter in this volume). Women-centred non-profit organizations have been "known for their stand on the protection of and need for advocacy" (Drevland 2007, 152), and non-profit organizations have provided a venue for women's political presence. As Randi Drevland suggests, "[t]his has positioned some women in potentially powerful political roles as protectors and advocates of public welfare, particularly by coupling the 'ability to link the practical and effective delivery of services to larger political questions ... making the local and community-based dimension of municipalities an important component'" (Andrew 1992, 114 cited in Drevland 2007, 153). At the very least, Drevland hopes that women's organizations can provide a "discursive political space for confrontation and negotiation" (154) and be a "moderating influence on neoliberal policy, one that acts as a buffer between the state and market forces" (152).

"Introduction to Women's Studies": Service-Learning, Feminist Praxis, and Activism

What does all of this mean for WGS students who work with women-centred non-profit organizations in service-learning placements? How do students experience feminist praxis and activism in their service-learning placements in the contexts that I have sketched here? To answer these questions, I draw primarily on my experiences of incorporating community service-learning into Introduction to Women's Studies courses at the University of Alberta between 2007 and 2011, and secondarily on informal interviews I conducted, for the purposes of an earlier conference paper and this chapter, with recent WGS graduates who have gone on to paid employment with women-centred non-profit organizations.[5]

Introduction to Women's Studies at the University of Alberta was a four-teen-week, semester-long course with an average final enrolment of between thirty and forty-five students. Although it was an introductory course, many students took it as an elective in the final years of their undergraduate degrees. One of the challenges of teaching the course was negotiating students' different academic levels. Senior undergraduates often bring well-honed critical thinking skills and an awareness of gender and feminist issues, developed in other courses and extracurricular activities, whereas first-year students often come to the course without a coherent understanding of gender, or with a conviction that feminism is (at best) passé. The community service-learning (CSL) component of the course—which required that students work with a women- or gender-centred non-profit organization for twenty hours over the semester—sometimes helped to level the playing field, so to speak, because it required students to think about how they were learning theoretical concepts through experience, which many of them had not done in any sustained way.

When service-learning was becoming institutionalized in North America in the early 2000s, feminist teachers pointed to a "natural affinity" between what was then largely called "women's studies" and service-learning: the method grew out of the same desire to address social inequalities that feminist pedagogy represents (Evans, Ozer, and Hill 2006; Washington 2000; see also Butin 2006b). In "Feminist Social Projects," Webb, Cole, and Skeen explain, "current debates in both areas study power relations.... Current examples of service-learning... [are] based in theories of activism that analyze power relations (as feminist theories do) *and* work to change current structures" (2007, 241). And as Mary Trigg and Barbara Balliet note, a central tenet of service-learning is that it teaches students "what it means to be citizens in a democratic society" (2000, 87). They add, "advocates of service-learning hope it will contribute to creating new generations of citizens who understand the way government [and, I would add, institutions and power] works, and who will feel and act on their sense of responsibility to their communities" (87). More specifically, service-learning and feminist pedagogies both strive for collaboration and non-hierarchical relationships, and both stress collective action rather than individualism (90).[6]

As I have explained elsewhere (Muzak 2011), while I appreciate these aspirations for service-learning, and I do think that both service-learning and WGS have transformative potential, my motivations for incorporating service-learning into my intro classes were more modest. I see service-learning as an opportunity for WGS students to understand the diversity of gendered experiences more fully; to develop a deeper understanding of the ways in which gender roles have had an impact on the life choices available to women; the ways in which gender intersects with racialized identities, ethnicity, class, ability, and sexuality; and then, ideally, to envision and engage in strategies that lead to social change. My broadest pedagogical goal is to have students learn how to revise theoretical frameworks on the basis of experience (Imagining America n.d.; Muzak 2011). Nonetheless, at the risk of re-inscribing the much-criticized separation between academic feminism and feminist political activism, I do hope that the women-centred non-profit organizations the course was paired with for the service-learning component offered students a chance to enact or witness feminist praxis and activism.

I always offered the CSL component as an option in my intro courses. Community placements were organized by the university's Community Service-Learning Program, which also arranged a meeting between instructors and community partners to discuss expectations before the semester began. Reflecting on these meetings as I wrote this chapter, I realized that, although I prepared for them by familiarizing myself with the organizations' missions and programs, I was never concerned with having the organizations demonstrate a feminist analysis of their programs or articulate an overarching feminist mandate.[7] Community partners, between five and eight per term, visited the classroom at the beginning of the course to introduce their organizations and projects. On average, about half of the class participated in the CSL option.

Service-learning placements usually involve a specific project or program (as opposed to generalized tasks like administrative support). I'll provide a couple of examples and then move into analysis of the outcomes.

Example 1

Students worked as child care assistants at an organization for pregnant and parenting teens. One student began to reflect on how often she heard the young mothers talking about the discrimination and sometimes abuse they faced in their dealings with doctors and nurses. For the final course assignment, she wrote a kind of working paper—a document that could be the beginning of a formal policy analysis—intended to help health care professionals better understand the pressures and discrimination teenage mothers experience, and then went on to write a report on how medicalized birthing procedures could be less negative for young mothers. In effect, she produced a document to help the organization advocate for policy change in the health care industry.

Example 2

Students worked with immigrant women to produce a cookbook as a fundraiser. The immigrant women got to practise their oral and written English by providing an accompanying story of why they chose the recipe; their ethnic and maternal traditions were acknowledged, validated, and enjoyed by other women, including the students; and the organization raised much-needed (albeit modest) funds.

Example 3

Students worked with an organization that prepared women for employment in non-traditional careers—namely, the trades. The organization also provided limited housing for women and their children while the women were in training. WGS students were tasked with researching opportunities to promote the organization's affordable housing, and with helping to reach out to potential students for the trades training. Students found the task too ambiguous; after basic orientation, the staff did not have time to teach them enough about the organization and its needs to be helpful. Moreover, students discovered that there was already a waiting list for the organization's housing and no shortage of potential applicants for the training.

In terms of feminist pedagogy, praxis, and activism, these scenarios yielded mixed results. It is sometimes difficult to convince students who are frustrated with their placements that they are actually learning something relevant to the course. This is, of course, where classroom learning comes in. Students in example 3 began their placements believing that the organization's mandate to help women gain employment in non-traditional careers was inherently feminist. Once they realized that the organization was too occupied with administrative tasks to supervise them properly, and we began in class to talk about sexism, the wage gap, occupational segregation, and so on, they began to ask questions: Was helping women find employment in these traditionally masculine jobs enough? What about the sexism they would invariably face on the job? Was it the organization's responsibility to advocate for better working conditions for women in the industry (for example, anti-harassment training and policies, wage equity, better maternity benefits, etc.)? These questions resonated in the classroom but not in students' placements with the organization, at least not during this particular semester.

Not surprisingly, as an interviewee told me, this organization was hesitant to explore advocacy that was not directly related to the provincial and federal governments' goals of "economic security." This emphasis on employment is a hallmark of the neoliberal mindset, where paid work is framed as a means to responsible behaviour and citizenship (Baker Collins et al. 2011, 299). This organization also received significant funding from corporations, and as an interviewee remarked, fear of losing funding meant that the organization worked to conform to funders' expectations, and funders wanted to see only information about what percentage of women who completed training were gainfully employed and in which sectors. This fear and the pressure to change mandates to match funders' expectations (and ideologies) are common in the non-profit sector (Drevland 2007), and I think that these circumstances do, in fact, decrease the probability that WGS students will witness and/or participate in feminist praxis and activism during their service-learning placements. In this particular case, I worried the students learned that social services provision is primarily a means to help women "meet their citizenship obligations to join the labour market" (Baker Collins et al. 2011, 303).

The organization does not have to be one explicitly centred on women's employment for students to learn this lesson, however. In my second example, where students worked with immigrant women to develop a cookbook as a fundraiser, they noticed that many of the women who accessed the services of the centre were also volunteers there. In fact, for many women, volunteering at the centre was their first work experience in Canada, and it was meant to help them secure paid work. In a sense, the organization helped newcomers to Canada become market citizens—"autonomous individual[s] whose receipt of short-term assistance is expected to lead to self-sufficiency" (Baker Collins et al. 2011, 299).

But, as students were quick to point out, the immigrant women's cookbook project also encouraged contributors and students alike to challenge stereotypes about ethnicity, religion, and class. Women who came from diverse ethnic and class backgrounds shared similar stories about how they learned to make a favourite dish, often with their mothers, aunts, and grandmothers. Shared experiences were unexpectedly discovered through food, and their stories and recipes destabilized barriers of ethnicity and religion that visibly divided women before the project. One student suggested that this kind of interaction was "at least potentially activist" because it revealed some of the factors that created social and cultural inequalities and discrimination. Collaboratively authoring a cookbook may not have been a deliberately feminist activist strategy, meant to bring about gender equality and structural change in society, but this project helped to build relationships based on connection (across difference), and students recognized these relationships as politically important. In turn, they repeatedly characterized the work of this organization as feminist, although they also admitted that the organization itself and its clients might not see (or at least openly describe) their work and the cookbook project that way. No one remarked on the organization's need or desire to produce a marketable product (arguably, a hallmark of neoliberalism) or even on the organization's need to fundraise, and we did not discuss the necessity of fundraising in class that term. What has stayed with me about this project is how powerfully students felt the women's connections to one another through their stories of food and the sharing of recipes. Students suggested that working within the conventionally feminine, domestic domain of food preparation and nurturance allowed the organization to perform a kind of stealth feminism. That is, they saw the act of a diverse group of women uniting to share meaningful parts of their cultures as the first, crucial step toward understanding and working for common goals. In short, food provided a guise for potential feminist organizing.

This organization also offered English conversation classes where discussions often focused on how to navigate various bureaucracies and everyday activities like grocery shopping. Several students who worked in the English conversation classes characterized these discussions as moments of feminist activism. A couple students likened these classes to consciousness-raising. This is a space where women realize that many of the difficulties they are facing as newcomers to Canada are not individual problems but instead rooted in larger structural forces, including sexist, racist, and classist policies and practices. In class, students' discussions of these experiences helped us cultivate a better understanding of intersectionality. The students' description of the English classes as "consciousness-raising" also raised the question of what constitutes activism. I suggested that the English classes might be appropriately called consciousness-raising if the group's realization of the "commonality and causes of oppression" led to some kind of political action (Bickford and Reynolds 2002, 239). The students who were working with the immigrant women in these conversation classes were not convinced that gaining this insight was "activist enough," at least for now. A student reminded me how profoundly strange it was for one woman to have to buy winter coats and boots for her children because she had never experienced a Canadian winter. It was not that students conceptualized the daily struggles of being a newcomer to Canada as impediments to feminist activism; it was more that they began to recognize how different social positionalities influence social structures, which I consider an important achievement in the intro course.

A few final remarks about the first example describing the student who, as part of her in-class work, produced a report that could help the organization advocate for policy change in birthing procedures and general treatment of pregnant teens and young mothers: from a pedagogical perspective, this report exemplified successful service-learning, as the student brought feminist theory to a problem she identified in the organization, a problem she also recognized as structural. She provided a sophisticated analysis of the problem and then recommended concrete actions that could be taken to make a real difference in the lives of young mothers. It was one of the finest examples of feminist praxis linked to a service-learning placement I have seen—or at least, it had the potential to be. As I generally do, I encouraged the student to share her final project with the organization. The organization did not want anything to do with the report. They objected to the criticism of caregivers and health care providers as sexist. They upheld the medical model as the best birthing model for all women. The student's supervisors had no interest in the kind of advocacy and activism that she had offered; and, yet, wanting students to use their service-learning placements to enact feminist praxis, I had encouraged her to produce exactly this kind of work.

I use this example not to criticize the organization or to suggest that my academic approach is superior to or more appropriate than the organization's, but to demonstrate an important disjuncture that can happen when we incorporate service-learning into our curricula. Overall, I think this placement served the student well; she was upset by her supervisors' response, but she stood by the report and the need for feminist activism in the organization and used parts of the report in her application to a midwifery program. I add this last bit of information hesitantly with a recognition that one of the most common critiques of service-learning is that it serves the student first and meets demand for higher education to provide "practical" or "transferable" skills, skills for the workplace. So how to respond to this well-taken critique?

The constraints of the neoliberal restructuring of the non-profit sector and the Canadian government's attitude toward women's advocacy at the time were particularly felt in this scenario. This organization serves pregnant teens— some of the most vulnerable women in our society. In a country and at a time when the federal government was demonstrating thinly veiled contempt for a woman's right to control her body, disdain for gender equality, and indifference to violence against women, this organization, we might imagine, had to (or at least appear to) toe the government's line. Moreover, with its mandate to help pregnant teens, its services are closely tied to medicine, an institution that largely upholds the neoliberal idea of individualized citizenship, in part by conceptualizing health issues as individual problems. This WGS student was implicitly asking this organization to link its service provision to larger political questions about a woman's right to control her body, the implications of sexism, and the pathologization of pregnancy, but the organization's inability or unwillingness to recognize and acknowledge these connections in their work can be seen as a symptom of the political climate it works within and the pressures of neoliberalism.

Service-Learning, WGS, and Anti-Feminist Political Climates

At the beginning of this chapter, I asked if praxis-learning in WGS curricula represents a possible intervention in anti-feminist political climates, and if service-learning helps re-politicize the work of women's non-profit organizations. When service-learning helps students make the leap from understanding issues as individual problems to understanding them as socio-structural issues (Parkins 2014; see also Parkins in this volume), as I believe it did in at least two of my examples (at the immigrant women's centre and the organization for pregnant teens), service-learning has the *potential* to intervene in anti-feminist political climates in some small but significant way, and it may re-politicize the work of women's organizations *in students' minds*, if not in the infrastructure of the organization (see also Gotell in this volume). In the classroom, I need to make more space to explore these questions—that is, to contextualize and politicize the work women's community organizations are doing and have done in Canada, so that service-learning students see themselves as part of a history of feminist activism and understand the current context of social services provision. For fear of being accused of indoctrinating students, I did not discuss at any length in class the Harper government's record of silencing women's non-profit organizations, for example. Yet this political context does affect how students make sense of and value their experiences in their service-learning placements, and community partners recognize that it affects the work of the organization. Collaborating more closely with community partners to understand how they are responding to the challenges of neoliberal restructuring of the non-profit sector and the "advocacy chill" could also deepen students' experiential learning. Another question to bring to class would be an analysis of how this context may be changing under the new Liberal government.

The restructuring of the non-profit sector to conform to neoliberalism and the federal government's changes to funding criteria have, without a doubt, severely limited the capacity of women's organizations to advocate, and this does have pedagogical implications for our students, but it does not mean that students are unable to witness or enact feminist praxis in their service-learning placements. It does mean that sometimes our desires or intentions for them to enact feminist praxis in these organizations are not fulfilled, but that's an important lesson too. One of the benefits of service-learning is that students' experiences in their placements become a kind of text inside the classroom, where we can explore what it means today to enact feminist praxis and activism and, moreover, expect it to be enacted in the non-profit sector.

Notes

1 The political activity audit was announced in March 2012 as a two-year, $8-million program, but was expanded in April 2013 to a five-year, $13.4-million program (Beeby 2014). See also Broadbent Institute 2014 and Kirkby 2014b.

2 Whether or not the non-profit sector as a whole has ever been an effective space of resistance is debatable, although the characterization of the non-profit sector as working for social change is a dominant one. Even critics who recognize the non-profit sector as a shadow state (Wolsh 1989, 1990; Gilmore 2009), or refer to the non-profit industrial complex (see INCITE! 2009; Mananzala and Spade 2008), hold out hope for non-profit organizations as sites of resistance or what Amara Pérez calls "a movement-building culture" (2009, 93). Early community service-learning literature largely represents the non-profit sector as a space of resistance, to support the argument that

service-learning too can be transformational—for the student, the school, the state, and the world (see Butin 2007). Arguably the most popular and longest-standing criticism of the non-profit sector has been that it is built on a charity model in which those with power determine how best to address the problems of those without (Morton 1995). Similarly, one of the most common criticisms of service-learning is that it is "too often infused with the volunteer ethos, a philanthropic or charitable viewpoint that ignores the structural reasons to help others" (Bickford and Reynolds 2002, 230). Certainly, all of these criticisms are at stake when we use service-learning as an experiential pedagogy in the WGS classroom.

3 "Unwittingly" was initially meant to characterize the students. Upon reflection, however, I realized that I was perhaps nearly as unwitting as the students when I began incorporating CSL into my courses. As a newly minted Ph.D., I was looking for innovative ways to engage students and to expand my understanding of feminist pedagogies and feminist issues in health care and social service provision. Although I had a cursory knowledge of the context that I sketch here, it was only when I took up a position as a postdoctoral fellow in CSL in 2008 that I began to consider more substantially how this context was affecting students' experiences. As my knowledge of the non-profit sector grew, I incorporated discussion of these contexts into the classroom. Sometimes these conversations felt awkward—like appendices meant only for students who were participating in the CSL component, or, worse still, like partisan indoctrination.

4 Tim Brodhead (2010) convincingly argues that the non-profit sector has long used "business" and marketing strategies without compromising their broader social goals.

5 Permission to paraphrase material from the informal interviews has been obtained from students via email. Efforts have been made to anonymize their experiences. However, for one student who might be identifiable, I obtained permission to include discussion of her experiences after sharing a draft of the chapter.

6 Whether WGS and CSL have a "natural affinity" is debatable and depends on one's understanding of the history and goals of both WGS and CSL. For discussions of the affinities and disjunctions between the two in the US context, see Trigg and Balliet 2000; Washington 2000; Evans, Hozer, and Hill 2006; Webb, Cole, and Skeen 2007; Brubriski and Semaan 2009; and Butin 2006a. When I began incorporating CSL into my WGS classrooms, I certainly recognized some affinity between the two—namely in their efforts to provide students with tools to create a political vision of a more just world.

7 In fact, I sometimes felt that using terms such as "feminist pedagogy" and "activism" unsettled community partners, and I likely tried to downplay the feminist work of the course. This is an unsettling realization for me now, particularly because of the emphasis on feminism(s) inside the classroom and my

instruction to CSL students to explore how feminism was or was not working in their organizations. I maintain that the partnering organizations do not need to be explicitly feminist to work well with the course, but some conversation between the instructor, students, and partnering organizations about how feminism(s) is at play or at stake in their organizations would probably be productive for everyone.

CHAPTER FOUR

THERE'S MORE THAN ONE WAY TO SAVE A BABY: NAVIGATING ACTIVISM AND ANTI-RACISM

SARITA SRIVASTAVA

I begin my social justice practicum course with a story about a river. Credited to legendary community organizer Saul Alinsky, the story tells of a crisis situation: we suddenly encounter a seemingly never-ending stream of babies floating down a river.[1] It is not clear how they ended up in the river, but the stream of babies continues at the same alarming rate, and the babies are in imminent danger. If they are not rescued from the river, they will surely perish downstream. Yet one person can carry only two or three babies in their arms at a time. At the end of the story, I ask the students: "You are standing on the riverbank—*what would you do?*"

I have now been teaching university students about social justice, social theory, and anti-racism for almost fifteen years.[2] When I first started teaching, I used the river story as it was first intended and is still often used by community educators—to vividly illustrate the differences between social service work and social change work. I hoped the story would encourage students to think about tackling the root of a problem, rather than managing it in the short term. Students grapple with the dilemma that while jumping in the river to grab armloads of babies saves a few of them, many more will continue down the river to their death. More importantly, rescuing individual babies does nothing to determine the underlying reason for why these babies are dying, or to remedy the fundamental causes of the problem. The river story is meant to highlight the importance of structural change over the band-aid fix—and to reinforce the importance of activism over service.

Teaching about social justice through community-based praxis learning has taught me, however, that there are a variety of legitimate ways to respond to and learn from this story. Rather than use the river story simply as a powerful parable, I began to use it as a spark to ignite discussion at the beginning of the course. Working in small groups, students were asked to approach the river story as a problem-solving exercise. I was initially surprised by the emotional intensity of students' responses to this story. Confronting this admittedly unsubtle parable for the first time, most of the students are stunned by their heart-wrenching predicament—they do not take it up lightly or abstractly. They are clearly invigorated by the discussion. More importantly, they come up with creative solutions and take the exercise beyond the either/or dilemma. They realize they do not have to confront the crisis alone, and ask: is there some way we could work together? Are there some creative solutions that allow us to jump in to rescue babies *and also* work collectively to stop the flow of babies?

The river exercise also allows some students to assert that their place is on the front lines, doing crisis and intervention work. Although they support long-term, structural approaches to challenging injustice, they feel they are better suited to front-line service work. Used in this way, the exercise not only challenges a simple service versus activism divide, but also situates participants as the thinkers and actors that they need to be in order to make a difference. In confronting the river dilemma, they not only begin to assert themselves as actors, but also to assert their own place in a social justice struggle.

My students' own responses to this story, and their innovative and creative projects, have enabled me to see the river story in a new light. I now view this story as a framework for learning about social justice through community engagements that are necessarily framed by creativity, ongoing reflection, theorizing, and discussion about how to navigate the continual ethical and practical dilemmas of social justice work. Using the river story as a starting point, my practicum seminar encourages students to develop their own approaches to activism and service, and centres the students as activists and theorists. The river exercise immediately galvanizes the students into placing themselves in the position of the active, engaged doer and thinker, rather than the passive learner. Challenging the activism versus service divide, my practicum seminar encourages students to find their own place and create their own project. It supports both original activist projects and more conventional service work, placing minimal structure, guidance, or frameworks on these projects. Creative and independent pursuits inevitably produce some messiness and angst, but these are ideal starting points for reflection and learning.

A social justice practicum course requires one to navigate not only these tensions between service and activism but also the tensions between multiculturalism and anti-racism. Indeed, critiques of service work are, to some extent, echoed by critiques of multiculturalism. Just as service work is criticized for failing to challenge the foundations of social inequality, multicultural approaches may encourage diversity but fail to challenge the structural foundations of racial inequality. By representing Canada as a country that values and celebrates ethnic difference, critics charge that multicultural discourse may submerge more critical discussions of racism. Activists and scholars who reject empty multicultural celebrations of diversity look instead to anti-racist and intersectional theory and practice. In practice, however, even where anti-racism is an explicit goal, liberal multiculturalism often provides a historical, institutional, and funding framework within many organizations and communities. The result can be a hybrid of multiculturalism and anti-racism, a complex interaction that often dampens anti-racist efforts, but sometimes also provides the wedge to open a space for more critical anti-racist change (see Srivastava 2007). Course readings and discussions that introduce students to these constraints of anti-racist practice then prompt them to reflect on how their work both reinforces and troubles the multiculturalist impulses of cultural exchange. In this chapter, I offer some examples of how students traverse these tensions (see also Margot Francis' and Ilya Parkins' chapters in this volume).

My experience in the classroom has taught me much about how to navigate these political and intellectual hierarchies. Nothing has prepared me for the diversity of responses students have not only to this story but also to the practice of social justice. I am continually awed and inspired by the work that my students produce, their connections to one another, the support and community they cultivate within the seminar, and the careful, critical analysis and theorizing they produce from reflections on their own projects. Whether students are creating independent documentaries, starting organizations, writing children's books, starting magazines, or volunteering at a soup kitchen or church, their final papers are a space for them to bring together theory, practice, and reflection, producing insights on contemporary social justice work. In this chapter, I outline some of the principles that shape my social justice practicum, describe the seminar design, and use examples from my own students' work[3] to demonstrate how they traverse the tensions between service and activism work and between multiculturalism and critical anti-racist theory.

"Doing Time" Is Not Enough

While many of us are concerned that our scholarship, activism, and pedagogy should be framed by an awareness of the structural foundations of social inequality, community-based praxis learning is often criticized for its heavy emphasis on community service and volunteerism. These tensions between activism and service are acutely highlighted within the institutional and temporal limitations of a twelve-week university course. Community service is how many students carry out their field projects, particularly since volunteer positions established in local organizations are a common way for instructors to organize community-based placements.

As other contributors to this collection have argued, concerns about service models of education should be taken seriously, particularly in a climate where "volunteerism" (Bickford and Reynolds 2002, 230) has become a central cog in the neoliberal machine (see also Joanne Muzak's, Amber Dean's, and Lise Gotell's chapters in this volume). As community services continue to be cut, individual contributions of time and money are often promoted as replacements for government funding (King 2004). Bonnie Zimmerman goes further to suggest if community-based learning emphasizes volunteerism, then it also may be reinforcing the neoliberal trend by "taking on some of the work that used to be considered the responsibility of the state" (2002, 188). Speaking about the "pitfalls" of community service, Forbes et al. also observe that it can "devolve into a cultural safari into the jungle of 'otherness'" (1999, 158). The moralism and racial innocence implicit in the "helping the less fortunate" approach also underlies my concerns with the volunteer placement as a form of education and community engagement (see Srivastava 2005; Heron 2007).

There are, in other words, a number of pitfalls within community work that activists, students, and educators need to navigate:

- "Volunteerism," or simply putting in volunteer hours without deeper engagement, learning, or commitment to social justice.
- Helping others without reflecting on our own relationship to them, or on the conditions of structural inequality.
- A "feel-good" impulse, one which we can find in both service and activism, and one which reinforces our sense of moral superiority, the sense that we are more enlightened or more radical.

So although I use the river story as an exploratory exercise, allowing students to place themselves at various locations on the riverbank, or on the spectrum of service and activism, I avoid steering students toward volunteerism. While they may decide to volunteer in an organization, I try to organize the course so that they are not just "doing time." By "doing time" I mean putting in a few hours of volunteer time at an organization, feeling good about it, and calling it a day—without developing a critical understanding of institutions, social inequalities, histories, and strategies for challenging the way things are. But how are we to navigate around these caveats?

Rigid dichotomies should be avoided. Divisions between service versus activism and community versus student flatten many of the complexities of social justice work, especially within the practicum seminar. For one, placing service work within the historical context of social movement organizing challenges this dichotomy. What may appear as service work—volunteering at a shelter or clinic, for example—exists today only as the result of a long, activist struggle. Secondly, many of the sites and practices that we should include in social justice activism—including writing, cultural production, community-building, and so on—may or may not be linked to conventional activist or community groups. Reinforcing a division between service and activism prevents students from valuing the diversity of practices that contribute to social justice. If the organizing principle is social justice, rather than any particular practice or mode or framework—"community" or "service" or "activism"—then we not only avoid the activism versus service trap, we also widen the scope of student activity to a greater diversity of creative, innovative, and everyday practices.

In his recent book, *Liberating Service Learning*, Randy Stoeker (2016) argues that service-learning should not be student-centred or learning-centred, as it often is, but community-centred. In his view, a conventional approach to learning, which allows for failure, experimentation, and mistakes, is not appropriate for community-based learning. According to Ellen Wexler (2016), Stoeker's book argues that "communities are not places to make mistakes." He illustrates with a metaphor, comparing service learning to firefighting: if firefighters fought fires the way we treat service-learning, then it would be irrelevant if those fires were put out. It would matter only if the firefighters learned something (see Wexler 2016). A striking, if flawed, metaphor; through it, Stoeker points out that students are often sent into communities without sufficient training, precisely because we want them to gain that training "in the field." Stoeker's distinction, then, is not between service-learning and activism, but rather between service-learning that serves the student, and service-learning that genuinely benefits the community. He raises important ethical questions and is right to ask universities to account for whether students are doing good or harm when they are sent into communities. His critique prompts us to ask: is a community better or worse off after the students have left it?

These are important questions, and I share Stoeker's concerns. For example, what is the effect of a required service component in a course that otherwise does not address the ethics, politics, theory, and history of social movements? However, unlike Stoeker, I orient the social justice practicum toward learning and theory rather than around immediate community benefits. What can I teach these students, and how can I guide them through a rigorous theoretical and practical learning experience? How might this experience make them more likely to engage with social justice work in the future? I see the contribution of the students as best assessed within a longer time frame—in terms of their future contributions, whether or not they end up in careers related to social justice or community development; whether they take away the skills to make a difference; experience building a feeling of community with other students committed to social justice and activism; and gain a knowledge of histories of change, the successes and the obstacles to change, and of theories of social movements and inequality and intersectionality. Certainly, many students do produce something of service to the community within a few weeks of a practicum seminar, but we have to assess benefits to the community with broad, reasonable, and long-term criteria.

Unlike firefighting, working for social justice is not a clearly defined task with a measurable outcome, nor one that necessarily requires a high degree of technical training and equipment. Despite its risks and messiness, finding one's own way through social justice practice is the only way any activist develops skills, connections, and experience. Most activists begin with a passionate desire to make a difference, and we learn through jumping in and getting involved, often with the help of mentors. Every year I am fortunate to teach a seminar for students who feel a passionate desire to make a difference. This needs to remain a starting point. I argue for a student-centred model—one that does not prioritize student over community, but rather recognizes that the best way we can serve the long-term cause of community-based social justice work is to focus on an inspiring, practical, and theoretical learning experience for students. Tammy Lewis' comment on her own university's community-based learning program is helpful here: "if the goal is community transformation and social justice, at least in the short run, the program is a failure. If the goal is student learning, the program is a success" (2004, 95). In my experience, where students are offered the latitude to develop creative projects, they critically navigate these poles of service, activism, university, and community with aplomb.

Often we are caught in an all-or-nothing analysis of our pedagogical strategies: if we are not rigorous enough then we are pandering, diluted, and anemic; if we are not critical and radical enough, then we are co-opted, neoliberal training institutes. I do not take these debates lightly, but I believe that it is precisely within the practicum course where students have the potential to creatively move beyond these dichotomies. However, the structure of the seminar must encourage a genuine attention to creativity, theoretical engagement, and on-going discussion within a supportive seminar environment.

Notions of "Community" versus "Student"

Many assessments of the success and failure of community-based learning rest on this central dichotomy, which pitches the imagined needs of "the community" against student learning. "The community" is often used to refer to a group separate from and usually unknown to the students, which students are sent into. Stoeker's concern about harm to communities arises from this imagined dichotomy between community and student. In my own practicum course, however, students often choose to work with organizations or create projects that are linked either to their own university community or to communities they are already active within. For example, one of the first practicum projects I supervised fifteen years ago involved a student who started a support group for queer youth of colour—a community she herself had once been involved in building. Another of my students was successful in creating a new scholarship for incoming students in the sexual diversity program; several other students have started new projects within campus groups working on anti-racism, sexual health, the Slutwalk, and so on.

Several years ago, two students carried out a striking project that researched the Queen's Women's Studies department itself. By the end of their project, they had successfully changed the name of the department. Using student surveys and an analysis of the department, their activist intent was to challenge the very framing of "women's studies" as a department and discipline. They used their research results to write a proposal arguing that the name, framing, and mission of "women's studies" did not reflect contemporary students, theories, and politics. At the end of the course, they were invited to present their results and proposal at a departmental meeting. At the very same meeting a motion was passed to change the name of the department to Gender Studies. Changing the name from "Women's Studies" had been long debated and fiercely contested, with a minority of department members arguing that the oppression of "women" as a group needed to remain a core disciplinary principle. While a majority of departmental members agreed that the department name needed to reflect contemporary theories of gender, change had not been possible without these students' activism.

All these projects trouble the implicit framing of students as outside "the community" and as potential burdens or sources of harm to communities. I am not dismissing the potential for harm to happen, nor the importance of ethical conduct. Instead, I approach the social justice practicum by framing instructors, students, and activists as learners who are already connected to various communities. If we take this approach, we might move away from the notion that we need to send students "into" communities to learn about others, and toward the notion that we are together learning more about how to build communities, connections, and creative paths to social justice (see also Amber Dean's chapter in this volume).

Indeed, one of the most striking aspects of the seminar has been the activist community that has been created among the students themselves. This past semester, the formation of an activist community became increasingly important to students, and an aspect of the course most students commented on. In the last class, many said they had not expected to create a community through attending a course, and they were struck by the experience of connecting with other activists on campus and receiving support for their own passionate causes.

A central tool in this effort was the course Facebook page, which I encourage students to create at the beginning of the course. For today's activist communities, Facebook groups and other online forums are a significant form of information, support, and community. As some students have noted in their papers, it is important to be mindful of "slacktivism," or substituting Facebook "likes" for activism. However, online connections contribute to meaningful feelings and practices of community, connection, and support, particularly for these students. Students may share the progress of their projects, post a finished documentary, link to a blog or online forum they have created, or share information and resources to help other students in their projects. It is clear that students have truly valued the support, sense of community, and knowledge that there are others in the university who care about activism online. I see the social justice practicum course as a place to continually cultivate these connections and contradictions between students and activists, universities and communities, and activism and service.

Rejecting the Field Placement Model

Often community-based praxis types of courses are modeled on what I call a "field placement" approach to community service learning. The instructor contacts or identifies a number of local organizations willing to take on volunteers. The students work for several hours a week in one of these organizations and write a report on their experiences. The advantages are control, expediency, and efficiency: the instructor, university, and community retain more control of what the students are doing, and little to no effort is required by the student to find or create a project. This approach makes sense in a program with the end goal of professional competence in the field: it finds students an appropriate work experience "placement" or "internship" so that they can get practical work experience and professional contacts. I rejected this model.

I have abandoned the "field placement" or "co-op" model because I found that it can limit creativity and support bland volunteerism, precisely because it does not sufficiently challenge students to find their own way to a practice of social justice. When placements are already organized for them, students do not have an opportunity to reflect on what they want to do, nor to act in ways that are not organizationally and institutionally based, and they have no chance to create new organizations. They also do not have an opportunity to understand the structural constraints of volunteerism: managing and training volunteers takes time and resources from organizations, and many are not as grateful as students might have expected. Organizations may not even have the time and staff to return students' emails. Exploration, openness, and creativity produce both beautiful projects and the possibilities of failure. My hope is that educators will encourage freedom to explore and create, and that students will take risks. Organizations that don't call back, school boards that block access, funding that doesn't come through—these are invaluable learning experiences about the institutional context of social justice that the student who takes a pre-arranged field placement avoids.

Bickford and Reynolds suggest that if we want to reclaim the "activist potential" of these courses, we should combine "critical consciousness with action and reflection," and encourage students to "envision themselves as actors" (2002, 230). If we take this approach, then a social justice practicum has the best chance of success when it is centred first around student learning, without expectations of "empowering the community." I believe a practicum course is most likely to be effective on these terms, however, if students have the freedom to direct or create their own projects and the space to theorize their own practice. This freedom and space are gained only when we abandon the "field placement" or "co-op" model. If we are going to produce students who are able to contribute to social justice, then we also need to help them cultivate the skills and knowledge that they will need to not only imagine a different world but also create the ways of getting there. We need to make the time and space for their imagination to thrive.

My practicum assignment allows students wide latitude. I suggest that they may volunteer within an existing organization, project, or initiative, or choose to plan or create an entirely new organization, publication, manifesto, scholarship, community initiative, and so on. In choosing their projects, I tell my students to ask themselves, "What will I contribute in terms of change?" and "What will I learn or contribute in terms of knowledge about organizing, advocacy, social change, and organizations?" There are only two criteria for choosing their project: it must be linked to social justice, and it must be community- or collectively-focused, although it does not necessarily need to be undertaken collectively. Their project might be based in an existing community (within or outside the university), be involved in creating a new community, or in speaking to a community. We discuss in class how we might define social justice and notions of community, but ultimately it is up to them to define and defend their project on these terms. However, they are primarily evaluated through their final essay, which must reflect an *integration* between their practical experience and theorizing.

In rejecting the field placement model, I am not discounting the value of service work, nor am I discouraging students from volunteering in a service organization, or even from devoting their lives to service work. Rather, my ambition is to cultivate a seminar environment, course assignments, and a classroom community that:

- Encourages students to figure out their own relationship to social change work: Where and how can they be most effective? Which skills do they want to develop? Where do they most want to act?
- Supports innovative projects that go outside of established organizations;
- Encourages creativity and cultural production;
- Encourages a critical perspective on the hierarchies of activism over service;
- Embraces the messiness, lack of perfection, and disjuncture between the theories and our practice;
- Uses seminar discussions, journal writing, and a final essay as a way of critically analyzing our practice in relation to theory and scholarship, using our own practice as a starting point for our own theorizing;
- Emphasizes that theory is not only something we read, but something we produce—theorizing is a *practice* we must engage in (Charlotte Bunch's [1987] model of theory-building is useful here).

Despite myriad constraints, students find creative ways to interpret both activism and service, gain a deeper understanding, and hone and contribute their skills and insights. I have been profoundly impressed and inspired by the passionate, creative, and arts-based projects that my students accomplished within a matter of weeks. One of the most impressive was the student who announced during the first class in September that she wanted to start a social justice theatre company. By March, Holly had founded a theatre company called *Acts of Resistance*, acquired funding and actors, collectively wrote a play and mounted a free production (Molaski 2016). Another student who was very passionate about challenging menstrual taboos produced a short documentary and used it in workshops with youth.[4] And the most unusual project, one that garnered a fair bit of attention online, was the production by two students of Cat Comics. They created an original series of graphic vignettes starring a cat that advocates feminist, anti-racist, and post-colonial theory with sly wit and style—including vignettes entitled "Intersectionality video game," "Cat colonialism," and "Cat performativity."[5]

When students create their own projects, we can most clearly see that the lines between service and activism, student and community, are not sharply drawn. Gillian's project grew out of her involvement with the United Church Sunday school—on the surface a fairly traditional project. Her aim, however, was to participate in a project of decolonization by turning the manicured lawns of the church into spaces to produce community-grown food. In designing her project, she aimed not only to teach community children how to grow food but also to challenge the very structure and purpose of the church as an institution.[6]

The Project Is Not an Endpoint

It is in the final essay that students are able to establish themselves as contributing to social justice as actors, researchers, and theorists. Kathryn, who directed a documentary and held workshops on menstrual taboos, wrote about how her political framing shifted as she more fully considered transgendered bodies, older bodies, and non-white bodies. After giving her first workshop, she began "to think about how being vocal about something that is typically taboo and historically shamed may have different connotations for people who do not identify or have social locations similar to my own. I began to examine the privilege I possess that allows me to be outspoken about a topic that is taboo and receive praise as opposed to receiving violence."[7] Most students' final essays show them to be similarly reflective, thoughtful, and inspired by their practicum experience—even, and perhaps especially, when the experience was not a wholly uplifting one.

Gillian used her essay, which she shared within her church community, to articulate the vision of decolonization that accompanies her community gardening project. She theorized the community garden not simply as a new use for church land or a way to occupy Sunday school children, but also as a profound shift in the way people relate to one another and to community. She argued that the community garden is a way of redirecting resources and funds "into practical tools to engage in decolonization and to embody the calls to action expressed in the truth and reconciliation commission."[8] She wrote,

> Repurposing space for intentional relationship with the earth, like Project Community Garden, can be one of a multiplicity of ways churches can cultivate embodied alternatives to colonized realities. It may help them embrace new structures and expressions of faith outside of the formal institutional constraints of the United Church and provide opportunity to revitalize community vibrancy and intention.[9]

Given her long-standing involvement within the United Church, both her activism and her theorizing will likely continue to make meaningful shifts.

Through an engagement with both practice and theory, and with all of us in the seminar, students develop their own ideas about and their own connection to social justice work. Rather than requiring particular forms of practice or theory, the practicum course should demand reflexivity, theoretical framing, and collective scrutiny. For example, students who volunteered in a local "soup kitchen-restaurant" were initially buoyed by the experience. They loved the concept as well as the feeling that they were serving people as restaurant patrons, and they loved the community. Yet as they progressed through the course, read material on community organizing, social movements, political theory, decolonization, and anti-racism, they also began to reflect on their own place and their own emotions in this process. While praising the organization, one student shared his concerns about the kinds of conversations that occur among the happy volunteers in the soup kitchen-restaurant. He wrote, "routinized conversations that homogenize identity of patrons as 'poor junkies,' or even descriptions in more respectful but equally boxing ways, such as calling them 'people with a messed up life' re-inscribe, and represent narrow assumptions about that marginalized group."[10] He advocated training for all volunteers: "The fact that dangerous, unitary assumptions are ascribed to a plural group of people...shows the necessity for volunteers to be educated, and trained in order to be self-reflexive and critical of their words— harmless as they may seem." Referring to an assigned course reading (Srivastava and Francis 2006) which highlighted the problems with anti-racist and anti-homophobia workshops, he clarified that he is not suggesting education *about* the patrons, but rather suggested that "examining one's own subjectivity through an analytical lens...continually reminding oneself of the...seductiveness of fulfilling a narrative founded in 'helping the poor,'...keeps volunteers reflexive."[11] It is possible that the continued involvement of practicum students could prompt the training that this student proposed; however, he will also carry these practical and analytical skills with him into future work.

Students often end up in a different place than they started, with many of their expectations challenged: they are not able to volunteer where they wanted, or the volunteer jobs are not as glamorous or as fulfilling as hoped, or the creative journey to produce a magazine/organization/documentary is (not surprisingly) difficult and circuitous. Navigating racial politics is one of the more angst-ridden aspects of practicum projects. As I have observed in my own research, efforts to engage with anti-racism often produce highly emotional and moralistic responses, tinged with self-examination and self-beratement (see Srivastava 2005, 2006). Some students experienced moments of doubt, wondering if their own anti-racist work was "good enough." They want to avoid the superficial or harmful efforts of multiculturalism and diversity, which are critiqued in the course material. My own and Jane Ward's (2008) work on anti-racism in organizations, for example, demonstrates that efforts at diversity and anti-racism may not only reinforce normative whiteness but also weigh heavily on participants and staff of colour.

One of my students began the course with the desire to produce a magazine for youth that more fully reflects their diversity. "Every kid deserves to feel represented," as she said.[12] Cecilia came into the class with an idea to "change the world" by leaving theory behind for something more practical: "I was ecstatic to start this course. I had never truly understood theory in the first place, so I was looking forward to focusing on practical applications, making a difference in my community, and essentially, changing the world! Hint, foreshadowing...."[13] As she progressed through the course and read critiques of diversity projects, she began to worry about how she could actually create a "diverse" magazine, particularly one that would avoid an empty celebration of difference. She expressed her initial thoughts in her field notes:

> Am I capable of making a magazine? Why didn't I volunteer with an existing organization? How do I address my privilege? How do I stop engaging in nonracism? Am I overthinking everything? How do I stop overthinking everything? Am I going to fail this class?

Ironically, while she began the course with the belief that she was leaving theory behind in favour of practice, Cecilia took her final essay in a more theoretical direction than most students, drawing on Bourdieu (1977) and Bonilla-Silva (2006) to discuss the concept of "white habitus." Feeling that her magazine project risked being framed by notions of liberalism and non-racism, she began to investigate a different theoretical framework for her work. In the end, she continued to feel strongly about her project, but argued for a magazine that could represent differences among youth and simultaneously attend to the production of white habitus in schools and family.

Confronting very similar tensions among diversity and representation, Rachel and Payal began the course with a desire to write a children's book that subverts conventional fairy tales by integrating queerness, gender and racial diversity, family diversity, disability, community, and solidarity. They ended the course with a draft of their picture book, *Ahana's Journey*, a story that follows a girl and her transgender, trans-species friends as she travels on a journey of artistic discovery and connection. The book itself is an impressive accomplishment, and they plan to donate proceeds from sales of their book to a local family shelter. However, in their essays Rachel and Payal also reflected on the immense difficulties of producing visual representations and narratives of diversity that are not merely "palatable." Rachel expressed some of her concerns with the book she created:

> A central motif of multiculturalism is the concept of a *cultural mosaic*. This concept in itself is contingent upon visuality. Within *Ahana's Journey*, the "happy 'colourful'" faces are Indian, Japanese and Black. Moreover, each of these characters inhabit a unique [physical] environment, which could be interpreted as a unique cultural backdrop. These illustrations, which signal diversity, seem to articulate race as something that is

a visual difference, not a social construction that endows certain bodies with privilege. Ultimately, in an attempt to create a visually engaging text for children, race is taken up in a multiculturally palatable way.[14]

Payal similarly wrote that problems arose as they tried to "get in as many identities as possible." For example, "the sole non-able-bodied character Nagisa was Othered by being left within a terrain on their own [the ocean] while the other two characters, Ahana and Phoenix, were…able to have more explorative roles."[15] Both co-authors remained committed to the project, planning to revise the text to reflect their concerns, but also to create a "toolkit" that would enhance the "pedagogical possibilities" of Ahana's Journey.

The students' own journeys through the practicum may be challenging and even circuitous, but for many it also takes them to unexpected places of learning, reflection, connection, and emotional strength. At the end of the course, Rachel was struck by the unexpected parallels in her own journey and that of Ahana, the main character in Ahana's Journey:

> Ahana and I, separated by reality and fiction, seem to have a few things in common. Both of us have embarked upon journeys to achieve a goal and have enacted our own agency in the process. The two of us also relied on support, from friends and classmates, to achieve this goal. Lastly, Ahana creates a painting to showcase her efforts while I wrote the final essay.[16]

Notes to Students

Many students echo Rachel's experience—the journey takes unexpected turns but brings them moments of insight, strength, or exhilaration. And yet it is also easy for students to falter, to feel alone, or be discouraged. In writing this chapter I have come to reflect more closely on the advice that I might give students or anyone that is contemplating this journey toward social justice and community work. These are a few guideposts I would offer my students as they navigate this challenging terrain:

1 *Abandon perfection, purity, and theoretical consistency. The corollary: Do not fear messiness and anxiety.*

   Whether you are trying to enter an organization or create your own organization, contributing to social justice is a challenging project and the journey will never be as you first envisioned it.

2 *Read what other people have written and listen to other people's ideas and feedback on your work.*

In those moments when things are not turning out as neatly as planned, remember that there are others who have been through this before, others who have either written about the experience or who may be willing to talk to you. Ask yourself: what can I read or who can I talk to help me think through this?

3 *Do not take existing theories and knowledge for granted.*

Read and talk to others, but also ask yourself: how does my own experience add to, challenge, or fill gaps in existing ways of thinking about social justice, communities, and organizing?

4 *The most "successful" projects are often those you have a strong connection to.*

It is always possible to start from scratch and cultivate a connection to a new topic and a new community. However, be realistic about whether you will be able to have the access and resources to do this. For example, while starting an organization in China may seem like an over-ambitious topic, one of my students was from the region in China where she wanted to organize and already had some contacts there. Conversely, one of my students was very excited about initiating a new arts project with youth in the local community but had no existing connections with any young people. She made considerable efforts to contact and recruit youth but had limited success.

5 *Redefine your notions of "success."*

No matter how challenging the journey becomes, you should always be able to answer the question, "What will I have contributed when I am on the other end of this experience?" Time, knowledge, analysis, theorizing? What connections, communities and relationships have I cultivated? What will I have learned? What have I taught others? How will this experience help to shape my future social justice work? What will I do differently next time? What could I teach others who want to do this work?

6 *Recognize the value of setbacks, challenges, and feelings of failure in facilitating deeper learning and theorizing.*

As one student wrote at the conclusion of her essay, "a central lesson to take away from this experience is to remain resilient during activism even when outcomes deviate from expectations.... Instead, it is useful to conceptualize how these issues might be addressed to create a more impactful and transformative result."[17]

Conclusions

Do some students undertake a mechanical "put in my hours" volunteer position? Yes, certainly they do. Do some students falter? Yes. But even in these situations, they are required to write papers that theorize some aspect of their project. They might reflect on why it was so difficult to find a volunteer position, and on how the presence of unskilled volunteers requires precious resources from small organizations. Whatever work they do, most students are also still gaining practical skills through their work, including video production, publishing, web design, and event organizing. Despite the importance of asserting that intellectual training is not the same as job training, we must also create spaces where we may integrate practical activist and organizing skills with theoretical, critical, and analytical learning.

Catherine Orr (2011, 11) suggests that we should be guided by the key principle that community-based learning "produces life-long learners" who continue to engage in "critical inquiry toward social transformation" (see also Orr's afterword in this volume). This is the best measure of the success for any practicum course, and it can be achieved only if we allow students the creativity, joyful connection, and uncertain journey that comes from open exploration of the possibilities for social justice, rather than suggesting volunteer field placements or privileging certain kinds of activist engagement over others. Much better to travel the messy, angsty path that ultimately produces deeper learning and commitment.

An elective practicum seminar draws students who are keenly interested in making a difference. It should support these students in moving toward creative and reflective ways of approaching social justice. If a practicum can accomplish this, then I believe it will have more lasting impact than any field placement. As a seminar progresses it becomes clear that, while I may be in charge of teaching them how to theorize, how to ask difficult questions, and how to practise activism, they are also teaching me, connecting me to their communities, and reminding me that they are the ones who will navigate the future of social justice.

Notes

1   Randall Shelden and Daniel Macallair (2008, 162) recount a similar parable, of people continuously falling down a waterfall, and credit it to Saul Alinsky.

2   I first taught a practicum course at the Institute for Women's and Gender Studies at the University of Toronto in 2003, and have taught one in the Gender Studies Department at Queen's University since 2007. Between fifteen and twenty-five students typically take the class, most of whom are Gender Studies majors. The course was originally a full-year, twenty-four-week course, but like all fourth-year seminars in Gender Studies it was changed to a twelve-week, double-credit course a few years ago. However, I have successfully proposed that the course should return to a twenty-four-week format to allow students more time to develop their practicum projects.

3   It is impossible to convey the range and depth of the diversity and creativity I have seen over the years using the few examples I discuss here. References to student work are taken from unpublished papers that were presented during

the Gender Studies 440 seminar, Social Justice Practicum offered by Queen's University, and are quoted here with permission and thanks. All the authors graduated from Queen's University before they were asked for permission to quote from and reference their work.

4 *Dear Me,* directed by Kathryn Blaikie (Studio Q, Queen's University, 2015), digital video. The documentary can be viewed at https://www.youtube.com/watch?v=SRoNSAqBXKk.

5 *Cat Comics and Feminism,* http://catcomicsandfeminism.tumblr.com.

6 Gillian R. McDonald, "Many Gifts One Spirit Permaculture Learning Circle Project: Alternative Modes of Organization and Relation for Embodied Transformation of Small Churches of the United Church of Canada," paper submitted in fulfilment of the requirements of Gender Studies 440, Social Justice Practicum, Queen's University, Fall 2015 and presented in a GNDS 440 seminar on December 3, 2015. Unpublished manuscript quoted with permission.

7 Kathryn Blaikie, "Just Add Privilege: How Activism Centered in Destigmatizing 'Taboo' Topics Excludes Marginalized Members of the Population, as Demonstrated Through Menstrual Activism," paper submitted in fulfilment of the requirements of Gender Studies 440, Social Justice Practicum, Queen's University, Fall 2015 and presented in a GNDS 440 seminar on December 3, 2015. Unpublished manuscript quoted with permission.

8 McDonald, "Many Gifts One Spirit Permaculture Learning Circle Project," 18.

9 Ibid.

10 Matthew Lumsden, "Martha's Table: Engineering a Trajectory Towards a More Comprehensive Systemic Support," paper submitted in fulfilment of requirements of Gender Studies 440, Social Justice Practicum, Queen's University, Fall 2014 and presented in a GNDS 440 seminar November 2014, 5–6. Unpublished manuscript quoted with permission.

11 Lumsden, "Martha's Table: Engineering a Trajectory Towards a More Comprehensive Systemic Support," 6.

12 Cecilia Wanan, "Liberalism, the beer goggles of theory: the necessity of understanding theory in eradicating racism in Canada," paper submitted in fulfilment of the requirements of Gender Studies 440 *Social Justice Practicum,* Queen's University, Fall 2015 and presented in a GNDS 440 seminar on December 3, 2015, 7. Unpublished manuscript quoted with permission.

13 Wanan, "Liberalism, the beer goggles of theory: the necessity of understanding theory in eradicating racism in Canada," 6.

14 Rachel Oster, "Integrating Theoretical and Practical Knowledge in *Ahana's Journey:* An analysis of tensions between multiculturalism and anti-racism in creative activism," paper submitted in fulfilment of the requirements of Gender Studies 440, Social Justice Practicum, Queen's University, Fall 2015 and presented in a GNDS 440 seminar on December 3, 2015, 7. Unpublished manuscript quoted with permission.

15 Payal Majithia, "An analysis of queerness, sexuality, and disability within *Ahana's Journey,*" paper submitted in fulfilment of requirements of Gender

Studies 440, Social Justice Practicum, Queen's University, Fall 2015 and pre-sented in a GNDS 440 seminar on December 3, 2015, 10. Unpublished manu-script quoted with permission.

16 Rachel Oster, personal communication via email to author, December 21, 2015, quoted with permission.

17 Oster, "Integrating Theoretical and Practical Knowledge in *Ahana's Journey:* An analysis of tensions between multiculturalism and anti-racism in creative activism," 13.

CHAPTER FIVE

COMMUNITY-ENGAGED PEDAGOGY, SEXUAL VIOLENCE, AND NEOLIBERAL GOVERNANCE

LISE GOTELL

In a recent article, Jennifer L. Johnson and Susanne Luhmann (2016) interrogate the long-standing embrace of university practicums by Canadian Women's and Gender Studies (WGS) programs. As the authors observe, feminist praxis-learning has most often been framed as activism for social change. In the context of the neoliberal university, however, practicums are increasingly promoted as enhancing the career readiness of graduates. Johnson and Luhmann are critical of both social change and instrumental rationales for praxis-learning. They contend that the view of community-engaged learning as social change represents a nostalgic feminist longing for an activist past. Yet rather than political activism, community work is very often engaged in managing the status quo. Moreover, when cloaked within rhetoric about skills and employment, praxis-learning concedes too much to neoliberal agendas and current preoccupations with justifying the liberal arts as employment training.

In this chapter, I also explore the contradictions of feminist community-engaged learning within the context of neoliberal governance. However, I argue that it is insufficient to see praxis-learning simply as the outward deployment of feminist teaching and learning beyond the boundaries of the university. Like Nan Alamilla Boyd and Jillian Sandell (2012, 252), I understand feminist praxis-learning as a practice of critical engagement that invites students to reflect on their own experiences, to theorize how community organizations see their work and constituencies, and to interrogate the interconnections between political economy, academia, and community organizations. Here I discuss my own pedagogical encounters with community service-learning (CSL) in a senior seminar course on the topic of feminism and sexual assault. Using the students' own reflections on their community placements written for a class blog, I argue that rather than seeing praxis-learning in WGS as feminist activism, it is more useful to think about how community work provides students with tools for understanding how the landscape of feminist politics has been constrained within a context of neoliberalism. Students' CSL work enables them to cultivate an appreciation of how neoliberal risk management technologies define governmental responses to sexual violence, creating would-be victims who are individually responsible for prevention, thereby obscuring the gender, race, and class power dynamics of sexual violence. In my class, by examining readings that explore the contemporary politics of sexual violence and their on-the-ground experiences working at agencies concerned with sexual assault and exploitation, students develop complex insights about identities, power, and possibilities for resistance in the context of neoliberal governance.

A Senior Seminar on Feminism and Sexual Assault: CSL as Activism or Institutional Ethnography?

I have incorporated a CSL component into my fourth-year WGS seminar several times. Feminism and Sexual Assault interrogates the contemporary construction of sexual violence. It analyzes how, as an effect of neoliberal governance and the rise of post-feminism, sexual violence has been re-privatized. Once constituted a "social problem" and a legitimate object of government intervention, sexual violence has been depoliticized and individualized, increasingly contained within discourses of abstract risk and individuated criminal responsibility (Gotell 2007). The necessity of rethinking a feminist practice of resistance in the present context is a thematic focus of the course. Resistance is a thread that weaves through the course content: the objective of the course, and the question we return to in seminars is "How do we fashion a third wave practice of anti-rape resistance in these challenging times?" Much feminist theorizing on sexual violence conceives of resistance within a limited debate about victimization versus agency that ignores how actions are constrained by power relations. We engage in the project of rethinking resistance through an examination of the strengths and weaknesses of past feminist strategies and by examining core texts posing innovative approaches to anti-rape theorizing and organizing. CSL offers a practice of discovery-learning that encourages crossing boundaries between classroom and communities, creating a dialogue between academic texts and embodied practices that is well suited to this theme of rethinking resistance. The second time that I taught Feminism and Sexual Assault with a CSL component, I obtained a Teaching Innovation Grant from the Community Service-Learning Program.[1] This grant provided funding for research assistance that enabled me to undertake an analysis of a class blog where students reflected on the relationships between course readings, seminars, and their work in Edmonton community organizations.

The context for my course is the well-established Community Service-Learning Program at the University of Alberta. The program works with instructors

COMMUNITY-ENGAGED PEDAGOGY   75

to arrange appropriate community projects, manages instructors' and students' relationships with community mentors, tracks student participation, offers pedagogical advice, and engages in rigorous evaluation. The model of curricular CSL developed by this program engages students in twenty-hour placements constructed as sites of learning, alternative texts, and community laboratories. Instructors are invited to go beyond seeing service-learning as the application of classroom learning by creating conversations between community work and academic texts. There were fifteen students enrolled in my seminar in the year that I undertook the analysis that forms the basis for this chapter (seven WGS majors, three WGS minors, and five other students). The course was partnered with eight organizations that offered placements to these students: three Edmonton and area sexual-assault/anti-violence agencies; one emergency shelter for homeless and transient women; one women's shelter; two sex worker support and outreach agencies; and one national feminist organization.[2]

To be clear, students in my class were doing "volunteer" work. The "service" in service-learning has connotations of traditional charitable work that props up the status quo. Because of this, many feminist scholars recommend a politicization of community-engaged learning (Bojar and Naples 2002, 3). Those who advocate for an activist or social justice approach often construct feminist praxis-learning as a mechanism for repairing the separation between academic feminism and feminist political activism (Bubriski and Semaan 2009; Dugger 2008; Naples 2002a, 2002b). In this view, engaging students in activism for social change becomes an antidote to the seeming de-politicization of WGS, a simple recipe for the de-disciplining of academic feminism (Messer-Davidow 2002; Naples 2002b). I am sympathetic to the argument that academic feminism has become too self-referential and isolated from social activism and materialist analysis. Nevertheless, the insistence that CSL can bridge the widening chasm between the classroom and activism rests on the flawed assumption that feminist political activism exists "out there somewhere" on the other side of the town/gown divide.

A WGS instructor seeking to connect academic knowledge to activism through the mechanism of community-engaged learning confronts serious problems in the context of contemporary Alberta. There are very few community placements that can provide students with experiences of anything clearly identifiable as feminist activism. Instead, students mostly participate in placements within Edmonton's expansive non-profit social service sector. Recently, I chaired a national meeting of feminist-run rape crisis centres and was the only person from Alberta sitting in the room. As many scholars have documented, Canadian feminism has been pushed to the margins of political influence as an effect of neoliberal governance (Brodie 2008; Gotell 2007; Muzak, this volume). Dominant political rationalities privilege self-sufficiency, stigmatizing public provision and claims-making on the basis of social disadvantage. Feminist organizations have been recast as "special interest groups," antithetical to a public good defined in terms of restraint, privatization, and personal responsibility.

This de-legitimization of feminism took a particularly vivid form in Alberta. The radical cuts to social programs and welfare eligibility requirements enacted by the Klein Conservative government in the mid-1990s was the model for neo-liberalization in other jurisdictions. This privatization of social responsibility occurred at a dramatic pace in Alberta, with the non-profit, voluntary sector left to shoulder the burden of social problems and inequality (Harder 2003). Feminist organizations found themselves not only silenced, but also under attack.[3] Gendered social problems like sexual violence were de-gendered and depoliticized. In fact, gender neutrality was adopted as an official policy stance, making it difficult for Alberta anti-violence agencies to draw attention to the power relations that underlie sexual violence. As a result of grants-based funding regimes and a push to professionalize, non-profits that work to address the continued realities of sexual violence and exploitation have been compelled to adopt an individualized and depoliticized lens (Beres, Crow, and Gotell 2009). There have been shrinking spaces for feminist activism and a restrictive emphasis on standardized programming, preventative education, and the provision of "services" to individualized "victims."

While it is certainly true that activism is an elastic category (Orr 2012, 90), WGS students doing placements at Edmonton women's shelters or rape crisis centres are only rarely engaged in anything approximating feminist politics. When I began to teach my course with a CSL component, I was concerned that making "volunteering" a course requirement would reinforce or even endorse the offloading of the social problem of sexual violence onto the non-profit sector—a sector that disproportionately relies upon the unpaid or underpaid work of women. Bonnie Zimmerman has expressed concerns about the role of community engagement within women's and gender studies teaching for precisely this reason. As she argues, the "emphasis...on volunteer activities...may actually reinforce current power structures and relations by taking on some of the work that used to be considered the responsibility of the state" (2002, 188). I worried that volunteering at professionalized rape-crisis centres and women's shelters would teach students more about the management of social problems than about feminist politics or resistance. Inserting students into the non-profit sector as volunteers can have the effect of deflecting energy away from broader social change. As Andrea Smith argues in *The Revolution Will Not Be Funded*, the "non-profit industrial complex" functions as a "shadow state," by providing social services that should be the responsibility of the state and by redirecting protest into service (2007, 8–9).

As I experimented with community engagement in Feminism and Sexual Assault, I began to understand that framing community experiences as activism not only fails to capture the contemporary realities of non-profits working in the field of sexual violence, it also misrepresents what students learn. Nancy A. Naples (2002a) contends that community-engaged learning in the field of WGS should be seen as a pedagogical deployment of Dorothy Smith's institutional ethnographic approach. Community engagement produces knowledge of local practices, expands what becomes visible in the everyday, and helps to map relations between local sites. According to Smith, the social cartographies generated through these explorations "mak[e] visible how we are connected into social ruling relations and the economy," and offer "a guidepost for activist interventions" (1999, 94–95). Instead of viewing community-engaged learning as an experience of activism, it is more fruitful to think about how it engages students in the practice of social mapping. As I demonstrate below, through their on-the-ground experiences and observations, my students come to understand how sexual violence is constructed and managed in the context of the present. Community-engaged learning is a powerful tool for developing concrete insights about the constraints on activism in a context of neoliberalism and can function as a mechanism for rethinking resistance.

Mapping Power Relations: Risk, Vulnerability, and Agency

You cannot teach a course called Feminism and Sexual Assault without grappling with the dichotomized construction of victim/agent that frames much contemporary feminist thinking on rape. Feminist scholarship on rape has come under increasing scrutiny by those who argue that the emphasis on vulnerability to sexual violence literally makes women into victims. This critique has been articulated in thoughtful work by feminist theorists, including by Sharon Marcus (1992) and Renée Heberle (1996). It has also been more publicly articulated by post-feminist writers, including Katie Roiphe (1993), and Camille Paglia (1991), who, as Rebecca Stringer has argued, "clearly couch their critiques of victim feminism as neoliberal celebrations of market individualism" (2013, 152). While these feminist and post-feminist critics are certainly not monolithic—there are substantive differences among them—it is the case that across these texts the broad message has emerged that to represent women as vulnerable victims hinders their agency and capacity for resistance. Proponents of this critique celebrate agency in a manner that mirrors neoliberalism's emphasis on responsibility and self-management.

Sharon Marcus' (1992) widely cited feminist theorization of the "rape script" is emblematic of this critique. Marcus, whose work is a core text in my course, argued that the feminist focus on women's vulnerability has the effect of re-inscribing a rape script that relies upon feminine passivity. According to this now-influential analysis of rape, feminists need to redraw patriarchal identifications of women with vulnerability through counter-images of female agency and resistance. At an individual level, theorists like Marcus contend women must disrupt the rape script by refusing feminine passivity and fighting back. In her important critique of this position, Mardorossian (2002) argued that feminist critics of victim feminism end up locating the cause of rape in women's non-combative responses, and leave us unable to acknowledge and theorize systemic vulnerabilities. The critique of victim feminism creates a binary construction of victim/agent that sees agency as good and liberating, while vulnerability is constructed as disabling and harmful (Stringer 2013). The effect has been to cast feminist analyses of vulnerability as theoretically and politically flawed. While giving a careful interrogation of these academic debates, CSL provided my students with multiple opportunities to engage in a complex analysis of situatedness and power relations that answers Mardorossian's call for renewed attention to vulnerability, and that deconstructs the limiting victim-bad/agent-good formulation.

The students' mapping of power relations very often began with their first journey to their placements. Two organizations partnered with my course were located in the inner city. At these placements, student engaged in front-line work with homeless and transient women, and women involved in the street-based sex trade. Like the social geography of Regina mapped so carefully by Sherene Razack (2000) in "The Murder of Pamela George" (a core reading in my class), Edmonton is a city rigidly divided by race and class. Colonization has imprinted itself on the social geography of western Canadian cities, creating stark boundaries between white, middle-class spaces like the university, ruled by norms of universal justice, and the racialized spaces of the inner city (and reserve), constructed as zones of naturally-occurring violence. Unmapping this colonial geography, according to Razack, involves asking questions about spatialized identities and power relations. Aided by Razack's concept of unmapping, and with critical awareness of myths of "stranger danger," my students reflected on their journeys into the inner city and interrogated their own unease. On the class blog, some described their conscious efforts to resist the fear that both limits women' mobility and reinforces the boundaries between white, middle-class spaces and the inner city. One student's blog post offered this reflection on her journey to her placement:

> [S]exual violence is spatialized. I can see how [the homeless shelter] is confined to a marginalized space consisting of Others and surrounded by peep shows and sex shops. I can almost feel the boundary drawing that occurs between 97th and 98th St. And walking home Tuesday night, I know that it appeared that I was wrongfully occupying this

space once I passed a group of men who yelled that I had better "watch my eyes." So I kept them down.

Another student commented on how the myth of "stranger danger" intersects with the space of the inner city: "The driver suggests that I 'be careful' parallel-ing and re-instating Russell's model of victim control ... these common-sense rules are futile and severely restrict women's freedoms and mobility."

Through these deliberations on space and fear, students gained a concrete understanding of how feminine gender identities reinforce the idea of public space as dangerous for women (Valentine 1992). It would be too simple to view reflections such as these as being about "observing Otherness" (Forbes et al. 1999, 162), especially since they are embedded in term-long conversations where students engaged in complicated negotiations of their own privileged identities. Instead, through multiple journeys into the inner city, students gained embodied insights into how fear limits women's mobility, and also into how mobility (or as Razack [2000, 107] puts it, the "license" to go wherever one pleases) is constitutive of white, middle-class privilege and of settler identity.

Journeys to middle-class neighbourhoods provided students with other insights about power, identity, and the contemporary construction of sexual violence. A group of students working with a suburban sexual-assault centre expressed a great deal of shock about deliberate efforts by schools to control disclosures of sexual abuse. One sexual-assault centre was engaged in deliver-ing a number of prevention programs for children and adolescents, including a program focused on the empowerment of "at-risk" girls that my students were involved in evaluating. Because disclosures of abuse often coincided with this program, several schools were reluctant to host it. One student commented on her anger at this suppression of disclosures: "What made me so mad—I am still in shock—is that some schools are hesitant to invite the program back because of the disclosures. ... This solidifies for me how sexual assault is supposed to be 'hush-hush.' If we don't talk about it, it doesn't happen." This "finding" became the subject of a conversation on the class blog, providing a tangible example of how sexual violence is reprivatized and erased through its active silencing. As Razack (2000) argues, the pervasiveness of violence against Indigenous women in the inner city disappears through its routinization. In white, middle-class suburbs, the disappearance of sexual violence directed at young girls takes a different form, erased through suppression.

Other powerful examples of silencing emerged through the students' CSL work. Engaging in outreach work with women doing street-based sex work provided students with concrete awareness of the ubiquity and ordinari-ness of sexual violence in the lives of marginalized women. As one student commented on the class blog, speaking specifically of the mostly Indigenous women who engage in Edmonton's survival sex trade: "[S]exual violence is far more systematic [for people of colour], ingrained in and normalized by our racist attitudes."

The bad date sheets that students helped to compile[4] and distribute for their CSL work not only documented this systematic violence but also demonstrated how sexual attacks against marginalized women are left ungoverned, placed outside law. As a student observed, "sexual assault can be commonplace. Because so many people involved in prostitution can't safely report to the police, [the agency] provides bad date sheets. . . . Information is published so that other people might be able to identify dangerous johns." Even though students know the statistical data that shows that very few sexual assaults are ever reported (H. Johnson 2012), they often assume that extreme acts of violence are nevertheless disclosed to the police. This student's blog entry, hypothesizing that the abysmally low rates of police reporting do not even reflect the experiences of street-based sex workers, is astute:

> these were serious actual incidents of crime reported by the women [on the bad date sheet]. . . . After reading through a multitude of cases, they all started to sound the same . . . I was surprised and frustrated to learn that [fewer than] 8 percent of sexual assault cases are reported [to police]. . . . What I wonder about now is whether even this low number is representative of marginalized women.

Razack demonstrates how "bodies in degenerate spaces lose their entitlement to personhood through a complex process in which the violence that is enacted is naturalized" (2000, 129). Through such spatial divisions and as an effect of colonial relations, Indigenous women and girls become legitimate targets of violence, particularly violence enacted by white men. In their work with agencies serving sex workers and homeless women, my students gained a concrete understanding of how repetitive and extreme acts of violence occurring in "degenerate" spaces against the bodies of marginalized women become normalized. For many of these students, this was the most troubling realization stemming from their community work.

The erasure of sexual violence from public discourse is a thematic emphasis of the course. The suppression of disclosures, low rates of police reporting, and the routinization of violence against marginalized women all function to obscure the pervasive realities of sexual assault and the power relations creating vulnerabilities. Sexual violence is individualized and decontextualized, represented as a series of isolated acts. Through classroom work, students learn about how technologies of risk management have come to define responses to sexual assault in a context of neoliberal governance. Women are responsibilized as individual agents of crime prevention and, in the process, altered forms of victim-blaming are created that are no longer specifically tied to sexual propriety (Gotell 2008). As responsibility for preventing sexual assault is placed onto would-be victims, social responsibility for rape is eroded (Hall 2004). In the class, students developed critical awareness of the disciplinary rules of sexual safekeeping that make women individually responsible for stopping rape. In blog entries and class conversations, students dissected the ways in which the prevention education materials they encountered in their placements were geared toward cultivating rape-preventing subjects. Many students were frustrated by these victim-blaming and responsibilizing messages, and wondered how to raise these critiques with their community mentors. As one student observed in a blog post: "'Do not go with someone new'/'Leave if things are not right'.... As I read these presentations, I felt there were forms of victim-blaming in the messages to youth.... I think it may be more ... challenging not to put the responsibility on women (or in other words, not to victim-blame)." As they grappled with the links between acknowledging women's/girl's agency on the one hand, and the assigning of "responsibility" on the other, students were actively deconstructing the binary construction of victim/agent. While acknowledging the victim-blaming logic of risk-management discourses, the following student blog comment nevertheless makes a strong case for empowering women and girls in order to interrupt the rape script (Marcus 1992): "boundary presentations to young kids, especially young girls are so very important ... I am not trying to victim blame here, but because women need to take back their voice." Just as classroom knowledge tentatively moved into the community, some students' positive experiences with prevention education also gave them tools to speak back to the academic critique of rape management discourse. Through commentaries like this one, students were, in effect, asking whether it is ever possible to separate empowerment from victim-blaming or agency from responsibility.

The connections between risk-management discourses and victim-blaming that we made in our classroom work provided a framework for understanding the contemporary hyper-responsibilization of marginalized women, especially the homeless women and sex workers that many students encountered in their placements. The discourse of "high-risk lifestyle" has framed criminal justice and investigatory responses to missing and murdered Indigenous women in Canada. Echoing yet hyperbolizing the safety pedagogies of rape prevention, the rapes, murders, and disappearances of women in the sex trade and Indigenous women are framed as problems to be addressed through strategies of risk avoidance and self-management. Women are counselled to avoid taking risky actions and placing themselves in vulnerable situations; and extremely marginalized women who are victimized become defined by and reduced to their "high-risk lifestyles." Risk—being "at risk," "living a high-risk lifestyle"— becomes inscribed onto the identities of very marginalized women (Gotell 2008, 883). An especially strong critical analysis was offered in a blog entry where a student described a conscious experience of active listening. This student was able to develop a nuanced analysis of how conceptions of agency are often tied to abstract liberal notions of "choice," thus ignoring how decisions are situated and constrained. Her analysis challenged the increasingly dominant discourse of a "high-risk lifestyle" that makes marginalized women individually blameworthy for the violence they experience, as though vulnerability were a choice:

> [T]he ongoing process of individualization…seems to not only be effectively silencing and/or dismissing social issues faced in the community, but also proving that women are solely responsible for the "situation" they find themselves in.…. Therefore, not only does K. possess no market value in the Neoliberal sense, she is also considered, under Canadian Law and the criminal justice system, to be engaged in a "high-risk" lifestyle. The violence she has endured and survived only perpetuates the stereotype that victims choose this type of "high-risk" [life] freely and willingly, as if the context of their circumstances and the inflexible and underfunded structure of social services have no bearing.

CSL locates the students in a liminal position between classroom and community, and from there my students produced important reflections on agency. One challenge of using community-engaged pedagogy is the loss of instructor control over pedagogical direction. Sometimes my students' community work pushed the class in unpredictable directions. Sex work was not a specific focus in this class, yet because so many of the student placements were with organizations supporting women involved in sex work, it entered through the side door. In their work at outreach agencies and at a homeless shelter for women, students engaged with a group of predominantly racialized and Indigenous women involved in street-based sex work. Through these encounters and in conversations on the blog, students developed an analysis of racial hierarchies in the Edmonton sex trade. Out of conversations with the women engaged in sex work and with experienced outreach workers, the students gained critical insights on the inadequacy of exit strategies and about the links between survival sex work on the one hand, and poverty, racism, and the ongoing effects of colonization on the other. Students were profoundly challenged by the vulnerabilities of the women doing street-based sex work, and this caused many to rethink their previously held feminist positions on sex worker agency and on sex work as a stigmatized "profession." Our classroom conversations were enriched by these insights about disadvantage and situated agency that developed out of the students' community work.

CSL and Activism Reconsidered

My students' CSL work contributed to the intellectual projects at the very heart of my class: rethinking resistance in a context of neoliberal governance and complicating the victim/agent dichotomy that has constrained feminist anti-rape theory and activism. As I have emphasized, however, to claim that community-engaged pedagogy is or should be thought of as activism both overstates the possibilities of praxis-learning and fails to acknowledge the complex social mapping that WGS students undertake through their community work. The idea that students are engaged in feminist activism simply because they are in the community working with non-profits ignores the constrained spaces for feminist activism in the present. In order to critically orient my students to the work they undertake in the CSL component of my class, I always begin with an explicit consideration of the gendered nature of the non-profit industrial complex. Drawing on literature about the institutionalization of rape-crisis and sexual-assault centres (Beres, Crow, and Gotell 2009; A. Smith 2007), we talked about how centres have been professionalized and depoliticized with the expansion of the shadow state. My students thus embarked on their placements armed with critical tools to interrogate how activism has been inhibited as agencies confront increasing pressures to redefine themselves as professionalized "victims' services." Under significant budget constraints, with staff often forced to undertake punishing workloads, and with the daily pressures of fee-for-service and project-based funding arrangements, space for social change activism has been eroded (see also Joanne Muzak's chapter in this volume).

Only one of my students was involved in a project that was recognizably activist. A local sexual-assault centre contributes to organizing Edmonton's Take Back the Night (TBTN) march, using this as an opportunity for "public education." This centre significantly relies on volunteers to plan and carry out the march, as protests like this one are rarely viewed as being eligible for state or corporate funding. One of my students—a smart, third-wave, and queer-identified feminist—chose to work with the centre, helping with that year's TBTN organizing. This student had incredible difficulties when it became clear that the march would be women-only. The inclusion of all genders in feminist organizing was a political commitment she firmly held; as she wrote at the beginning of the term, "*Fuck gendered spaces!*" She struggled to communicate this position to other members of the TBTN organizing committee. Although this was a difficult learning experience for her, this student stayed involved with the organizing committee and designed a fantastic TBTN 'zine. Through this political work, she managed to ensure that the women-only march would include self-identified trans women. This was an undeniably uncomfortable experience of feminist politics, and as this student struggled through it, she came to appreciate feminism as a space of political contestation. As she wrote in a blog post:

> I feel very strongly about gendering spaces, as it is an exclusionary practice and has more to do with identity than addressing a problem. I feel particularly strongly when that gendering excludes transgender persons. . . . When I mustered the courage to email TBTN my concerns, it was explained to me that making a women-only event recognizes that sexual violence is gendered and rooted in misogyny. I was glad to hear that there was consideration for transpeople in their definition of sexual violence, as transpeople are disproportionately affected by sexual violence.

When thinking about politics and activism in relation to their CSL work, students adopted diverse positions. In our classroom discussions and blog exchanges, some were harshly critical of agencies that seem trapped within professionalized and depoliticized approaches. One student, charged with redesigning a prevention campaign directed at men and boys, reflected on the agency's refusal to take risks and believed there was great need for a more radical approach: "They don't take enough risks, they don't get in the community's face about violence against women, and so the message seems distant, prepackaged. . . . I do realize this is for a reason, namely funding and reputability. . . . A grassroots, in-your-face approach is needed. None of this prearranged presentation stuff. . . . We need a public outcry where the message is loud and clear instead of safely nestled behind the walls of privileged spaces."

With the neoliberal re-privatization of sexual violence, the political project of breaking the silence around sexual assault and rape, one first undertaken by second-wave feminists, must now be repeated. This student was insightful in his insistence that this should be done loudly. Students know that their interactions with community mentors must always be respectful and framed by an awareness of the constrained political context. Although many community partners enjoy students' critical feedback, the audience for this reflection was other members of the class. We can and do have different kinds of conversations in our classroom interactions, as well as on the class blog. Experiences of on-the-ground work in the non-profit sector can also have the effect of challenging a tendency for students to think that there can be a pure space of feminist politics, always politically correct, and untainted by pragmatic concerns. The political conversation enabled by CSL can be dialectical.

If some students were harshly critical of the depoliticization of sexual violence and the shrinking spaces for feminist activism, others highlighted how workers in agencies enact day-to-day resistance in the face of constraints. With critical awareness of the non-profit industrial complex, students documented the underfunding and lack of resources facing Alberta non-profits working against violence against women. Students emphasized the incredible commitment of the women who work in this sector for too little pay. As one student commented on the class blog: "The terrible irony of non-profits is that the women working for them are following their clients to the food bank. Until it has adequate resources and staff, [the agency] will not be able to translate its outreach work into a social and political shift in terms of how Canadians understand women working in the sex trade."

Using terms like "silent activists," some students wrote about how activism and service provision cannot be neatly separated: "They are *silent activists* providing essential services to women who are marginalized and ignored." The concept of "silent activism" encapsulates much of what my students learned about activism against sexual violence in the context of their CSL placements. Though constrained and forced to adopt an outwardly depoliticized stance, committed workers and volunteers in Edmonton non-profits engage in daily acts of political resistance.

Conclusion

Wrapping up this chapter is a tall order, both because I have tried to provide an overview of the substance of my course, and also because there are no simple answers to the complex questions of praxis-learning in WGS. While CSL rarely engages students in experiences of explicit feminist activism, it teaches them a great deal about the non-profit industrial complex and the depoliticization of sexual violence in a context of neoliberalism. While feminist theorizing on rape seems trapped within an endless debate about victim feminism and agency, the social mapping my students engaged in allowed them to deconstruct this binary construction of victim/agent and to generate complex insights about situated agency. While sexual violence has been individualized and decontextualized from the power relations that constitute its very dynamics, CSL enabled my students to re-contextualize and re-emphasize the systemic character of sexual assault. The social maps that my students drew across neighbourhoods and through social geographies anchored in colonialism enabled them to see the diverse ways sexual violence has been re-privatized and individualized in a context of neoliberalism, and to pierce through the discourses of risk that personalize the problem of sexual assault and obfuscate vulnerability and disadvantage. These maps also situated these students, enabling them to interrogate their own locations within colonial landscapes. The connections that students made, and the ways in which they were able to draw on their community work to offer new insights on academic texts, have enriched and complicated the shared project of my class, allowing us to imagine new ways of intervening in the contemporary politics of sexual violence.

Notes

1 I would like to acknowledge the support of the Teaching Innovation Grant (2008–2009), Community Service-Learning Program, University of Alberta. In addition, I am grateful for the research assistance of Cole Caljouw.

2 For their blog assignment, I asked the students not to refer to organizations by name in order to preserve anonymity and allow for honest discussions. Here, I also follow this advice.

3 Two workers at the Alberta Status of Women Action Committee were criminally charged with fraud for collecting Unemployment Insurance while working voluntarily. ASWAC was disbanded in 1997 (Harder 2003, 200).

4 Bad date sheets are compiled based upon sex worker reports of violence. These disclosures were made to agency workers and sometimes to the CSL students themselves.

CRITICAL APPROACHES TO PRAXIS /
IN AND OUT OF THE CLASSROOM

CHAPTER SIX

RELATIONS WITH THE DEAD? ETHICS OF FEMINIST MEMORIALIZATION IN SERVICE-LEARNING

ILYA PARKINS

In a hushed classroom, forty-four students presented memorial biographies of women who had been murdered by men in the Okanagan Valley in the previous thirty years. The presentations occurred in my first-year course called Introduction to Gender and Women's Studies II, at the University of British Columbia's Okanagan Campus. As I listened to the culmination of my students' service-learning project, I was struck by their solemnity and commitment to the task we had set for them in partnership with a local women's centre. Staff would use these biographies as part of annual memorial services on the National Day of Remembrance and Action on Violence against Women. While the students' dedication to the work was clear, I became uneasy as I listened to the biographies. A majority elaborated at surprising length upon the details of the murders, with some evidencing a sort of forensic attention to times, places, suspects, killers, and investigations. While a few used this information to indict the justice system for its failures to respond to violence against women, turning their biographies into hybrid political-memorial documents, most did not make such a link. The decisions of most students to focus on the killings eclipsed the details of lives lived—the ostensible focus of a memorial project—and in some cases meant they foregrounded women's "risky" behaviours rather than offering pictures of a whole life. The result was an odd convergence between some of the biographies and the obsession with criminality that is a strong feature of the media coverage given to various social issues in the Okanagan Valley. Thus I concluded that the project was limited in its reach and impact, even though it generated extraordinary affective investment. As one student wrote in a reflection paper afterward, "I have never felt so emotionally connected to a school project."

This chapter considers what limited this project, which was so promising in its response to a need articulated by a local women's organization. I use this retrospective analysis to locate in the framework of service-learning an incommensurability with the kinds of reflective engagement demanded by an ethical memorial practice. Two problems arose, which I consider in turn: the failure to adequately apply concepts of structural oppression in the memorial process, and the failure to witness the women's lives with appropriate care, which meant that they were strangely absent from their own memorial biographies. Here, I suggest that what links these failures is the lack of an operative concept of the relational subject, which would have provided students with a way to navigate the complex relationships they had to the women they were memorializing and to the social structures in which they were mutually implicated.

The question of what it would mean to have this project "work" gets at the heart of ideas about what service-learning might be. There is an apparent tension between the memorial work this project engaged in, and the critical or political insights that service-learning is meant to generate. The tension between memorial and critical political work at stake in this project has an analogue in other kinds of service-learning projects also caught between the imperatives of "helping" and providing critical learning for students (see also Margot Francis', Lise Gotell's, and Sarita Srivastava's chapters in this volume). But the tension I am exploring here suggests an ideologically laden opposition between emotional labour (helping, remembering) and the intellectual labour of critical analysis. This project made clear that these two pieces of the service-learning puzzle must be considered together. The emotional labour of memorialization requires an intellectual foundation in critical theories of power and difference, and methods that are sensitive to complex social positions and the importance of reflexivity, if it is to have a transformative impact. Such work cannot be ethically undertaken without acknowledging one's complex and sometimes contradictory and uncomfortable relation to others across layers of communicative media and difference, and negotiating this terrain requires critical, intellectual engagement. My reflection on this project, then, makes a case for the sustained integration of concepts of relationality in service-learning; it asks for critical intellectual work about power, difference, and social location to be at the heart of it. As Amber Dean argues in a reflection on the ethics of memorializing murdered women, "critique can be a way of caring for, or enriching, or expressing concern for one's subject" and therefore need not be considered antithetical to memorial practices (2008, 236). Indeed, in a context such as this one—a Women's and Gender Studies (WGS) classroom, and a service-learning project, with their twin orientations to the project of social change—intellectual work is fundamental to connecting memorialization to the possibility of social transformation. As Judith Taylor suggests (in this volume), sometimes the suspension of critique is warranted in order to be sensitive to the needs of a service-learning partner; there is no singular formula for integrating service-learning in WGS. In this case, however, I suggest that critique would have enriched both the project of memorialization, and the project of teaching and learning in WGS.

The Project

The project was initiated at the request of the Kelowna Women's Resource Centre (KWRC). Their director approached University of British Columbia's service-learning office with a request to partner with a relevant class to conduct research into the lives of murdered women, in order to create memorial biographies for ongoing display at memorial services on December 6, the National Day of Remembrance and Action on Violence against Women. My course, as an introduction to WGS, was a good fit and I agreed to participate, pleased that the impetus had come from the community organization. The project was not the focus of the course but was related in the sense that it asked students to think through course topics—including, most importantly, gendered violence—in a unique way. Students were put in pairs or threes to conduct the research, and randomly assigned a name from a list of nineteen women compiled by the director of the KWRC, who had immense knowledge of the history of violence against women in the valley. As the instructor, I played no part in this process and deferred to the local knowledge of the director. The list was not selective; it was not meant to privilege one "type" of murder or murdered woman, but to be as accurate a reflection as possible of all the murders that had taken place in the valley in the preceding three decades. For this reason, the lives and social locations of the murdered women were quite varied, and it was not possible for the class to position themselves in one particular way in relation to these women.

Three class meetings were devoted in whole or in part to the project. First, the KWRC's director and the community service-learning officer came to class a few weeks into the term to introduce the project, provide context, and answer questions. Several weeks later, we devoted part of a class to a check-in, in which we discussed the process, any challenges—practical or emotional—that were coming up, and questions. Toward the end of the class, an entire session was devoted to the oral presentations of the biographies. As well, there was an online discussion board created on the class website, and students were encouraged to post there with questions and reflections on the research. There was little use of this web space, though, which reflected the ways that students approached this project in general: they worked mainly in their pairs or trios, and there was limited opportunity for them to make connections with other groups or discuss the difficulties they were navigating as they worked on the project, which might have provided some fodder for reflexive work. The work of writing the biographies was not graded, but students were required to write a reflection on the process of the research, which accounted for a small percentage of their final grade.

Since there is a well-recognized potential for service-learning projects to benefit only students and the institution rather than community members, the fact that the project had been requested by a local organization was crucially important in my decision to have the class participate (Green 2003; Hui 2009; Himley 2004; Meisel 2008; Williams and McKenna 2002). My participation in the project was affirmed when, after the KWRC director and I gave several interviews to local news outlets, we were both contacted by members of the families of some of the murdered women. Every family member who contacted us expressed gratitude for the project, which felt like a blessing to proceed.

The day of the presentations was emotionally draining for all involved. As the service-learning coordinator said, it was as if we held "nineteen funerals" in the short space of eighty minutes. This turn of phrase stuck with me. A funeral is usually attended by mourners who knew the deceased; in this case, we were forty-five strangers, people who had come to know the victims through the distancing lens of the media. What, I wondered, was the bond that linked us in presenting these lives? What were these frames we were attempting to fit them in? And did we have the language or the critical capacity needed to begin to interrogate these frames? Carrick, Himley, and Jacobi note that "[a]s students meet people and enter places that put pressure on their sense of who they are and how the world is, we set in motion processes of identification and disidentification, moments of comfort and discomfort" (2000, 57). Given the particular histories that this project negotiated, these processes were intensified, and to make such an undertaking successful, the classroom had to face them head-on.

Successes: Individual Epiphanies

The students' critical reflections demonstrated that they were moved by the project and showed a critical capacity that could have provided the seeds for a much broader and more transformative process. Here is D., who came—as did several other students—to talk with me in my office about the distress he was in as he worked on the project: "This project has helped me to decide that anytime I hear or find out about injustice that I will stop and take time to remember. That I will care and stand vigil because it is a responsibility each of us shares as a human being." I also observed that many students talked about making connections between the personal stories of the murdered women and the larger structures in which they were embedded. I was encouraged to see so many of them making connections between these individual lives and deeper structures of misogyny and violence. They responded to the outrageous failures of the justice system in so many of the cases. They also responded to the press's discounting or dehumanization of the women when they came from working-class backgrounds or were members of a marginalized community including Indigenous women, drug users, or sex workers. K. wrote, "because the murder…was spoken of in isolation to the thousands of other murder cases regarding women, I had to challenge myself to recognize that [the] murder was much more than just a random, disconnected incident." K. narrates an important, extended moment of awareness, which highlights the way that insights about violence against women unfold in a process over some time, and points to the intersection of learning from this particular project with broader principles in the discipline of WGS. Since making the leap from individual to socio-structural is a paramount goal of the gender studies classroom, this is no small achievement and speaks to the very real successes of this project.

Despite such evidence, though, the day of the "nineteen funerals" emblematizes the limits of our memorialization efforts. That day was the ultimate opportunity for the class as a whole to make that move—from personal to structural—in both their narrations of the women's lives and their constitution as a "community of memory" (Simon and Eppert 1997). However, the narrative choices made by many of the groups, their consequences, and the ways that the biographies were structured reveal that a layer of inquiry about representation was conspicuously absent. This level of representational analysis would have provided a means to implicate the students *themselves*—as subjects in relation to the dead women—in the structures that the project was pushing them to confront. Instead, most chose to focus on lurid details about the crimes, which effectively displaced the focus from their own implication in structures of misogyny and violence, and their own relationship to the women.

Structural Analysis, Representation, and Under-Theorizing in Service-learning

What took place on the day of the biography presentations can accurately be described as a public remembrance practice. Sharon Rosenberg writes, "[a]s a memorial address, a public remembrance practice can be understood as attempting to bind the living in a particular relation—not only to the dead, but to each other" (2003, 10). Rosenberg's work underscores that remembrance is relational and that, hence, it always includes an ethical dimension—if we are bound to others, including the dead, then we are bound to do well by them. The ethics that public remembrance foregrounds are not only those of doing justice to the memory of the dead but also the ethics enacted in the community bound together by the acts of remembrance; they are, thus, relational.

Researching the life of a murdered woman and providing a snapshot of that life to honour her in a public memorial context inevitably brought up issues of representation. First, most students were relying on the Okanagan Valley's local media to find out about the lives of the women they were researching. Their glimpses of those lives were thus filtered through the rhetorics of gender, race, class, marginalization, and violence that dominate this culturally and politically conservative area. The students were sensitive to aspects of the media filter on the women they were researching; for example, a number noted they were shocked to find more information about the murderer than about the murdered woman and her life.

A second layer of questions about representation, however, remained inadequately addressed during the process. This would have involved questioning what it meant to be in charge of re-narrating the lives the students had seen so poorly mediated by the media. The sort of questioning required by this second layer was not adequately addressed—not even by me, as a facilitator of the projects. Just one student brought up the question of the ethics of such representation. She wrote on the discussion section of the course website: "I feel frustrated and unsure about how best to represent these women's lives. As the ones telling the stories, we are given a certain power, and we must be very careful when writing these pieces that we do not turn the write-ups into a police file case report, nor a spectacularized media sensation about the murder." This student's response is productive and contained the potential to move this project into a more meaningful register. The reaction is marked by its interrogation of positionality; it considers the political implications of the relationship between students and the women they were researching. This recognition of the situatedness of students in relation to the murdered women emphasizes difference. The danger of recognizing difference, of course, is to fetishize it. As Donna M. Bickford and Nedra Reynolds (2002, 237) write, "[i]n most service-learning situations, relationships are clearly based on difference: I'm homeless; you're not." (Their concern is that service-learning projects often foster "attitudes [that] overlook...the structural mechanisms that make difference different in the first place" [233]). In contrast, this expression of concern about the ethics of representation through difference recognizes that such difference is produced by power. In this case, the power differential is underscored by the fact that the women's deaths bring the classroom "community" together, in what might be considered a rather grotesque form of opportunism. Of course, the possibility of ethical relations with the dead is structured by the layers of communicative media: this was not just about the choices that students made in telling their stories, but about the texts they accessed in their research. Their sense of the women's social locations was developed, in part, through the lens provided by the local newspapers. For example, as one student noted in a private conversation with me, there seemed to be evidence that at least one of the women was Indigenous, but the media—acting without a structural analysis of the white supremacist dimensions of violence against women—never noted women's ethnicities, with the exception of the case of Rajwar Gakhal, who was murdered by her ex-husband along with eight members of her family, and whose murder was framed as "culturally" motivated. In general, this silence in the media about race and ethnicity foreclosed a conversation about the very particular contexts of gendered violence. Indigenous women, for example, face shockingly high rates of racist, sexualized violence and murder in Canada, an issue that had been important in the class's introduction to the issue of violence against women. But the representational regime students were navigating focused on the lives of murdered women in a way that divorced them from this context.

Thus, the students were constructing their own narratives of women's lives in a representational regime untouched by the important, feminist critical work of grounding identities in social practices, communities, cultures, and relationships. What is more, because identity is relational, when students did not have a sense of the women they were writing about as socially located, they themselves were abstracted from their social locations, allowing them to take up a kind of meta-critical "God's-eye view" in their narrations, which both reinforced the power relation imbalance between them and the dead women, and added to the difficulty of locating their own positions in relation to this violence. For example, students seemed unable to deal with their peer's discussion-board challenge to them around issues of representation and power. This is not to say that they were neophytes in feminist critical practice. Although this was a first-year course, students had encountered issues of power, privilege, difference, and representation more broadly. More importantly, they had seen such an approach reflected in the work we read about violence against women, much of which explicitly interrogated the normative, feminist frames of reference for understanding gendered violence.[1] As many of the other chapters in this book explore, though, what was missing were critical frames to implicate the students themselves in these structures of power and domination in a relational network with the murdered women (see in particular Margot Francis' chapter for further examination of this problem).

In effect, the class was missing a theoretical dimension; the project seemed to displace the earlier learning we had done together not only about privilege, power, and difference but also about violence against women. Given the greater comfort level of students with "doing," rather than critically interrogating the very frames "doing" occurs within, it is not surprising that theoretically inflected reflection became a casualty of this process. Yet, as S. Mei-Yen Hui points out, "[s]ervice-learning for social justice requires that students not only become informed on social issues but also critically observe how they are positioned in relation to them" (2009, 23). That is, for service-learning to have a transformative impact, it must not only incorporate theoretical dimensions but also must offer ways for students to work through the implications of theory in their own lives.

Hui's assertion about the importance of reflexivity in relation to positionality and power also resonates in important ways with the goals of feminist pedagogy more generally, highlighting the points of potential intersection between service-learning and feminist work. Tamara Williams and Erin McKenna note that "[t]he development of feminist pedagogy and of experiential learning coincide historically. They also converge in their shared insistence on the authority of experience... and their challenge to dualistic accounts of theory/ practice, public/private, self/other, and knowledge and experience" (2002, 137). And yet the authors also foreground conspicuous silences in feminist classrooms undertaking service-learning projects. Somehow, it is as if "the novelty and excitement of service-learning" has precluded doing the difficult, reflexive work that feminist epistemological principles demand (Williams and McKenna 2002, 143). This was certainly the case in my classroom. The students were enthusiastic and animated in relation to the project they undertook, and I heard many expressions of gratitude for its difference, its novelty—but I did not hear, from the vast majority of them, connections made between what we were doing and the kinds of reflexive, critical work that we had also read together. The assumption that structured my service-learning classroom and most others relies on an immediate equation of experience with authority, bypassing the difficult work of thinking through the relationship of experience, knowledge, and power. These were, in this instance, largely questions of representation, as students were both using written narrations of women's lives and constructing their own narrations. In order to facilitate considerations of power and privilege in a narrative context, discursive fields, stereotyping, constructions of objectivity through particular authorial voices, and the representational play of social difference are crucial additions that must be made to the syllabus. All of these were issues that could have been introduced by mediating them through historical examples and applications, facilitating a recognition of the research process as relational and power-saturated.

Allowing for Haunting: The Ethics of Memorialization in Service-learning

Of course, to recognize the research as relational in a way that decentred students is much easier said than done in a project with research "participants" who are no longer living. In reconstructing what worked and what did not about this project, I have continually come up against an impasse generated by the uniquely sensitive matter of working with nothing but the ghostly traces of the women being memorialized. Avery Gordon (2008, xvi) defines haunting as an "animated state in which a repressed or unresolved social violence is making itself known," and the students' reflections attest that this is what happened for them, though some lacked the analytical tools necessary to leverage that haunting into the recognition of the structural nature of the violence the women experienced. Gordon (2008, 64) suggests that "the ghost is alive, so to speak. We are in relation to it and it has designs on us such that we must reckon with it graciously, attempting to offer it a hospitable memory out of a concern for justice." Her framing of the ghost as relational draws out its ability to make claims on the living, to move them in some way—as my students were moved by the project. More, her framing of haunting as a phenomenon that occurs in and highlights the interstices between presence and absence, visibility and invisibility, is deeply resonant with the odd status of both researchers and research subjects in this project. In perusing news reports of the women's deaths, students encountered the simultaneity of these states, as the women's murders were spectacularized, even though many of the women lived lives otherwise rendered invisible to and forgotten by many in our community. In fact, students were dwelling, for the most part, on the hyper-visible remnants of the women's lives. Gordon (2008, 16) writes that "[h]ypervisibility is a kind of obscenity of accuracy that abolishes the distinctions between permission and prohibition, presence and absence. No shadows, no ghosts." Further, she notes that such "hypervisibility is a persistent alibi for the mechanisms that render one un-visible" (17). This is precisely what the students confronted in their encounter with the ghosts of the women they were researching: an "obscenity of accuracy" about their deaths and sometimes the circumstances of their socially marginal identities, which subsumed the possibility of encountering the "mechanisms" that rendered them invisible.

But Gordon also expresses reservations about her *uses* of ghosts. Addressing the ghost of Sabina Spielrein, an early twentieth-century psychoanalyst, she writes, "Dear Sabina, I'm uneasy about using your story, or the story of the places you were between…about needing or seeming to need a dead woman to enliven matters, to make them have material force" (Gordon 2008, 59). She thus sounds a note of caution vis-à-vis the kind of project my class undertook, in which students' educational and citizenship needs were ultimately prioritized over the lives and deaths of the women they were researching. Of course, it is difficult to know what it might look like to prioritize the "needs" of dead people. But, though the students were clearly haunted by the women they researched, the question remains whether they actually "offer[ed] [them] a hospitable memory out of a concern for justice" (Derrida cited in Gordon 2008, 64). If we conceive of justice, in this case, as a construct that knits together the individual and the social by excavating the broader conditions which structured the women's deaths *and* makes clear to researchers that they sit in these same structures themselves, then it seems that the process of producing the memorial biographies did not meet these criteria.

Gordon's focus on ghosts also allows me to frame what was at stake in this project, in order to imagine what it might have needed in order to memorialize the women in a justice-oriented framework.[2] Students were being asked to hear the women's stories, though these were terribly distorted through their mediation, and to retell them. If this task were framed as the witnessing and re-narration of historical trauma, then there would be a range of analytical tools available to facilitate the kind of inquiry that admits the personal and social dimensions of gendered violence. As Roger Simon and Claudia Eppert (1997, 178) argue, "witnessing is first and foremost an ethical concept [which] . . . should be distinguished from other possible responses to testimony, such as mimicry, voyeurism, or spectatorship." If we understand what students were partaking in as a kind of witnessing, then the necessarily relational, ethical dimension of their project could perhaps be conveyed to them in a more meaningful way.

Telling It Differently: Witnessing Context as Communal Knowledge-Making

The service-learning impulse, which emphasized the needs of the students, encouraged them to dwell on what they knew about violence against women, about women, and about community. In these cases, older knowledge patterns, which dated from before the course curriculum's attempt to trouble what we think we "know" about gendered violence, persisted, indicating that most students were not able to truly "listen" to the testimony of the ghosts they were researching. Simon and Eppert argue for the importance of "learn[ing] the limits of what one can and needs to say as a witness and to try to respond to what lies beyond what one already knows; the task is to acknowledge and remember the person, while not always speaking about her or his testimony but to her or his testimony" (1997, 179–80). For the students to learn from the stories of the women they were researching, they needed to first refuse the perpetuation of universalizing narratives about violence against women. And in order to do that, they needed to be aware of the situated nature of their assumptions about gendered violence.

Such work involves delving into issues of representation, as I note above. What, specifically, does that critical analysis of representation entail? First, the students should have been equipped to talk about the *context* of the women's experiences of violence. Arguably, they already were given some of the tools to allow them to approach context: they had been prepared with the rudiments of feminist theory, and with the paradigm-questioning work we had read about gendered violence in the course. Yet they seemed not to have absorbed this knowledge in a way that allowed them to apply it to their constructions of the women's representations in their projects. To make "context" real, one could ask the students to investigate multiple levels of it: they could reconstruct the context of Kelowna, and they could ask what structured the media's silences around particular aspects of the women's lives, and their spectacularizing presentation of others. They could also reconstruct the context of gendered violence in a classed, colonial, and white supremacist province and nation. Thinking about this information in the context of the women's lives and deaths might "ground" it in a way that it was not grounded when they encountered it as abstract theorizing. In the context of service-learning, it would also displace the tendency to reduce the relationality of the situation to a researcher–subject dyad in which the researcher is privileged over the "subject," by forcing students to recognize the multiple relational networks that structured women's lives, and to confront those aspects of the networks that exceeded what the students themselves knew or experienced. Further, attuning students to the contexts that structured the media's coverage of the women's lives—prompting them to pay attention to the absence of objectivity in any discursive event—would help to open a discussion about their own positionality and knowledge, their own bias as they attempted to represent the women's lives. This would ensure that the conversation did not begin and end from the students, but rather figure the students as one node in a network of situated actors reconstructing these events.

Simon and Eppert (1997) consider the absences that structure the witnessing and reconstruction of historical trauma, and their incitement to dialogue with and about these absences seems an important beginning point for reimagining my class:

> The inevitable translational betrayal of the testimonial act means that narratives and images of historical trauma are commonly shot through with absences that, in their silence, solicit or "ask" questions. Actively to remember such testimonies entails not only repeating them but also posing difficult and often unanswerable questions which press for responses that could help decipher what is to be heard when one listens to a testimonial account. The explanations sought in such questions typically are not attached to something in the text but rather to something missing from the text. (183–84)

This absence needed to be recognized as an important part of another, related context for the students, the one in which they came into mystified contact with the traces of the women's lives. Part of the work of our classroom community should have been to confront the absences we were working with, and to reflect on what kinds of responses they elicited and what those meant. Such labour would entail dwelling on the meeting of social factors that determined both the women's lives and their representation by the media, with the students' affective responses to the haunting they were clearly experiencing. This would have transformed the psychic work that students were doing into communal work; it would have moved the reckonings with what this learning meant out of my office and into the space we shared, what Simon and Eppert call a "community of memory."

Indeed, in retrospect, had the project been guided by a conception of a community of memory, I believe the work that needed to be done would have been more easily accomplished. Given that the community the students were partnering with for this service-learning project was ambiguous, working explicitly to identify and define a community that the project spoke to would have been a productive, critical practice. It may well have troubled the assumptions commonly held about the "community" in community service-learning, and that troubling is a useful strategy. For Simon and Eppert, "communities of memory designate structured sets of relationships through which people engage representations of past events and put forth shared, complementary, or competing versions of what should be remembered and how. Within these relationships people make topical the significance of their understanding of past events, arguing over the reworking of narratives and images that embody and elicit living memories" (1997, 186). An important element of their description is its orientation to process. In my classroom, we could have initiated an ongoing, relational dialogue over how to represent the women. Simon and Eppert further note that the conflicts and struggle generated in a community of memory "cannot be worked through without taking into account the realization that historical knowledge depends on those whose histories have prevailed" (1997, 186). That is, this community of memory would have taken root in the realization that the histories of the women they found in the media were partial and reflected the voices and interests of the dominant constituency in conservative Kelowna. This theoretical idea about the perpetuation of ideology could then be connected to students' experience by asking them to consider their own role vis-à-vis hegemonic representations of marginality and gendered violence—their own inclusion in structural oppression—and asking them to stake out a position that might tell a different story than the local media told.

To construct such a community of memory requires an understanding, as I note above, of relationality as its structuring principle. In retrospect, were I to construct such a project again with a view to the establishment of a community of memory, I would be guided by the principles theorized in feminist work about relationality. This work helps us recognize that there is more at stake here than just the relationship of one individual with a particular social location and history, and another individual who was, during her life, differently located. Because of community service-learning's tendency to produce a binary framework, whereby the only two registers are "us" and "them," we need to give students tools to think through the complex, non-binary "web" of relations that their project engages in—a web that, in this project's case, included more than just them and the murdered women, but also the community partner, the women's families, the media, and the university's service-learning office. As Carolyn Pedwell argues, building a "relational web" as an analytic tool "provides a framework for unravelling and integrating some of the historical, discursive-material processes through which such figures have been constructed and reified, rather than simply taking their 'nature' for granted. Indeed, a strong focus on teaching constitutive connections *between* particular entities produces a shift away from thinking of set and coherent 'figures' and practices and toward contemplating the *relationships* produced in and through various encounters with specific contents" (2008, 99).

Pedwell's approach effectively links to the ethics and politics of belonging that are sketched by Aimee Carrillo Rowe. She argues that, useful as it has been, the concept of a politics of location retains a curiously static and atomistic "I" at its core—accounting for one's location is only ever precisely that, a view of the individual. But as Carrillo Rowe (2005, 16) puts it, "the meaning of self is never individual, but a shifting set of relations that we move in and out of." For this reason, "the very conception of 'location' might be reimagined in ways that make community and belonging central to its interrogation" (Carrillo Rowe 2005, 25). Her framework suggests that tracing this "politics of relation" should be central to an anti-oppressive and transformative teaching practice, subtly moving away from a "politics of location." It is precisely this kind of genealogy that might have made a difference in my CSL project, for it would have troubled the solipsism that can be activated by centring the students' needs and experiences.

Pedwell's and Carrillo Rowe's emphases on relationality in transnational or transracial research and coalition are indispensable theoretical tools for reimagining such a project. Yet, they do not necessarily take into account the particular, affective dimension that is inherent in memorializing the dead. But Sara Ahmed's early work considering feelings generated in transnational feminist dialogue allows us to think through the "intimacy" that seemed to emerge through the project, the sense students had that they had a relationship with a particular woman. Ahmed (1997, 32) writes, "a politics of becoming-more-intimate is a politics bound up with responsibility—with recognising that relations between others are always constitutive of the possibility of either speaking or not speaking." This has a special resonance with the memorial project, which effectively relied on a kind of ventriloquism. Ahmed suggests that an ethical intimacy is about the ongoing recognition of difference without subsuming it—which might help mitigate the tendency to assimilate the murdered women's lives to the students' own frames of reference. Such a relation "gets closer in order to allow the difference between us, as a difference which involves power and antagonism, to make a difference to the very dialogue between self and other" (Ahmed 1997, 32). What might it mean to let difference make a difference, in a project like this, when confronting that difference would require a confrontation with structural oppression? Ahmed's questions about relationality and intimacy—mediated for a first-year class, of course—would have let us begin the task from a more sensitive position, one that brought together the complex dimensions of witnessing with a structural analysis that foregrounded difference.

It is, indeed, relationality that links the limits to understanding structural violence, and the associated but different problem of what it meant to witness and provide an account of specific instances of violence against women. The absence of tools to understand the subject in relation, whatever those might look like for first-year students, meant that they had an ambiguous relationship to the women they were researching. Putting themselves in relation, forging a careful but not voyeuristic intimacy, would have required acknowledging that the students themselves were not so different—in terms of the possibility of being violated—from the women they were researching. As our course readings and discussion emphasized, violence against women cuts across class and ethnic lines. It thus is not solely the tragic lot of "bad girls" or the particularly marginal, although, as I note, certain marginalized communities are at significantly increased risk. Acknowledging the contours of their relationship with the murdered women, then, demanded of these mostly female students that they recognize the points of potential contact *as well as* incommensurability, a balance that Ahmed's reworked concept of intimate relations could help us achieve. A complicated dance was necessary to accommodate both structural oppression and the demands of ethical witnessing; students needed to learn to both avoid assimilating the murdered women to their frames of reference, in arrogant intimacy, *and* to recognize potential points of contact that would lead them to reckon with the reality of structural violence.

To accomplish such work would have required a thoroughgoing accounting with several layers of theory and this complicated the task of facilitating the service-learning project. It would be especially challenging for the staff member from the university's service-learning department, who is not likely versed in the theoretical work I have argued is imperative. It would, though, be work usefully undertaken by me as part of the core curriculum of the course.

By integrating these questions into the core curriculum, too, the relational work of service-learning would effectively become integrated into the course, and not hived off as something anterior to intellectual inquiry. This would be an opportunity to enact the transformational promise of service-learning by according it a primacy that matched the other concepts we were studying.

It is clear that this project gave something concrete to the communities it was designed to assist, the Kelowna Women's Resource Centre and the family members of murdered women. This is important, and my intention is not to suggest otherwise. Perhaps I remain haunted by the collectivity of ghosts that the project stirred up, all these murdered women who remain imperfectly represented. Gordon (2008, 183) writes, "[t]he ghost is...pregnant with unfulfilled possibility, with the something to be done that the wavering present is demanding." Had we approached the project been differently, more attentive to the complexities of power and privilege in the representational regimes that structured it, I believe this possibility might have been fulfilled in a way that both did justice to the women being memorialized, and constituted a more meaningful "something to be done" than it turned out to be.

Notes

An earlier version of this work appeared as Ilya Parkins, "'Nineteen Funerals': Ethics of Remembering Murdered Women in a Service-learning Classroom," *Review of Education, Pedagogy and Cultural Studies* 35 (2014): 127–43. Reprinted with permission.

1 The list of readings included Vickers 2002; Valentine 1989; Ristock 2005; and Morales 2007.
2 In the context of the service-learning classroom, Gordon's (2008) interest in haunting can be read alongside Margaret Himley's (2004) work on the way that service-learning is "haunted" by the "strangers"—community members—that students encounter in their work, who are figured as ontologically distinct from the students by the conventional rhetoric of service-learning (see also Amber Dean's chapter in this volume for further discussion of this point).

CHAPTER SEVEN

QUICK TO THE DRAW: SHOOTING FROM THE HIP IN FEMINIST NGOS

JUDITH TAYLOR

Many pedagogical puzzles centre on the cleavage between what students want to learn and what professors want to teach. We might alternately say the cleavage rests between what professors teach and what students already believe they know. My experience of teaching feminist service-learning is well captured by both of these maxims. Like many other contributors to this book, I aim to give students a greater appreciation of two things: the dynamics of complex organizations, and the challenges feminist social movement organizations face in their efforts to create social change (see in particular Joanne Muzak's, Lise Gotell's, Ilya Parkins', and Rachel Alpha Johnston Hurst's chapters in this volume). Doing either involves staving off students' quick and unflattering assessments about organizations they have only just glimpsed. My own students often seemed to be hanging out in the clouds, and as I will explain, the rarefied air up there precludes seeing a goodly portion of what is taking place on the ground. It also veils the humanity of the people there. This chapter is about the stakes of paying attention to our students' political and intellectual instincts, so they may push past them and really learn outside the classroom.

Since 2002, I have taught a fourth-year Women's and Gender Studies (WGS) course at the University of Toronto in which ten undergraduate students find or initiate a group or organization that does work they conceive of as feminist and that is of interest to them. They typically volunteer in homeless shelters, rape-crisis centres, food security organizations, or reproductive justice campaigns. They begin with a set of interests, and I recommend organizations or groups I think they might have quality learning experiences within. They volunteer from September to February, spending March and April reflecting on and writing about their experience. The readings for the course cover subjects such as movement NGOization (Bernal and Grewal 2014), strategic decision-making and problems of financial buoyancy and government oversight (INCITE! 2009), organizations' efforts to think through race and racism (Scott 1998), and strategy formation and how to gauge efficacy (Whittier

2009), to name just some. For a final paper, I ask students to write a case study of their organizations focusing on the explication and resolution of a dilemma. This assignment grew out of my experience teaching the course, because I began to find WGS insufficiently attentive to problem-solving. Students in my classes did not seem keen to problem-solve—rather they wanted to unpack and unravel, rolling out proverbial spools of thread with no thought as to what such unravelling might generate. One of my pedagogical goals is to show students that unravelling is often more fun to produce than to live with, or clean up. What is unravelled must be ravelled again. This and other learning patterns indicated to me I needed to conduct some research to figure out why students were approaching service-learning in the ways they were.

Kim de Laat (a doctoral student) and I interviewed twenty-five students who had taken the WGS service-learning course with me and other faculty members, to better understand their experience of it.[1] We found that WGS, as the broker between young feminists and organized feminism, is helping to curate a particular kind of experience which may not be conducive to positive feminist intergenerational relations and activism (Taylor and de Laat 2013). In these internships, students see NGO staff as bosses, not comrades; they often feel neglected or segregated when doing menial tasks rather than understanding them as core to the daily work of the organization. Rarely do mentors in organizations engage students in expansive conversations about the history, multiplicity, and challenges of feminist work. Without the intimacy and camaraderie of such conversations, service-learning mirrors professional work more than activism. Many placements introduce students to what is now a highly institutionalized era of feminist work for change.

Yet, on the contrary, one could argue Canadian feminism is in a period of deinstitutionalization: Status of Women has been both curtailed and co-opted, feminist NGOs have experienced steadily diminishing resources, and the advocacy umbrella voice for these disparate NGOs, The National Action Committee on the Status of Women, is defunct (see Lise Gotell's and Joanne Muzak's chapters in this volume for further discussion about the impact of government changes and funding cutbacks on feminist NGOs in Canada). The loss of umbrella advocacy too shapes students' experiences, as the organizations they volunteer within often appear disparate and fragmented, operating more as silos than members of a larger cause with a shared set of commitments.

In our study, we asked the instructors of women's studies programs engaged in service-learning and feminist organizations that take student volunteers to consider what we perceived to be the depression of young feminists' political imagination as a consequence of interning (Taylor and De Laat 2013). Seven of the twenty-five former students we interviewed had overwhelmingly positive experiences. Their mentors were consultative, told pedagogically useful stories of challenges and change, and included them in meetings and the core work of the organization. The staff members in those successful settings were cooperative and social with one another and not disproportionately invested in protocol and hierarchy, and the students admired the work they were a taking part in.

The rest, however, felt somewhat taken advantage of, unrecognized, and disheartened. They expressed some disinclination to join a feminist group after graduation, and came to find WGS implausible in terms of its usability. For most students, the internship, in other words, had a chastening effect. Learning experiences need not all be positive nor inspiring. Professors teaching service-learning courses ideally co-mentor students with someone in the placement organizations, but mentoring is hard to come by, and it is arguably beneficial for students to hustle—to make themselves useful and memorable, even if they are uncomfortable or unsuccessful. But in their placements, more often than not, students cared less about their own inclusion and more about diagnosing their placement organizations and checking off the insufficiencies they found. Initially I reasoned that students need not share the kind of admiration I experienced as an undergraduate observing seasoned activists at work. Not all mentors are inspirational. But over time, I came to conclude students were "too quick to the draw." They often wanted to ferret out errors rather than first understand how the work was being conceptualized by those doing it. From what did this collective inclination arise?

In this chapter, I would like to think more about both feminism's predilections and habits, and the way in which these habits produce particular kinds of learning orientations that students adopt in the communities they choose to engage. My hunch is that part of students' "quick draw" learning experience comes from the "quick draw" toolkit feminist studies equips them with in the classroom prior to entering organizations purporting to do things in the world. By "quick draw" I mean a kind of rapid-fire inclination to discount, dismiss, judge, distance, and hold in contempt rather than question with the aim to learn more than their observations can reveal. Left to their own devices, my students very often engage in what Eve Sedgwick (2003) calls "paranoid readings" of the organizations they join. Paranoia as a political orientation is centred on exposure—discovering the problem, and then shining a light on it. Such an orientation has an almost videogame quality to it, shooting monsters as they jump out from behind hedges, and experiencing the anticipation, exhilaration, and calm of cartoon annihilation. It is a "relational stance" students can use to engage with and understand the world, predicated on its de facto nefariousness. Paranoia elegantly predicts and elucidates the worst, *as though finding the worst is the best thing feminism can do.*

This relational stance is also one that is, in Sedgwick's understanding, deeply pedagogical. She writes that paranoia "represents a way, among other ways, of seeking, finding, and organizing knowledge," which is "nothing if not teachable" (Sedgwick 2003, 136). While it requires a terrible alertness in adherents, it actually prevents them from seeing many things. Anxiety can heighten our observation, but it also usually delimits it. And thus, paranoia produces observations that do a particular kind of corroborative work, showing that things are, in fact, *just that bad*. But this singular focus, for Sedgwick, narrows the field of what's possible to know. It obscures alternative ways of understanding, or alternative things to understand (Sedgwick 2003, 131).

Paranoia not only frames feminist scholarship, it conditions the feminist classroom as well. Students engage in both paranoid readings of their field sites, and of one another. One of our participants described her classroom this way: "There [were] definitely some value judgments I felt, being passed on what students did. Not necessarily by the prof, but she allowed other students to make comments and that sort of thing. So I didn't find the discussions were that helpful." Judgments among students mirror students' judgments of the organizations they join—all are in some way insufficiently feminist, however defined. Upon entering their organizations of choice, students appear poised to see the worst, observing until they find fault. The same suppositions emerge in classroom discussions: a lesbian organization is racist; a mental health organization labels and medicalizes clients; a trans youth program is inaccessible; a food security organization has class pretentions. And this paranoia is "infectious," in that it expands to how students read one another. These analyses represent a troubling disingenuousness, or bad faith. They also curtail learning. That said, these judgments also cohere with broader feminist reflexes. When did we become the ones who delight in the quick draw, externalizing our damage with such ease? If the state is always pernicious, the NGO always compromised, students need not leave campus for the rape-crisis centre, the child care advocacy organization, the labour union, or the food security organization, because no experience will be found in service of learning. They already know, and what they know negates anything that might be learned or accomplished in these settings.

The quick-draw impulse might be animated, in this case, by a set of underlying anxieties that are less often expressed. In the case of service-learning, students' judgments can calm the underlying causes of anxiety that often animate them. Judgments of one kind mask judgments of another—desires to earn more than NGO workers, fear of women on the street and domestic abuse victims, fear of hard work, fear of failure, fear of too much responsibility for others, fear of being, or not being, middle class or working class, fear of wanting something, fear of losing, fear of the economy, fear of numbers, fear of not "already knowing" or being seen not to know, fear of being disliked or judged by NGO staff. Our students themselves have chauvinisms and do not necessarily want to be proximate to front-line work. Said one, "I thought doing a women's studies practicum would position me to go into some sort of underpaid social work type place and I didn't want to do it. And I probably thought in a very snobby way that it wasn't high theory enough, like it was something people who weren't smart did. Something that people who wanted to just work did."

Students' engagement with front-line workers is complicated by their own class and status anxieties. Types of apprehension shift across students—while some see front-line work as low-skill or low-wage, others posit that NGO staff profit monetarily and in status from neoliberalization, by advocating on behalf of the truly disenfranchised. Students who already assume that NGO workers are benefiting parasitically from the populations they work with might find a specific narrative to tell once they are in their host organizations. For example, a student might notice that at a drop-in centre, the staff use a coffee maker located behind a staff partition that is different from the one the folks use who come into the centre. She might draw immediate inferences about classism and professionalization of the staff. Judgments replace inquiry. She does not think about the ecosystem of an organization: about what it is like to work on the front line for decades, how to prevent burnout, and the needs of privacy or autonomy for both staff and participants, all of which might be enabled by separate coffee spaces. In short, observations that should be the starting point of inquiry for "Why is this?" become the cynical lens through which all other organizational behaviour is read. The phrase "when your only tool is a hammer, everything looks like a nail" aptly fits here.

Discovering or suspecting organizational imperfections risks short-circuiting the curiosity that should accompany the learning forays that internships represent. Even in the cases when such suppositions are true, these problems ought not provide sufficient cause to disconnect from the learning experience or discount the social and political worth of the organization. As Sedgwick (2003, 136) writes, "anticipating negative affect can block entirely the potentially operative goal of seeking positive effect." She elaborates that paranoid readings block anything that could be read as positive, as reformist, or ameliorative, or about pleasure, as if only bad feelings are substantive, and only revolution is desired (144). We learned in our research that students are aware of how a WGS pedagogical approach encouraged their search for the negative. When asked if WGS helped her come to an understanding of civic engagement, one participant confessed, "I am so tempted to say yes, but in all honesty when I think back to women's studies it seemed very antagonistic. I learned how people were screwed over. I didn't learn how to participate in the resistance against that." What this and similar reflections suggest is a kind of one-dimensional classroom, where we train students to identify oppression but not to understand the myriad ways one might respond to it. It could be said WGS values critique over creation. To value creation is to tread into territory of self-celebration, something Robyn Wiegman (2002), in her introduction to *Women's Studies on Its Own*, cautions against. To her, a central tenet of women and gender studies' vibrancy is its ability to "challenge every impulse to celebratory self-narration" (Weigman 2002, 2). If this is the case, it should come as no wonder students' first instinct in the grassroots is not to appreciate.

Some of WGS' most treasured contemporary concepts, such as Sara Ahmed's (2010) killjoy in *The Promise of Happiness*, deepen students' convictions that they must be suspicious rather than observant. In her explication of the killjoy and the cultural uses of happiness as an aspiration, Ahmed elegantly outlines for students the political utility of their lack of cooperation, but I fear they keep the sulk rather than the larger implications of Ahmed's analysis. Telling young feminists to be killjoys is not exactly a spiritual or emotional stretch for them. It would be a stretch instead to ask them to differentiate between Ahmed's killjoy and Sedgwick's paranoid reader. Where precisely does productive non-cooperation cross into scourge? Answering this relies on revisiting what we mean by praxis. Praxis as a concept can feel old-fashioned, and today appears less frequently in the indexes of books about WGS than ever before. Feminist scholars such as Nancy Naples (2002c, 383) bemoan the idea that WGS is itself a kind of activist practice, thus not requiring specific pedagogy on community organizing outside the academy. That said, many others would like to complicate the dichotomization of the university and the "real world," activism and scholarship (Gunew 2002).

More commonly now we have arms-length analyses of feminists at the grassroots like Aiwa Ong's (2006) chapter on NGOs and domestic labour in *Neoliberalism as Exception*. In Ong's work, the feminist scholar observes the feminist NGO to reveal how it is trapped in the logics of the market and the state (see also Lise Gotell's chapter in this volume), trying to articulate compromised humanity's deservedness through moral suasion. Because NGOs work within moral and economic regimes, she writes, they "thus directly or indirectly subcontract for states and work with market interests" (Ong 2006, 216). NGOs experience what Ong (2006, 216) calls "enmeshment in normative structures," which sounds compromising, even if she argues such enmeshments can lead NGOs to be more efficacious in their grassroots work. Ong is in fact correct, of course, that NGOs must work within the economic, cultural, and ethical frameworks of the dominant societies they are aiming to change, and that this negotiation can make feminist claims look a lot different on the ground than they do in a classroom. But one of the implications of

Ong's analysis is that feminist politics stay perfect in the academic mind, yet are compromised in civil society because they are situated within these larger ethical regimes. Such analyses, too, lead our students to assume academia is pure, but work on the ground is tainted, partial, to be avoided.

Additionally, WGS must revisit what we mean by inquiry and research. WGS is between a rock and a hard place. The rock is its certainty; the hard place is the ethical and scholarly obligation to find something out. Most disciplines have a recipe for this conundrum: we do research and read theory, we explore some problem, and then we reconcile what we have read with what we ourselves have observed, and try to stick with the puzzles such reconciliation produces for longer than most outside of academia care to do. Some call this empiricism, others scientific method, and still others just academic work. WGS practitioners vary in what they believe constitutes exploration, and the journey from having a question to a considered answer, but none would say a journey should not be had. Even so, we might have an interesting discussion about whether the journeys are too scripted, and the end destination fully known at the moment of departure. We might usefully ask whether the journey is curtailed by the conflation of discernment and critique. Or is it that critique comes to pass for discernment? This problem has led me to accept Janet Halley's (2006) invitation to periodically "take a break from feminism" and encourage students in my class to do the same. It is less gratifying to sequester feminism in our minds, but it is more edifying. It allows for the questions "What are people doing here, and why?" and "What might they know, that I don't?" Such questions lead to better research, and also enliven what might be thought of as an *ethics of service-learning.* Perhaps we would want students to approach the front-line work of NGOs that open their doors regularly to them for the purposes of learning in the field on different terms. We might want to disabuse the heady notions that we, or they, know more, when NGO workers have in fact seen and done quite a lot.

For me, this is about a kind of golden rule we need to have in WGS that is something inelegant like "Don't judge the practitioner." Scholarly enquiry must be more nuanced than admonishing feminists who are trying to produce social change through real negotiations with the state. At minimum, students need to understand the "chilling conditions" under which feminist non-profit organizations in Canada have been labouring (for further discussion, see Lise Gotell's and Joanne Muzak's chapters in this volume). Teaching and research do not themselves constitute such challenging negotiations, which may contribute to what I perceive as a misalignment between feminists within and outside of academia. Tenure, academic freedom, and exceptional occupational autonomy have produced scholarly work environments which, for those scholars who are part of the tenure track, produce an unfettered relationship to structures outside academia. Such working conditions, which have not always been the case for feminists in the academy, now put feminist scholars in markedly different positions from NGO feminists.

As a way of concluding, I turn to examples from two books: one judges the practitioner in a way that appears too quick to the draw, and one gives an empirically rich and ethical account of the practitioner. In her book *In an Abusive State: How Neoliberalism Appropriated the Feminist Movement against Sexual Violence*, Kristin Bumiller (2008) makes the case that feminist lawyers, social workers, international advocates, and policy analysts, through partnering with the state, have emboldened the state's war on vulnerable men, particularly those of colour, and medicalized and legalized the terrain of assault in a way that harms victims as well. Many of her analyses do not appear to build on evidence, and her portrayals are often cringeworthy. Anyone who has worked in a shelter, a police division, or a crisis care unit knows there are some pretty thoughtful people engaged in victim services. But none of them are featured in the examples Bumiller gives of lawyers and social service workers who appear heartless and cold. The question is fundamentally whether feminist scholars can ask questions about the limits of legal justice strategies for women who have experienced violence, without making those involved in criminal justice and victim services appear as unthinking people complicit in the revictimization of those on the margins.

For example, Bumiller makes the case that the state has aggressively prosecuted men accused of sexual assault to increase its power, and focused more on punishment than the possibility of rehabilitation. But from there she argues that part of this prosecutorial logic is to over-invest in the treatment of women victims. She writes, "[t]his victim focused agenda has contributed to the growth of administrative power exercised over clients who have experienced sexual violence. The primary objective of these services is to turn women who have experienced the trauma of violence into successful survivors. This generally involves retraining women to protect themselves from future violence as well as to seek help from professionals who can guide them through the process of psychological recovery" (Bumiller, 2008, 64). In her effort to show the state's aggression, Bumiller implicates any feminist in the violence against women movement who coordinates with the state to counsel women, teaches them self-defence, advises them of sick leave rights and procedures, and finds them alternate homes or sources of support. Who are these countless but uncounted advocates wearing jeans and runners, answering phone lines, feeding their own children cereal before heading to hospital emergency rooms or sitting in legal clinics listening intently to women who are, suffice to say, not having an easy time in their lives? While Bumiller's approach forecloses such questions, WGS service-learning courses need to begin with them.

By contrast, in her book *The Politics of Child Sexual Abuse, Emotions, Social Movements, and the State*, Nancy Whittier (2009) analyzes survivor advocacy work in the US to better understand the goals, challenges, and effects of such politicization. Whittier's project appears not dissimilar to Bumiller's: tracing the work of feminist movements and the public integration, or adoption, of feminist ideas. But her analysis does not blame people who sought to work with the state or gain state recognition. Rather, she carefully asks what practitioners and activists tried to do, and what became of their work. Whittier shows that arguments that cohere with popular conceptions of a problem will achieve the most success, and those that are more challenging do not find their way into policy, newspaper articles, or sex education classes. For Whittier this is about the circulation of ideas, not the failure of activists. How ideas circulate and get adopted is quite important to understand, and such understandings are helpful to practitioners, students, and scholars alike, to say nothing of everyday people. But it is also important to note that practitioners cannot always predict what the integration of their ideas and state logics will produce, nor should scholars cavalierly, or in a determined fashion, blame social change advocates for the unintended consequences of their activism. Such scholarship ultimately is more than cautionary—it is a smug deterrent that is effectively a pedagogy of inaction. Such a pedagogy coheres with WGS' move away from praxis and activism as programmatic foci. We can see in scholarship such as Ong's and Bumiller's how students might come to judge rather than align with feminists in NGO settings. Such scholarship implicates feminists in a web of ruling relations our students cannot help but want to avoid.

In her book *Curious Feminist: Searching for Women in a New Age of Empire*, Cynthia Enloe (2004) maps thoughtfully and plainly the stakes of asking questions one genuinely does not have answers for. For Enloe, what makes curiosity *feminist* in particular is a commitment to taking women's lives seriously, not with the assumption that they are always good, but that the conditions of their lives indicate how power operates, and the places the work of social change can be found. Absent genuine questions, Enloe (2004, 4) argues that power will "glide right by us like an oil tanker on a foggy night." For me, taking vulnerable people's lives seriously as a starting point of feminist service-learning guides students to think about the big picture rather than stop at initial, knee-jerk observations. No matter how imperfect, NGO failings did not lead to the development of WGS—the problems NGOs struggle to address did. But students may find it easier to fault practitioners than trace power and ponder the sheer durability of unacceptably high levels of inequality and suffering.

WGS need not be the arm of social movements, nor train students to activism. That said, service-learning, be it fashionable now for universities, or a central part of WGS history, can give our students exceptionally rich exposure to complex problems that have no easy solutions. It can give them access to practitioners who have a great deal to offer in knowledge and experience about how people, and the world, work. The NGOs that work with our students offer numerous and changing lessons in organizational dynamics, political constraints, the generation of ideas, and strategic action. These will benefit our students whatever their life intentions and can never be completely understood—there will always be new puzzles and unanswered questions. Learning in an advocacy organization can be both useful and intellectually rich. However, we hollow out such connections and opportunities when students choose to discover the ways in which supposedly justice-oriented people are actually oppressive. Students can produce nuanced understandings that are also compassionate with their hands in the dirt, rather than tucked carefully under crossed arms. When students must contend with real-life dilemmas in an organization, they potentially develop empathy, a key facet of undergraduate education that is often learned, rather than inherent in people (Nussbaum 1998). Open-minded observation also enables students to be receptive to what Sara Ahmed (2010, 219–20) calls happenstance, the idea that what happens may be good or bad, may lead to boredom, awe, determination, joy. Respect for practitioners, and being open to happenstance, make for better research, better learning, and better relations between the feminist academy and those who graciously allow our students a seat at the table.

We can ask students if they are too quick on the draw, if they shoot from the hip without fully understanding, if they imagined themselves in the role of the staff they observe, and if their analysis makes them the prophet and their research subjects the dupes. Such habits and cynicism can be outgrown, but not easily. They are the raw materials with which we build bridges between universities and the feminist organizations in their midst. And they can become learning orientations that prevent our students from working through their initial discomforts and suspicions in favour of a more substantive and empathic observation after graduation.

Note

This research was supported by a grant from the Centre for the Study of Post-Secondary Education, Ontario Institute for Studies in Education, University of Toronto. The research received approval from the Office of Research Ethics, University of Toronto.

CHAPTER EIGHT

EVALUATING THE EFFECTS OF COMMUNITY-BASED PRAXIS LEARNING PLACEMENTS ON CAMPUS AND COMMUNITY ORGANIZATIONS IN THE "DOING FEMINIST THEORY THROUGH DIGITAL VIDEO" PROJECT

RACHEL ALPHA JOHNSTON HURST

Community partners provide the foundation for community-based praxis learning (CBPL) in Women's and Gender Studies (WGS) programs. This chapter analyzes interviews with community partners of my undergraduate assignment, "Doing Feminist Theory Through Digital Video" ("DFT-DV"), in order to better understand the effects of CBPL on community organizations. Curiously, the vital contribution of community partners remains poorly understood, because research on CBPL has tended to focus on assignment design and implementation, or on evaluation of student learning outcomes. This lacuna in scholarship has a number of consequences for instructors, students, and community partners. Specifically, the distance between "the classroom" and "the community"—likely one that all CBPL assignments endeavour to shorten—is maintained by this persistent focus on the classroom, reinforcing student assumptions that the classroom is a space removed from "the real world."

In my experience teaching a third-year undergraduate feminist theory class required for all WGS degree options at St. Francis Xavier University (StFX), even when students enjoy the intellectual challenge of grappling with abstract concepts (and especially when they do not), they characterize the work we are doing in the classroom as removed from "the real world." As a result, students tend to evade acknowledging relations of power and exclusion, erroneously coding our classroom—and by extension, the university campus—as safe and protected. Such an understanding of the (WGS) classroom and university campus dangerously erases the relations of racism, colonialism, heterosexism, transphobia, ableism, and classism that structure these spaces. When I interviewed students who completed the first iteration of "DFT-DV," over half of them commented that the assignment challenged their preconceptions about the classroom as removed from "the real world" or "real life," because it required them to create a digital video. Students noted that "DFT-DV," was unique because they had to integrate ideas from course texts with ideas from community organizations, and because they were able to share their coursework with others—many students chose to upload their videos to YouTube or share them on Twitter or Facebook, for example.

"DFT-DV," is designed to offer an opportunity for all students doing a degree option in WGS at StFX to complete a CBPL assignment during the latter half of their degree. Based on my prior experience, however, I designed this assignment to be quite different from community service-learning (CSL) assignments that I offered in past versions of my introductory course. These past assignments were shaped by the institutional context at StFX.[1] In particular, I wished to dispel a widespread student belief, namely that in doing community "service" they were making a significant contribution to the organization. Instead, I wanted to highlight the organization's generosity in agreeing to supervise students and offering an opportunity for them to learn.

After discussing the assignment in context, I move into an analysis of interviews with individuals who supervised students for this assignment since its pilot semester in 2012: Carmen, Coucou, Ellis Bell, Fern, Nicky, Isabel, Macy, Maria, and Veronica.[2] These interviews were conducted in the fall semester of 2014. Some individuals supervised students for all three versions of "DFT-DV," others supervised students for only one version (new partners joined the project in 2013 and 2014), while others still have left and/or returned, based on availability and staff turnover at the community organizations). I interviewed nine representatives from nine of the eleven organizations or projects that participated over the past three years.

Two things connect the organizations that participate in "DFT-DV": first, every organization does some type of facilitation or education outreach activity, and second, every organization provides services for students in some capacity, as the majority are campus-based. The community partners for this project include or have included the Aboriginal Student Advisor, the International Student Advisor, the Black Student Advisor, the Positive Spaces training program (a joint StFX–Antigonish endeavour), the Human Rights and Equity Office, the Antigonish Women's Resource Centre (on four separate projects: *Healthy Relationships for Youth*, *Preventing Violence Against Women at StFX*, *Resisting Violence*, and *Responding to and Preventing Violence in Mi'kmaq*

Communities), the Student Life Office, the Residence Life Office, and Social Justice Radio/Radio Ada.

The interviews confirmed some of my assumptions about the positive and negative impacts of CBPL on the organizations, particularly regarding the effects of student (dis)engagement and the additional time burden of supervision. However, the interviews also engendered a number of unanticipated and significant insights about CBPL, namely that several supervisors conceptualized student supervision as a part of their work, that there still exists a disconnection between the organization and the university in spite of attempts to bridge that gap, and that several of the organizations rely upon student supervision as a means to connect their organization with the student body as a whole. And finally, these interviews were a wellspring of ideas to strengthen the assignment and the collaboration between my feminist theory course and the community partners who supervise "DFT-DV."

Overview of "Doing Feminist Theory Through Digital Video"

Drawing upon a diverse set of literatures and arts practices—including digital storytelling, participatory video, and critical feminist perspectives on service-learning—"DFT-DV" was designed as a creative CSL project.[3] Something that links these literatures and practices is an interest in challenging boundaries that often promote exclusion, like envisioning art and theory as rarefied and elite pursuits; technology and theory as inaccessible; the university as separate from the community; and activism as solely large-scale projects of structural change. Further, these literatures also emphasize a need to broaden conventional learning activities and evaluation methods by incorporating new knowledge sources and ways of communicating that go beyond the essay or exam.

"DFT-DV" replaces a learning portfolio assignment that invited students to write a final paper reflecting on one or two of their major insights that emerged and persisted in the feminist theory course (for example, the ethics of speaking about an experience that is not one's own was a popular choice of insight). The course is structured thematically using a contrapuntal reading approach. We meet twice a week, and during our first meeting we read short excerpts on the week's broad theme (for example, power) and I facilitate a class discussion on that theme. In the second session, students read a longer text (a book chapter or journal article) that approaches the week's theme from a decolonizing, queer, or trans theory approach, and two students give a presentation on the longer text. This approach is heavily concept-oriented, as we analyze how concepts can move (or not) across and through divergent histories and geographies.

For "DFT-DV," students select a relevant concept with a community partner (for example, transgender, decolonization, or power) as the subject of a short, non-documentary video that will support the facilitation and education outreach activities of that community partner.[4] The assignment is divided into four sections, which span the duration of the semester-long theory course. First, students engage in a "research and concept exploration" phase, where they learn about their chosen concept through their community placement and course readings. The second phase, "planning and writing," requires students to write a script about their concept and consider how they will bring it to life using voices, sounds, music, and images (still photographs and video). At the beginning of the third phase, "shooting and editing," students hand in their script and a list of materials that they have or will produce to support it, which will be a guide for creating their video. The fourth and final phase is reflective, where students write a paper about how the process of "DFT-DV" shaped their understanding of their chosen concept, as well as a response to the bigger question: "What have I learned about feminist theory in this course?" The latter question is anchored by the videos and encourages students to identify recurring questions and themes in their work. With the students' permission, the videos are uploaded to the "DFT-DV" Vimeo site, so that the community partners and others can use them in their work: http:// www.doingfeministtheory.ca/.

Differentiating "DFT-DV"

My previous attempts at offering optional CSL assignments in the introductory course were not particularly successful. It was extremely difficult to facilitate reflection that produced a structural analysis of privilege and oppression, in particular. Even students who were capable of writing an excellent research essay on the feminization and racialization of poverty in Canada and who received a critical introduction to CSL from the Service Learning Program faltered when attempting to apply that knowledge to a service-learning placement with the local women's centre or community food bank.[5] When asked to make connections between course material focused on structural explanations for the feminization and racialization of poverty, most students produced reflections that emphasized the individual conditions of the lives of people their paths crossed with.[6] In addition, there were a small number of major violations of trust between a few students and me, and as a result between the organizations and me (as well as the university that the students and I represented). Some students lied to me all semester, reporting fictional experiences at their placements. Journal reflections were not handed in by some students, only to be written up the night before the final paper was due and misrepresented as ongoing reflection and analysis. Meanwhile, because the StFX Service Learning Program organized the placements, I was one step removed from the relationship between the students and the organizations and did not have a means to connect with the students' placement supervisors.

When I was conducting research to design "DFT-DV," I was interested in pinpointing exactly what it was that commonly "went wrong" in service-learning assignments. I engaged in this research skeptical of the widespread assumption by students and some members of the university community that the service provided by university students is valuable. Instead, I suspected the opposite might be true (Stukas et al. 1999, 13). As Eleanor M. Novek (1999, 235) remarks, often CSL assignments are perceived by students (and some-times, instructors) as an opportunity to be "exposed" to social problems in the community where they attend university; such an approach facilitates a "paternalistic 'feel-good' benevolence." Amber Dean (2007, 352) remarks that students come to understand community-based learning as teaching them to be advocates on behalf of individuals and communities with whom they have no relationship, rather than as a way of understanding the structural privilege and oppression that configure their lives and the lives of those they work with.[7] In my own experience, this distancing manoeuvre enables privileged students to protect and even reinforce their privilege, while sometimes simultaneously performing a shallow critique of that privilege, or at other times, responding irresponsibly to the service-learning placement.

While it aligned with the university's CSL practice, the way I initially offered service-learning did not promote the kind of learning I intended, inspired as I had been by Paulo Freire's (1970/2000, 51) visionary dictum of praxis as "reflection and action upon the world in order to change it." As Donna M. Bickford and Nedra Reynolds (2002, 233) caution, even off-campus projects that have been meticulously planned can go awry—for example, by amplifying the difference between the student and the communities served by the orga-nization offering the CSL placement—without producing critical insights into the structural foundations of these differences. Bickford and Reynolds (2002, 233) comment that while community-based projects theoretically have the possibility of helping students become better critical thinkers, readers, writers, and community members, this happens only when "their social and cultural biases [are not] further entrenched" by their community involvement.

The CSL component of "DFT-DV" was inspired by Bickford and Reynolds' (2002, 244) argument that students do not need to leave campus in order to "experience geographies of exclusion," and that leaving campus, rather than bridging, can further ensconce the presumed distance between campus and community. So instead of seeking out inequalities in the off-campus commu-nity, I turned the students' critical lens upon their campus. Staying on campus and with community partners that share a common commitment to serving the student population in some way was an attempt to compel students into a confrontation with the relations of exclusion and oppression within their own university community.

Further, I agree with Bickford and Reynolds' suggestion that it is not necessary for students to engage in extensive projects (both in scale and time) in
order to glean significant insights about and from activism. In fact, smaller-
scale projects have the potential to be more accessible to students who are not
accustomed to considering themselves as activists (Bickford and Reynolds
2002, 244). A CSL component of a smaller and more task-oriented order also
relieves some of the burden from the community placements, as they do not
have to devote as much time to supervising students. Thus, the other major
element I changed for "DFT-DV" was to limit the amount of time spent in the
placement to ten hours. I worked more closely with organizations to identify or
even design a small task that would be useful to them, while being manageable
for a student, allowing the students to complete the tasks independently without draining further resources from already limited staff time. An unanticipated benefit to smaller scale placements is that students are generally unable
to assume a position of mastery in relation to their work with the organization.

I have used this assignment in four iterations of my feminist theory course.
Each time, only a handful of students possessed prior experience in expressing
ideas through art and music, so the process of developing a digital video was
one that often radically decentred the student's framework for what academic
work looks like, as well as the process of making meaning. Students commonly
vented their annoyances and disappointments about using the technology and
the difficulty of expressing their ideas creatively. While the process of working creatively often manifests in frustration and anger, which in turn I need to
hold and tolerate for my students (Hurst 2014b, 342–43), I recognize that these
emotions emerge in response to having their expectations unsettled regarding
what "helping" their organization might look like, as well as a deeper emotional investment in their work.

Interviews with "DFT-DV" Community Partners

Overall, the community partners I interviewed expressed appreciation for these
efforts and the "DFT-DV" assignment, and yet the interviews also confirmed
my concerns that the community-based portion of the assignment negatively
impacts the organizations, particularly in terms of time spent mentoring students. The community partners all noted that service-learning supervision
is a complicated yet crucial component of their work, because it provides a
connection to students that they otherwise would not have. Several of the community partners agreed to participate in "DFT-DV" because they desired a
deeper connection to the WGS program generally and the feminist theory
course specifically. Also, they assumed the videos would be useful to their work.
But community partners also identified the drawbacks, especially regarding
time. Some hoped that they would receive more support from the students,

and were disappointed with the lack of attention and care that students put into the work they did.

I asked the community partners to reflect on the concept of praxis, and they discussed it in relation to their work, the placement, WGS, and the university more broadly. The video that the students produced was offered as an example of praxis, and the community partners emphasized the importance of process and movement in their definitions and explanations of praxis. As the interviews unfolded, I realized that the interviews themselves are another valuable tool for making student involvement more meaningful to community partners. In the conclusion to this chapter, I argue that incorporating a structured and formalized process of debriefing with the organization and the student could be a valuable way to continually improve the quality of student involvement *and* student learning in "DFT-DV," and I offer some suggestions for how this process could be embedded in the assignment.

1. Community Service-Learning and the Work of "DFT-DV" Community Partners

Wishing to establish and strengthen connections to students was the most common answer given by community partners when asked why they agreed to be a supervisor for "DFT-DV." Fern's response captured this motivation well: they noted that their organization is interested in "bringing in different perspectives, different angles" to their work, and that the mission and values of the organization are strengthened by "branch[ing] out and work[ing] with as many people as possible." Half of the interviewees echoed Coucou and Carmen, who characterized their day-to-day work as "disconnected" or "removed" (respectively) from students, even though their organizations directly serve that population. Isabel, Jane, Carmen, Macy, Ellis Bell, Veronica, and Coucou all commented that service-learning is another opportunity to engage students in the work of their organization that simply makes sense. Thus, the decision to supervise students was based on the assumption that it will benefit the organization through learning more about the students' perspectives on the issues that the organization addresses. Yet while these student perspectives are useful for the organizations, supervision requires additional time and work.

I was surprised to hear several community partners describe student supervision as just another expectation of their jobs. While only three of the interviewees (Macy, Coucou, and Maria) noted that they receive very limited administrative support and/or have no volunteer coordinator to assist with their work, I know that all of the organizations are in a similar situation. In fact, Coucou, Macy, Maria, and Isabel commented that one of their hopes when agreeing to participate was that they would receive additional support of the sort that an administrative assistant could provide. As Maria said, the students worked on tasks that "would have been really time-consuming for [her]," and her organization really needs "boots on the ground" and "extra hands to do the work." However, when I commented that I was concerned about the potential drawbacks (such as time commitment) for organizations, Carmen responded by saying, "well, and no offence, we're an academic institution…we need to make time to create these learning opportunities for our students," thus articulating supervision as an expectation of her workplace. In a related discussion, Jane commented that her organization is "interested in student learning so [they] want to support maybe a more hands-on way or a more practical way for students to gain some knowledge." Ellis Bell noted that she was "definitely encouraged" by her employer to supervise students when the opportunity arose. Hoping that students would be able to help make up for a lack of administrative support is one reason that supervision was characterized as an expected part of their job, but so was an understanding of their work as being connected to student learning.

I did not expect that community partners might participate in the assignment to establish a deeper connection to the WGS program, the feminist theory course, and/or me. The interviews showed that community partners have an attachment and an expectation of the formative role of WGS. Veronica wondered, "What are they doing in women's studies class that is different…that allows those women to become, emerge, with voice and leadership?" Similarly, Fern and Nicky hoped that their involvement in the "DFT-DV" project would connect them to a "feminist theory perspective" and enrich their work.

Very few of the community partners come from a WGS background. Isabel said, "I myself have never taken a WGS course, so all of what I know is through lots of practice, and through lots of failed workshops that I've led [laughs], and just keeping up to date and uh, running with it," and that she "really did appreciate…being able to share what you were learning in class and those readings because it helped, I've read some now, so I feel a bit more comfortable with the theory aspect of it." Maria shared this feeling, and said that she "expected to kind of enjoy the opportunity to share with them the work that I do, you know, which has been the case, but I'm also learning something myself through it." To me, these hopes and expectations suggest a parallel assumption of the distance between classroom and community to the one articulated by students, and a desire to close that distance through learning more about WGS and teaching students more about community organizations.

2. Drawbacks to Participation

The interviewees generally under-emphasized the drawbacks of supervising students working on the "DFT-DV" assignment, which I expected, as most of them are colleagues and friends. However, I coaxed out some interesting reflections on the drawbacks to participation. Time constraints were a major factor, both in terms of the time required to create a project and mentor students through it, as well as the amount of time they had to work directly with the students. Isabel commented that her organization, which used to supervise several CSL students a year, currently works only with my project and another professional program because of the significantly higher workload required for CSL supervision. Fern remarked that "[I] had feelings at times where I just thought, oh, I could have done this myself faster, and it wouldn't have taken so long," which they found "frustrating" especially when they felt "like you're putting a lot of effort in and that's not always the same amount of energy or effort, isn't always coming back." Maria even met with my students on days when she was off! While her enthusiasm for the project buoyed her along, I was concerned to learn about this during our interview. Time was a major consideration for Macy when deciding whether or not to participate, and she said, "it's kind of like when you can't give away a project because you're actually not organized yourself enough to do that." Likewise, Carmen thought the time commitment to the project was a "big responsibility" that she took very seriously. However, Macy also added that she felt the project was well set up, and that as the organizer, I was "really mindful of, of who people are that you're asking to do it…I'm surprised at…how much [was] already done for us." I appreciated Ellis Bell's insight that unlike practicum placements for professional programs such as education and nursing, service-learning placements are often more onerous for the organization. CBPL students are rarely equipped to work independently for the organization, which may be different, for example, from an education or social work student doing a placement. As a result, the supervisor has a heavier workload, rather than additional time freed up to mentor students.

Several supervisors commented that the shorter placement time is an incentive to participate, because agreeing to do so is not a significant risk; however, it also is a major drawback because students are limited in the types of tasks they can do for the organization. Isabel and Veronica noted that "DFT-DV" students could realistically plan only one event, given the time available. Veronica, Isabel, Fern, and Nicky all commented that it would be beneficial to have additional time to orient the students, particularly to the organization's mission and values, and teach them the specific skill set needed to work there. Coucou also remarked that the placement is short, and that they had a difficult time understanding the limited time commitment for the work the students do with the organization. Isabel made an interesting comment, stating that while she felt the placement was too short, she could also understand that it was a less-threatening "bridge" toward future activism that "makes it less scary to act" and provides a way to get students to be more vocal or visible "outside of class" regarding what they are "thinking about in class."

Individual supervisors identified a few other drawbacks, which, while not common to the group, are significant to understanding the impact that this assignment specifically and service-learning more broadly has on community organizations. Veronica and Ellis Bell commented that theirs were contract or sessional positions, which was the case for several of the community partners I interviewed. This job instability leads to a lack of continuity, impedes momentum, and limits the ability to establish a coordinated plan for integrating CSL students into their respective programming. Ellis Bell also noted that, in the end, the materials that students produced as a part of their placement were not useful for the organization, because they did not reflect its values. Fern said that they "hoped for more service" than what they received from the students. Nicky commented that the amount of time it takes for students to mesh with one another and the organization (and the unpredictability of whether this will happen or not) was a drawback. Macy, on the other hand, felt the work that students did for her organization was not celebrated, which seemed like a drawback to her. So, the organizations overall were more positive about their involvement with students than I expected, and I would describe their involvement as crucial to the organizations' work because it provided much-needed student connection. Yet this involvement was also complicated, primarily due to time factors, and because students did not always fulfill expectations. The work of supervision was not well-supported internally by all of the organizations.

3. Praxis as Process

I enjoyed discussing the concept of praxis with the community partners by using questions about how they understood praxis in relation to "DFT-DV," and if they had examples of students "getting" the concept. In addition, I learned a lot about how they conceptualized their work outside of our relationships as friends and colleagues, which often spoke to the "everyday" nature of their work in contrast to committee work or extraordinary events. The community partners offered a range of definitions and examples of moments when students seemed to be really grasping the concept of praxis. In this section, I describe the understandings of praxis offered by the community supervisors and analyze the frequently made comment that the videos themselves were a method and product of praxis. To conclude, I reflect on the argument that praxis needs to be understood as process. I suggest that while these interviews were conducted for the purposes of research, "DFT-DV" could benefit significantly from incorporating elements of the interview process into the arc of the reflective process to better connect the community partners, the students, and me as the course instructor.

Ellis Bell defined praxis as "that whole other level of complexity, even if it's just people's schedules, and their transportation, and their kids," which she suggested was another "layer" on top of lengthy discussions "about one or two words in a piece that we're putting out." Maria made the interesting comment that supervising students for this assignment gave her an "opportunity to reflect on praxis." For her, this was valuable, because she felt she had lost sight of the theoretical underpinnings of her work:

> I find it easy in the role that I'm in to sort of forget about the theory.... The sort of, mundane details of the work...just...occupy a lot of space in my brain and even though the connection to theory is always there, I lose sight of that connection, and I'm just thinking about like oh, I have to get these things laminated, and I have to set up this meeting, and um, I have to do the dishes in the lunchroom, and mailing things off, and like all of this stuff that you know, somebody might take a look at what I'm doing and think, well, how is *that* feminist?

Many of the community partners understood praxis in a similar manner, and commented that the integration of theory and practice is more complex and less "clean" or "pure" than a discussion of theory alone (the terms Isabel and Ellis Bell used to describe theory). The choice of these words suggests an assumption that the classroom is a safe and protected space, this time protected from the "mundane" details of work, like time management and disagreements between colleagues. This is significant because it means that it is not just students who make this assumption about the classroom.

Coucou described this integration of theory and practice as something that is fuller, an understanding that goes beyond the "superficial level" to really "illustrate...visualize... [and] communicate a concept" because the student would be equipped to explain that concept to those with no prior knowledge of it. Fern noted that they understood praxis as a "process" that "honour[s] where you're at in your own learning, your own experience." This understanding manifests in the way that their organization works through issues of inclusion, intersectionality, and accessibility. Carmen said that praxis involves "find[ing] out where they're at." In a similar vein, Isabel described praxis as "hard" and a "process" where "you're required to motivate yourself to move along in that process and challenge things and still act, and act and challenge things," to realize that "action is a longer process" that requires time to make mistakes and adjustments along the way. Most of the community partners answered the question about praxis by articulating their hope that students would become invested in an ongoing engagement with their organization. They shared the hope that the assignment would be a catalyst for the students to engage in a longer process of reflection and action. Veronica was particularly impressed by students who had completed this project the semester before a faculty strike at the university, when she saw these students go on to "take great risks" and "go outside of that comfort zone and express themselves in a way that is...so clear." She said, "When people say the strike was a terrible thing, it was beautiful! It was a beautiful thing to see these students engaged in some sort of governance" that challenged the university administration. These definitions of praxis are different from those in the previous paragraph because they do not conceptualize the classroom as separate from the community; instead, "DFT-DV" was presented as a way to facilitate deeper connections.

Some, though far fewer, of the community partners identified the process of creating a video as an example of a process of learning through praxis that breaks down the classroom/community divide. Macy responded that the students begin learning through praxis "the minute you put the camera in their hands" because they are "seeing...this thing that [they] wouldn't have normally seen." To her, the video camera was a "tool" through which students integrate what they have learned by "standing back." When asked about the usefulness of the videos, Coucou said that they were "not disappointed, I was impressed by the product, because if I would receive this assignment... maybe I wouldn't choose these difficult concepts to illustrate, oppression or colonization, whoo they're hard; so I was impressed that they were able to." In Coucou's view, the video itself was proof that students were fully able to "seize the concept," because "when they produce something there's no way to cheat—they did understand or not!" Several interviewees (Veronica, Macy, Coucou, and Carmen) also stated that creating videos with local relevance was valuable, not only to the work that their organizations did but because it demonstrates to the students that there are "opportunities right here" to become involved in social change.

These discussions about praxis were valuable, as I learned the assumption that the classroom is a distanced and protected space is not only held by students: community partners also hold them. Encouragingly, community partners noted that "DFT-DV" helps weaken these divisions for both students and supervisors, affirming Sara Ahmed's (2000, 180) comment that difference "necessitate[s] the dialogue, rather than disallow[s] it—a dialogue must take place, precisely *because* we don't speak the same language" (emphasis in original). Ahmed speaks to the context of transnational feminist organizing, though her comments can be extended to think through the responses of "DFT-DV," where students, community partners, and I share a commitment to dismantling systemic oppression yet draw upon sometimes intersecting, sometimes divergent vocabularies of experience to do so. Chandra Talpade Mohanty (2003, 191) defines theory as the "deepening of the political...a distillation of experience, and an intensification of the personal." This idea emerges not only in student learning about praxis in "DFT-DV," but also in community partner understandings of the video as praxis (a "distillation" or "intensification"). Further, the desire to bridge the perceived gap between the classroom and the community on the part of both students and community partners is an expression of Mohanty's definition of theory *as* praxis, a process of building community rather than assuming a pre-constituted one.

Conclusion

It was heartening for me to interview the community partners, particularly those who frequently supervise CSL students, and to hear that in spite of the drawbacks of the project, they appreciate my greater involvement in coordinating the "DFT-DV" placements in comparison to other CSL placements organized by the Service Learning Program at StFX. Coucou said that in their experience supervising CSL students, there is often a big disconnect between the placement, the professors, and the course; this was echoed by Maria, Isabel, and Ellis Bell, who commented that it is usually very difficult to supervise students, because as community partners they are required to create a placement from scratch without knowing what the students are learning in the classroom.[8] Because the interviews took place while some of the community partners were supervising students, they ended up being a valuable space for clarification and reflection for both the community partners and me. At the end of our interview, Nicky remarked that the kind of "meta-level of analysis" that we engaged in during the interview was "very useful." They suggested that it would be interesting and valuable to expand the Service Learning Program at StFX in general in order to build in "ongoing processes of reflection with organizations, with students, with faculty…beyond questionnaires." Informal conversations and email exchanges in the aftermath of the interviews suggested that our conversations were mutually valuable for better understanding the position of CBPL in partner organizations. I shared a number of insights about the placements from the interviews with students enrolled in the course at the time, such as the parallel understanding of a divide between community and classroom.

While it would be unrealistic and a significant time burden for both the community partners and the course instructor to repeat the interview process every year, I suggest that it would be valuable to build in a multi-year cycle of formal check-ins as a part of this assignment. Further, it would be even more valuable to present and discuss these check-ins with the students working on the assignment, to facilitate deeper structural reflection that moves away from the individualized analyses discussed earlier in this chapter, or to even have students themselves conduct the check-ins. For example, students could organize individual or focus group discussions with community partners as a part of "DFT-DV" and integrate this feedback into their final reflective paper. Based on the effects of the interviews I conducted, I suggest that this type of "meta-analysis" and ongoing reflection could strengthen my relationships with community partners and make student involvement more meaningful. Carmen described student involvement as a "golden nugget" or the "pearl in my oyster." This is something that so many community organizations hope for when they supervise students, particularly in the face of institutional structures (decreased administrative support, for example) that limit the amount of time community partners have to spend with the students their organizations serve.

Notes

I am grateful for the research assistance provided by Rory Begin and Holly Chute in the early stages of this project in 2012–2013, and thankful to the community and university partners for their enthusiasm about the project and the trust they put in me since it began in 2012. This research was supported by funding from the St. Francis Xavier University Service Learning Program through the J.W. McConnell Family Foundation.

1   At StFX, there is a long-standing Service Learning Program, which coordinates virtually all CSL opportunities at the university. This institutional arrangement exists not only to provide support to faculty offering CSL assignments, but also to ensure an even and equitable distribution of available opportunities across departments and programs in the context of a rural community where there is a finite number of community organizations to draw from for such placements.

2   All names and identifying information (like the location and names of the organizations) have been changed to protect the interviewees' anonymity. I also use the gender-neutral pronouns "they" and "their" when the chosen pseudonym is non-gendered or gender neutral for the same reasons.

3   While I am aware of the debates about whether or not "service-learning" is feminist (see Bojar and Naples 2002, 3), the boundaries between what is called "service-learning," "community-based learning," "experiential learning," or "praxis learning" are often quite blurry and porous in my experience. While I feel that "community-based praxis learning" actually describes "DFT-DV" best, I often use "service-learning" to describe my assignment because it fits best within my institutional context. StFX has the oldest Service Learning Program in Canada, and currently, those who work for the program promote a reflective and critical approach to service-learning based on intersectional understandings of social justice. When presenting this assignment to students, naming it as "service-learning" has the potential to defuse their anxiety about community-based learning because they are familiar with the program, even if they have not completed a service-learning assignment.

4   Describing examples of student assignments would take this present chapter too far afield; I describe and analyze two "DFT-DV" videos in my article "How to 'Do' Feminist Theory Through Digital Video: Embodying Praxis in the Undergraduate Feminist Theory Classroom" (2014a). More detail about

student responses to the assignment can be found in my article, "'A Journey in Feminist Theory Together': The *Doing Feminist Theory Through Digital Video Project*" (2014b).

5   This critical introduction endeavoured to differentiate CSL from charity and other forms of volunteering. The second purpose was to familiarize students with the concepts of privilege and oppression in order to situate their CSL experiences.

6   For example, students were asked to reflect on questions like "Is the importance of intersectionality taken seriously in the work I am doing?" and "(How) do the tasks you are doing with your organization address the larger structural reasons for inequality?"

7   Intriguingly, students who come from or have prior relationships with the communities being served do not select those organizations for their placements, in my experience. Speaking anecdotally, I can recall no student who selected such a placement, and in several instances, students who could have worked with an organization or community they were familiar with chose other options in order to branch out into new organizations and communities.

8   Fortunately, since I conducted these interviews, the Service Learning Program at StFX created questionnaires for professors and community organizations to bridge this gap in understanding.

CHAPTER NINE

INTERROGATING FEMINIST PRAXIS *INSIDE* THE CLASSROOM: "STORYING UP" RACE, INDIGENEITY, AND ALLIANCE-BUILDING

MARGOT FRANCIS

This chapter offers a preliminary reflection on the complex dynamics at work in teaching and learning from Indigenous perspectives about settler colonization, race, and diaspora in the undergraduate classroom.[1] Framed as a case study, I develop a reflective analysis about teaching a fourth-year course in Indigenous Social and Political Thought cross-listed with Sociology, Women's and Gender Studies (WGS), and Indigenous Studies.[2] I frame my study as an interrogation of feminist praxis *inside* the classroom. This focus invites a shift from the more common notion that praxis emerges in relationship to student placements with community organizations where one learns about "others" who are presumably not in the university. Instead, I suggest that the process of challenging settler colonization happens not only "in the street" or in activist efforts toward local/ global Indigenous solidarity. Drawing on the work of Indigenous and anti-racist feminist scholars, I argue that everyday practices of teaching and learning can also illuminate, complexify, and unsettle the colonial field of relations we are all situated within.

My interest is in foregrounding a series of student interventions that grappled with experiences of racial ambiguity, the erasure and persistence of Indigenous affiliations, and the continued power of imperial and colonial projects in students' everyday lives and familial histories. Drawing on Stó: lo writer Lee Maracle's analysis of stories as a form of "oratory," I explore how a wide range of students used their own familial and kinship narratives to "story up" their interlocking histories of racialized and colonial relations (Maracle 2007, 60). These oratories, I argue, profoundly influenced the classroom dynamics while also exposing the complex intersections of complicity and alliance-building in attempts to de-colonize the classroom. Maracle (2007,

61) suggests that Stó: lo notions of oratory encourage the telling of stories that bend the light toward the unseen, and that only through engaging with shadow knowledges can we develop an intimate appraisal of history and the conduct of others in relationship to ourselves. I argue that Maracle's notion of oratory as a form of "storying up" these hidden knowledges could also be seen as a form of *praxis* that is engaged, productive, and that holds the potential to enlarge theory. As Dian Million (2014, 35) has argued, narratives are "always more than telling stories"—they are about the desire to link paradigmatic knowledge, to "seek the nooks and crannies of experiences, filling cracks and restoring order." Indeed, Million suggests that in Indigenous epistemologies, theory and stories converge through articulating "a strategic felt comprehension that has the power to change a paradigm, or reinvest a political movement with a new vision to act" (2014, 37). In the context of my class, students used the process of "storying up" their contradictory relationships to colonial and imperial history in ways that drew connections between racial, gendered, and colonial projects that are often assumed to be distinct; hence, narrative worked to produce praxis. Students also drew on course readings that mapped local Indigenous resurgence and the diasporic movements set in motion by global colonialisms in places that ranged from North America, to India, Palestine, Chiapas, and Afghanistan.

The assignments for the course included a research essay, a student presentation, and a take-home exam. However, my introductory exercise invited a different form of analysis by asking students to make links between their own familial history and local/global forms of colonial power and Indigenous resistance. Here I drew on the experience of Victoria Freeman and Lee Maracle who co-taught a course on Indigenous Studies at the University of Toronto.[3] In this context, Freeman and Maracle found that students frequently made productive connections between their own familial history of migration, racialization, and settlement and their position as settlers and/or Indigenous people in contemporary Canada (Freeman, personal communication, 2012). In the hope that I could prompt similar self-reflexive analysis, I asked students to engage with the course material not just as reflections from movements "out there," but also as analyses of relations of power that have profoundly shaped all our kinship histories and forms of identification. In short, I was interested in inviting students to investigate their own location in relationship to the material benefits and losses associated with colonization, race, and diaspora. Hence, in week three of the class I asked them to complete the following one-page assignment:

Reading Response:
This response should draw connections between the history of colonization and resistance in the articles assigned for the first two weeks of class

and your own family history. In preparation, I ask students to engage in informal conversations with your family/kinship network to assess how your history is connected to Indigenous history in North America and/or in your country of origin.[4]

On week four, when students handed in this reflection, I asked them to participate in an informal roundtable where they each spoke about what they learned from this assignment. Student narratives about familial and kinship relations brought the "elsewhere" which we often associate with praxis-learning experiences with/about "other" people directly into our classroom. Indeed, many students "storied-up" their complicated connections to settler colonization in ways that paid close attention to the multiple histories, borders, and spaces that have been mobilized to uphold and challenge colonialism in Canada and internationally.

This chapter starts with an overview of selected debates on de-colonization between Indigenous, feminist, and anti-racist scholars. These materials provide a context for my writing and also highlight issues discussed in the course I am reflecting on here. I then turn to three themes that emerged from student discussion that constitute the focus of my analysis: (a) the labour of Indigenous survivance and knowledge practices; (b) diasporic perspectives on imperialisms, colonizations, and racialization; and (c) interrogating whiteness.

Framing Praxis

As I did in the classroom, I begin by briefly locating myself and my own familial and kinship relations.[5] I am a white settler, living on Indigenous territory, of English and Scottish origin, whose earliest ancestors first arrived in this territory in the 1750s and who benefited from Indigenous dispossession in a myriad of ways, including through land grants for farming. In my work as a scholar I have been publishing about the cultural politics of Indigenous–settler relationships for twelve years. The course discussed here was taught at Brock University, which is located on the territory of the Anishinaabec, Haudenosaunee, and Wendat people, and I was raised in Anishinaabec territory in what is now Ottawa. Brock University is just over one hour away from the most populous Indigenous community in Canada, Six Nations, where several centuries of anti-colonial conflict over land erupted in what is known as the Six Nations/Caledonia dispute in 2006.[6] In my teaching about Indigenous perspectives on contemporary feminist thought, I frequently encounter white students whose views were shaped by the aftermath of this conflict—indeed, these are some of the most racially charged discussions that have erupted in my classrooms. My own familial history positions me as necessarily implicated in the contemporary politics of white settler colonization at the same time as I claim networks of affiliation shaped by feminist, queer, and anti-racist scholarship and activism. In all of these contexts I am centrally concerned with the politics of alliance-building and with challenging settler colonialism piece by piece.

The work of Mi'kmaw scholar Bonita Lawrence and anti-racist scholar Enakshi Dua constitutes a key and contested intervention in Canadian scholarship on Indigenous–feminist relations. In "De-colonizing Anti-Racism," Lawrence and Dua (2005) draw attention to the failures of anti-racist feminist and post-colonial theory to attend to contemporary practices of colonization and struggles for de-colonization by Indigenous people. They critique feminist scholarship for neglecting to address the genocidal violence against Indigenous communities, which provides the foundation for white settlement, and more recently, for the multicultural state. Anti-racist "rights"-based arguments for inclusion, they suggest, ignore the contemporary targeting of Indigenous people for legal and cultural extinction, while neoliberal state processes continue to appropriate their resources. At the core of Lawrence and Dua's analysis is the differential relationship that Indigenous people and settlers have to the land. As they argue, "to acknowledge that we all share the same land base and yet to question the differential terms on which it is occupied is to become aware of the colonial project that is taking place around us" (Lawrence and Dua 2005, 126). In this regard, the authors contend that any analysis of white settlement, multiculturalism, and nation-building must include an explicit awareness of the intersection of state "settlement policies, with policies controlling 'Indians'" (Lawrence and Dua 2005, 136). This analysis clearly sacrifices any notion of innocence on the part of settlers.

A second widely discussed article on settler colonial relations comes from Nandita Sharma and Cynthia Wright (2008/9), who provide a very different analysis of who constitutes a settler, the definition of colonization, and the nature of nationalist attachments. Of particular interest to me is their critique of Lawrence and Dua's ideas about settler colonialism, enslaved labour, and immigration. They point out that migration is often one of the few avenues of escape for those who have been dispossessed of their former homes and livelihoods, and that some migrants are Indigenous to other territories; in addition, many migrants have been forced out by colonial, capitalist and neoliberal violence, and are unable to return to their home territory (Sharma and Wright, 2008/9). Highlighting an alternative vision in anti-capitalist movements toward a global commons, they articulate a very different understanding of colonization:

> By understanding *colonization* as the theft of the commons, the agents of decolonization as the *commoners*, and decolonization as the gaining of a *global commons*, we will gain a clearer sense of *when* we were colo-

nized, who colonized us, and *how* to decolonize ourselves and our relationships. By comprehending colonialism as occurring each time the
commons is expropriated and the commoners are exploited, our understanding of colonialism and who has been colonized should expand.
(Sharma and Wright 2008/9, 133, emphasis in original)

Sharma and Wright's analysis is of particular value for its detailed attention to
the frequent demonization of those from "elsewhere" that often goes hand in
hand with the neoliberal policies constraining the movement of people while
simultaneously enabling the freer movement of capital, ideas, information,
and technologies of securitization. Yet their argument conflates the theft of
the commons with colonization, and Indigenous sovereignty with state-based
nationalism, arguing that any form of national attachment is racist—a perspective that is troublingly universalizing in its global sweep (see Smith 2008).[7]

In response to Sharma and Wright, Bonita Lawrence collaborated with
Zainab Amadahy (2009) to write about the politics of alliance-building
between Indigenous peoples and Black settlers. Lawrence and Amadahy
explore the potential connections between racialized people who have been
forcibly displaced from their homelands through slavery and Indigenous
people forcibly displaced by state settlement policies in North America. In
particular, they highlight the possibilities and importance of shifting from a
discourse of racial inclusion toward an anti-colonial solidarity framework—as
did groups such as the Black Action Defense Committee, Palestine House,
the Coalition Against Israeli Apartheid, No One is Illegal, and the Canadian
Islamic Congress during conflicts over land during the Oka crisis in 1990 and
the Six Nations/Caledonia dispute in 2006.[8] More recently, there has also been
a shift to acknowledging Indigenous leadership in environmental struggles, as
is evident in the No Dakota Access Pipeline (NDAPL) protests and grassroots
protests against the Trans Mountain Pipeline in Canada.[9] For anti-colonial
coalitions to continue, Lawrence and Amadahy highlight dual challenges; first,
the importance of Indigenous leadership in developing "a vision of sovereignty
and self-government that addresses the disempowered and dispossessed from
other parts of the world who were forced and/or coerced into being here on
Turtle Island," and at the same time, the significance of settlers choosing to
"modify their value systems, worldviews, and practices to enable the original
vision of the Two Row [wampum]" which requires them to reimagine the
terms for sharing this territory (Amadahy and Lawrence 2009, 131).

Beenash Jafri's 2012 analysis elaborates on how discussions about the
responsibilities of settlers on Indigenous territory frequently conflate notions
of "privilege" and "complicity." She argues that for most racialized people,
"systemic inequities, underemployment and the racialization of poverty" mean

that "there are few 'benefits' associated with being a settler." Jafri's analysis of the politics of alliance-building draws on Sarita Srivastava's work on the emotional responses evoked by a therapeutic model of unlearning racism within social movement organizations (see also her chapter in this volume). Such an approach "defuses anti-racism critique into 'issues of individual emotion...' while foreclosing the possibility for structural transformation."[10] Rather than an individualized focus on settlers, Jafri suggests that readers reflect on the ways non-Indigenous people may be complicit in a system of hierarchical power, while accruing few of its benefits. This framework shifts our thinking toward understanding settler complicity as "a field of operations into which we become socially positioned and implicated." Instead of aiming for moral reform for individual settlers, or the individual absolution of responsibility ("checking" privilege), Jafri suggests that we re-examine how we become accountable in fields of relations still saturated by colonial power.

Shaista Patel's work provides one example of what it might look like to dismantle settler colonialism "piece by piece." Patel's focus is on the imperative for de-colonial critique in light of the post 9/11 labelling of Muslim bodies as terrorists. Drawing connections between these seemingly disparate experiences, she notes that contemporary anti-Muslim discourse is founded in "the legacy of a white supremacist settler-colonial governmentality that continues to label Indigenous peoples...as terrorists" (Patel 2012). In recognition of this link, Patel argues for the importance of mapping out how complicity and alliance-building structure seemingly different modes of representation. In her own words, "[h]ow could I live on this land that did not ethically belong to me, and talk about violence directed at my body, and at my people, without situating that violence and my work for social justice within the history of a nation-state literally founded on the dead bodies and erased nations of Indigenous peoples?" (Patel 2012).[11]

The Idle No More movement of 2012/13 extended this process of connecting seemingly different struggles through its foregrounding of recent Canadian government legislation that weakened environmental protection and facilitated corporate resource exploitation. The movement emphasized Indigenous leadership and modes of activism while also assessing the impact of these legislative changes on both Indigenous and non-Indigenous people. Grounded in notions of Indigenous sovereignty, one particular catchphrase epitomized this focus: "we are *all* treaty people."[12] It summed up a strong critique of the historically popular idea that treaties were one-sided agreements made by Indigenous people to give up their land to a white-dominant state. Instead, the notion that settlers and Indigenous people are *all* implicated in treaty relations implies that Indigenous ideas of sovereignty require *everyone* to participate in the difficult work of navigating respectful treaty relationships.

Haudenosaunee treaty practices, for example, were governed by the notion of a "covenant chain" of relationships, or the Two Row Wampum, which included attention to culture, diplomacy, and trade (McNabb 1999, 11). Robinder Kaur Sehdev (2011, 70) extends this analysis by noting that treaty relationships were understood to be recursive—in other words, the treaty process required the frequent return to negotiations about the shared use of land, the intersecting space of cultures, and equity in trade relationships. As the Chicksaw scholar James [Sákéj] Youngblood Henderson argues, Indigenous people have "distinct notions of how to live well with the land and with other peoples by consent and collaboration," and the frequently tokenistic ideals of Canadian multiculturalism usually undermine Indigenous sovereignty and instead serve to construct spaces "where ethnic difference is paraded in the service of 'Euro-Canadian self-congratulation and individualism'" (Youngblood Henderson quoted in Sehdev 2011, 269).

In the next section I highlight the themes that emerged from class discussions of these ideas and texts, and recount how students used Maracle's method of "storying up" their kinship histories to place themselves in conversation with these debates. Here narrative became praxis insofar as students drew from theory to mobilize critical and reflexive stories about their own positioning within colonial and racial power. These narratives were not about "others out there"—but instead drew connections between the systemic organization of colonialism and the intimate spheres of familial and friendship relations.

Indigenous Knowledge and Survivance Practices

A central theme that emerged from the three Indigenous students (in a class of twenty) was the labour required for sustaining Indigenous survivance practices in the face of ongoing overt and insidious racism and state efforts at assimilation and erasure. The contributions of an Oneida student who spoke early in the class roundtable illustrate the commitment necessary for this process: she introduced herself in the Haudenosaunee language—which she was now painstakingly relearning, after her grandparents had been forbidden to speak it in residential school—a process she identified as a means of de-colonization. Drawing on the scholarship of Bonita Lawrence (2002), she assessed her experience with Western primary and secondary school systems that represented Indigenous people as vanishing into the past, a process that diminished her existence at the same time as it established Canada as a benevolent and benign nation. This student's critique drew from her engagement with Oneida culture, and she honoured the role of her mother, grandmother, and great-grandmother in maintaining that knowledge. However, other Indigenous students described a more tenuous set of relationships and different kinds of ruptures in their affiliation to culture and identity. For example, a Métis student described how he grew up assuming that he was white, and realized only later that he had strong ancestral ties to a Métis community in southwestern Alberta. His connection to this heritage was fostered in conversation with his aunt, uncle, and grandmother, other Métis and Indigenous people, and more problematically, in his application for status from the Métis National Council. While he began his application feeling like a "fraud"—a feeling exacerbated by their exclusive criteria—he used this affective sense of dissonance as the starting point for investigating the history of racialized Canadian assimilation practices that aimed to prevent as many Indigenous people as possible from gaining status, based in part on whether they "looked" white- or dark-skinned (Scudeler 2011, 192). Drawing on his sense of dis-ease and alienation as sources of knowledge themselves, this student undertook research that made connections between post-colonial ideas of hybridity (Bhabha 1994) and Indigenous theories of Métissage (Donald 2012, 536), which hold together the "ambiguous, layered, complex and conflictual character of Aboriginal and Canadian relations without the need to deny, assimilate, hybridize, or conclude." This emphasis on the ways the body holds the contradictions of history was also evident in the remarks of an Algonquin Pikwakanagan student whose contribution to the roundtable began with the following comment, "I knew my Dad was Algonquin, I just didn't know what that meant." Highlighting her estrangement from Algonquin Pikwakanagan culture after her parents' separation, she went on to complete a final essay that emphasized Indigenous resistance to Bill C-31,[13] with a particular focus on the significance of critiques arguing that this legislation will result in the extinction of Indigenous status within four to seven generations (Cannon, 2005; Rutherford and Lawrence 2010). I recount these brief examples from Indigenous students in order to highlight how familial and kinship relations hold crucial knowledges about state-legislated erasure, familial and community-based practices of continuity, regulation, and rupture, and to highlight the connections between national narratives of benevolence and concrete personal losses. Students' narratives "storied up" the impact of government, educational, and legal policy, and in doing so brought the implications of these larger systems into the classroom in direct and tangible ways through oratories about the demanding labour and commitment necessary for resurgence.

Diasporic Perspectives on Imperialism, Colonization, and Racialization

There were also common themes that emerged from students whose families had migrated to Canada as a result of colonization, war, imperialism, or racism in their countries of origin (four in a group of twenty). These narratives highlighted the connections between white settler colonialism in Canada, and different but related experiences of exclusion/expulsion elsewhere. For example, early in the roundtable a student whose family had fled Sri Lanka during the civil war talked about the impact of British colonialism on the conflict between Tamil and Sinhalese communities. Drawing on Lawrence's (2002) analysis of British military strategies which pitted Indigenous communities against each other during the early years of trade and warfare in Atlantic Canada, this student argued that similar practices were used by the British to divide ethnic groups and control the trade and governance of the colony of Ceylon, later Sri Lanka.[14] While this is a complex history, her comments emphasized parallels between British strategies to control colonial outposts in widely different global locations and the ways this legacy still lives in the present in experiences of war and traumatic displacement. The intergenerational impact of a colonial legacy also emerged from others who used the exercise of speaking to their family to learn stories they had, prior to this, never known. To illustrate, another student's family first migrated to Canada after the partition of India (in 1947) with their remaining relatives arriving after the Sikh Massacre in the Punjab (in 1984), both events deeply influenced by British rule in India. Interestingly, this student had focused her academic work on Canadian studies and women's and gender studies, and until this class had never before spoken to her family about their reasons for leaving their homeland. As the term progressed, she interviewed her grandparents about their experiences in "convent" day schools run by British missionaries in the Punjab whose aim was to inculcate them in British language, values, and culture—a process their parents attempted to reverse every night by teaching them Punjabi, Urdu, and Hindi, and passing on oral traditions. The objective of this project, which she presented to the class later in the term, was to compare and assess the impact of convent schools for Sikhs in India with residential and day schools for Indigenous students here in Canada. While there is limited research on this topic, her familial interviews and discussion of these issues in class opened up an important set of connections for students to learn about parallels and differences between missionary strategies of British rule in India and Canada and their continued intergenerational effects.

While the long reach of the British Empire was the most dominant theme in these discussions, other forms of racialized rule were also in evidence. A student of mixed Roma and Bulgarian heritage highlighted the brutal discourses employed to label Roma people as backward and uncivilized which had, in her family, caused a deep schism, so that she had avoided any contact with her Roma grandparents in Bulgaria prior to her family migrating to Canada. Her discussion highlighted the segregation of Roma into ghetto-like "slum" areas and compared this with the reserve system for Indigenous people in Canada. While the histories that produced these practices of exclusion are very different, the civilizational discourses employed to construct certain communities as primitive, lazy, and untrustworthy can productively be put into conversation. This student's contribution also opened up space to discuss how anti-Roma discourse is evident in recent changes to Canadian immigration policy that have made it increasingly difficult for Roma people to apply for refugee status in Canada.[15] Finally, the lingering influence of the Soviet Empire was also evident in our classroom discussion, prompted by another student's analysis of the corrosive impact of Soviet rule in Poland, his family's flight prior to the fall of the Berlin Wall in 1989, and his own commitment to retain, in his words, his "tribal" affiliation with the Polish language, dance, and traditions.

All of these examples illustrate classroom conversations about the impact of different kinds of colonialisms, imperialisms, and racisms for students who are now settlers on Indigenous land. As highlighted above, racialized and newcomer students were well aware that the benefits that accrued to them as settlers on Indigenous territory were contradictory and tenuous. The everyday impact of racism *in* Canada as well as prior to their migration was also an intermittent theme. Perhaps one of the best examples of this came from a racialized newcomer student who had just returned from working in the oil industry in Alberta. While he was critical of the devastation caused by tar sands development and the takeover of Indigenous lands, he accepted this job in the context of limited employment options and the need to cover his university tuition costs. In the opening roundtable he highlighted witnessing overt anti-Indigenous racism, which he assessed as considerably worse than the racism he encountered. He drew on this experience to develop a critique of Canada's "benevolent" legacy in relation to Indigenous people at the same time as it also illustrated forms of settler complicity we are all implicated within. Thus, student contributions to this course provided complex forms of narrative praxis that highlighted the local/global scope of colonial power, and the contradictions and connections between multiple kinds of imperialisms and racisms.

Interrogating Whiteness

The themes that emerged from other students who were born in Canada interrogated whiteness as a space of racial appropriation/amnesia at the same time as they problematized the binary of Indigenous versus white settler identities. Only one of the students in this group highlighted what must have been a more common anxiety: What does my family history have to do with the themes of this course? Most voiced a different kind of concern, namely: Why don't we know the history of the land where we were raised? And, why are the stories of Indigenous land dispossession so difficult to uncover? These were highly productive anxieties, and resulted in students scrambling to track down the intersection of familial histories, Indigenous dispossession, and state appropriation of land. The very opaqueness of the knowledge available to them prior to this course spoke volumes about the invisibilized mechanisms the state used to accumulate territory, exclude Indigenous people from legal status, and establish white dominance and a racial apartheid between Indigenous people and white settlers, particularly in southern Ontario.[16] While most students did not present definitive answers to these questions, perhaps the questions themselves and the process of having to respond to them at the roundtable began to break through at least one of the defence mechanisms that protects settlers from an awareness of the colonial *present*: namely, the indifference to Indigenous dispossession.

Several other themes that emerged from this group were equally important as they "storied up" students' contradictory implications in systems of colonial rule. For example, feminist students identified kinship networks that included activist work in local shelters and highlighted the disproportionate impact of gender-based violence on Indigenous women *and* significant conflicts between white versus Indigenous feminist approaches to anti-violence advocacy. In particular, one student critiqued the feminist-inspired law reforms that have promoted mandatory charges against male abusers, as these have done little to help Indigenous women who continue to experience high levels of violence and incarceration. Another student whose aim was to work in the Ontario Provincial Police stressed his alarm at the high rates of criminalization for Indigenous people and the normalization of the death of Aboriginal men in police custody. In both cases, students foregrounded the violence of the state as foundational through genocidal schooling practices, the breakup of Indigenous families, and police violence, and considered how their activist and career aspirations needed to be rethought in light of the ongoing impact of colonial power. Again, there were no obvious or easy answers, but the questions themselves, posed at the roundtable, were then taken up repeatedly and continued in the students' research and presentations throughout the term.

Finally, other white students returned to racial and colonial connections that cut close into familial histories. For example, a student of Italian-Canadian heritage who was raised on Anishinaabec and Wendat territory on the Humber River investigated her grandfather's migration in light of the Canadian state solicitation of southern European immigrants as sources of "cheap" manual labour. The eugenic hierarchy, which represented southern European men as inherently ignorant and prone to violence (Harney 1993) had significant repercussions for her grandfather, who faced discrimination in establishing his place as a newcomer in Canada. However, he and subsequent generations of his family still benefited from the centuries-long state processes of eroding Anishinaabec and Wendat claims to that same territory. These points of comparison resulted in this student interviewing her grandparents to learn more about the conditions they faced when they came to Canada after the Second World War and then investigating the very different kinds of discrimination faced by Indigenous communities who had been forced off that same land. Another white student, whose family was originally from Quebec, also interviewed her grandmother, who expressed relief that "someone finally asked you to ask" about her own Indigenous heritage. Her grandmother confirmed that, like many Québécois families, they had several Métis ancestors whom the family had never spoken about. In a related vein, a student whose family was from northern Ontario investigated the background of his grandmother who had been rumoured to be Anishinaabec, but who refused to speak about her heritage. As she had recently passed away, this student looked up the census records to confirm her status and found that prior to her marriage to his grandfather she had been listed as Anishinaabec. His dedicated work to uncover how his grandmother lost her Anishinaabec status under the Indian Act (until 1984, Indigenous women lost their status if they married non-Indigenous or white men) was a vivid example of the gendered discrimination faced by hundreds of thousands of Indigenous women and their children—the impact of which still lives in his own sense of dissonance, estranged from, but related to, the local Anishinaabec community in and around his hometown of Sault Ste. Marie, Ontario.

Conclusion

I offer these preliminary reflections on teaching this course in a collection on feminist engagements with community-based learning in WGS in part to explore how the classroom itself can serve as a site for feminist praxis through inviting the "elsewhere" of students' own familial and kinship networks into our discussions. As the analysis highlighted at the start of this chapter emphasized, Indigenous feminist scholars have critiqued the field of women's and gender studies for its failure to address the genocidal violence that is the foundation for white settlement and the contemporary multicultural state. In the context of this course, non-Indigenous students were asked to explore their implication as settlers who are complicit in the appropriation of Indigenous land, and to investigate the relationship between the history of their kinship networks and intersecting imperialisms, racisms, and gendered colonization.

In a class of twenty students, the Canadian state policy of assimilation was brought startlingly to light by several students' narratives about Indigenous heritage that was legally erased, silenced, or simply not spoken about. From my perspective, these stories were not told by students in order to appropriate an Indigenous past. Quite the reverse: students undertook research within their families, and then narrated their discoveries in ways that illustrated the intimate reach of state policy and the felt sense of disorientation and loss that results from being both estranged from and related to this legacy. These oratories became a mode of praxis that unsettled the assumed homogeneous operation of whiteness so that racial categories were reassessed as very far from "natural." Student narratives, then, illustrated how "race" is shaped by place, history, and legal fiat and the concomitant production of silence and shame as emotions that obfuscate, at the same time as they serve, state power. In a related vein, Indigenous and Métis students emphasized the labour of confronting these colonial paradigms and the difficult work of retrieval and relearning in order to bend the light toward resurgence. While these students also highlighted state practices of assimilation and erasure, they did so in a context that seemed to implicitly mobilize Gerald Vizenor's (1998, 93) idea of survivance as "a native sense of presence, the motion of sovereignty and the will to resist dominance... not just survival but also resistance, not heroic or tragic, but the tease of tradition, and... [a way to] outwit dominance and victimry." Here student oratories emphasized the active desire for language acquisition and the deeply nourishing and deeply conflicted process of learning and reimagining complex Indigenous cultures.

Consistent with the scholarly literature cited at the start of this chapter, in particular Jafri (2012), Patel (2012), and Kaur Sehdev (2011), students of colour were differently positioned in relationship to settler colonization in Canada, at the same time as they were implicated in the settlement of Indigenous land. This was particularly evident in the ways they highlighted parallels between British policies in governance, trade, and schooling in a range of global colonies from Sri Lanka, to India, to Canada. These themes were also picked up by a Roma student who highlighted productive points of conversation between the civilizational discourses (in Bulgaria and Canada) that constructed Roma and Indigenous people as primitive, lazy, and untrustworthy; and again by Sri Lankan and Indian students who discussed the racism they faced, and they saw Indigenous people facing, in everyday and employment contexts. The parallels and differences between colonial and racial regimes around the globe highlighted how de-colonial critique might intersect with analysis of racial and gendered power.

Dian Million (2014, 37) argues that theory is an essentially "social process" insofar as it links "certain ways of intuiting/feeling/thinking towards... other ways of intuiting/feeling/thinking." In the oratories I have documented above, students engaged with their kinship relations in ways that drew on the "social process" within and outside of the classroom in order to *do praxis through story*. Using what Million (2014) would call "felt-embodied narrative practices" they made astute connections to chart widely disparate and unequal legacies, highlighting the local/global reach of colonial/racial ideologies, the contradictory complicity of settlers, and the sustaining and difficult labour of Indigenous survivance. Through these risky narrative practices, and in conversation with Indigenous theoretical analysis, they began to enact the always unfinished business of de-colonial learning. There was no need to look elsewhere.

Notes

1 This cross-listed class had twenty-one students, twenty of whom were fourth-year students and one of whom was an M.A. student who completed extra assignments in the class for a graduate credit.

2 This chapter refers to unpublished material including in-classroom conversations and essays produced by students. I have anonymized this material as much as possible. In addition, I also sent a draft copy of this chapter to each student in the class for their feedback. Those who might recognize themselves have responded to provide explicit permission for my use of their material.

3 The course was titled The Politics and Process of Reconciliation in Canada, and was offered in the Aboriginal Studies Program at the University of Toronto (2010–2012).

4 This assignment was worth 5 percent of the final grade.

5 I have included a more extended reflection on my own positioning in settler colonial contexts in the Acknowledgements and Introduction of my book, *Creative Subversions: Whiteness, Indigeneity and the National Imaginary* (Vancouver: UBC Press, 2011), and I discussed this material in the classroom at the start of the course.

6 For further information see DeVries (2012) and http://www.sixnations.ca/LandsResources/LCMap.pdf.

7 For further analysis of the relationship between sovereignty and the state see Andrea Smith (2008).

8 For further analysis of the Six Nations/Caledonia conflict, see DeVries (2012). Regarding the Oka Crisis, see Simpson and Ladner (2010).

9 For further information on NDAPL see: https://www.thenation.com/article/the-lesson-from-standing-rock-organizing-and-resistance-can-win/; https://www.huffingtonpost.com/dave-pruett/standing-with-standing-ro_b_12048806.html. On the Trans Mountain Pipeline see: https://www.newswire.ca/news-releases/indigenous-leaders-shut-down-construction-on-kinder-morgans-pipeline-679065693.html; https://www.huffingtonpost.ca/2018/04/15/kinder-morgan-pipeline-first-nations-block-trans-mountain-indigenous_a_23411828/.

10 Quoted in Jafry. See: https://www.ideas-idees.ca/blog/privilege-vs-complicity-people-colour-and-settler-colonialism.

11 See Shaista Patel (2012) for further discussion on this point. See also Andrea Smith (2016).

12 Earlier reflections on this dictum can be found in Epp (2008). For a populist reflection, see Cree scholar and activist Tara Williamson's blog: http://decolonization.wordpress.com/2012/12/24/we-are-all-treaty-people/

13 For further analysis of the problems associated with Bill C-31, see http://Indigenousfoundations.arts.ubc.ca/home/government-policy/the-indian-act/bill-c-31.html.

14 For scholarly assessments of this period, see Spencer (2004).

15 See for example: "Canada Pays Thousands of Roma to Abandon Refugee Appeals, Leave Country," http://globalnews.ca/news/1618256/canada-pays -thousands-of-roma-to-abandon-refugee-appeals-leave-country/.

16 Three useful sources recommended to students were Hill (2009); Freeman (2010), available online at: https://tspace.library.utoronto.ca/bit stream/1807/26356/1/Freeman_Victoria_J_201011_PhD_thesis.pdf; and the first story blog, available at: https://firststoryblog.wordpress.com/category/ places/.

CHAPTER TEN

THE DE-TERRITORIALIZATION OF KNOWLEDGE PRODUCTION IN CANADIAN WOMEN'S AND GENDER STUDIES PROGRAMS

JENNIFER L. JOHNSON

This chapter explores how we might de-territorialize the sites most frequently chosen for feminist praxis components (for credit) by applying spatial concepts from feminist geography and geographies of education. In it, I draw upon examples from an assignment where students had to integrate theoretical knowledge with an account of their own pre-existing paid and unpaid work experience to suggest that feminist praxis can be a part of many different kinds of in-class learning. Some might consider this a form of work-integrated learning (WIL), a term currently supported by the Higher Education Quality Council of Ontario (HECQO) and put forward in various forms at many institutions as a way of preparing "work-ready" students. However, according to the ways in which most institutions seek to formalize experiential learning, it probably would not qualify as such.[1] In the context of liberal arts-oriented Women's and Gender Studies (WGS) program commitments to social justice and the practicalities of student life, I make the argument that there is great value in the types of practical or experiential learning offered within many WGS programs beyond the context of formalized placements. A spatial understanding of teaching/learning practices includes movement outside the traditional classroom alongside a critical analysis of power relations in place, and need not necessarily require sending students "out to work." Students should decide for themselves, based on their goals, lifestyles, and finances whether they want to choose a program of study with unpaid experiential components, and if for some reason they cannot commit to more unpaid labour, there are other ways of responding to feminist praxis, as I explore here. In order to examine the benefits of examining student's existing paid and unpaid workplaces as potential sites of feminist praxis, I discuss two examples provided by students from one of my own undergraduate courses. Finally, I suggest that critical notions of student and teacher place-making assists our students in translating their efforts for their own purposes, whether that be to the job market, family responsibilities, voluntarism, or elsewhere, and also retain the integrity of WGS as a politically transformative field.

Is WGS "Territorial"?

What words come to mind when you first hear the phrase, "My women's and gender studies program is sending me on placement…"? Where will this student be spending their time, and what will she/he be doing during the semester? Very likely many will assume, and not incorrectly, that the student will contribute to the work of a local women's shelter or sexual-assault crisis centre. One could also assume that a faculty member or course leader, an organization representative, an administrative assistant, or the student him/herself (or all of the above) spent a fair bit of time negotiating, conceptualizing, and arranging the placement (as evidenced in the chapters of Muzak, Gotell, Hurst, Parkins, and others in this collection). In this chapter, I work from the premise that WGS has purposefully, and with good reason, valorized certain "places of learning" as appropriate sites for students to learn about and practise feminism outside of the classroom. I take as a given that most programs offering formal praxis components want to, even if they may lack resources to do it consistently, combine placement, practicum, and activist experience with critical and reflexive research and debate in a supportive setting. But the valorization of such a limited set of appropriate places for WGS students to engage in praxis is also subject to market and policy forces as described by Muzak (in this volume). I also agree with Taylor and de Laat (2013) that it is correct to exercise caution in assuming placements expose students to activism, when more often internships might overly shape these experiences through an employer/employee relationship instead of a practice leading to critical feminist consciousness. Assumptions about the proper place of feminism explored through experiential learning merits investigation, one I question here as a kind of territoriality associated with the sourcing of placements.

By raising the issue of territoriality for WGS placements I do not intend to revisit the discussion of whether some sites or issues are feminist enough to be considered sites of praxis, helpfully explored elsewhere (Braithwaite 2002; Detore-Nakamura 2012). Rather, I argue it is important to recognize the larger policy changes taking place in Canadian post-secondary education, and how these changes affect the kinds of administrative work faculty do to prepare for offering these courses. For example, in my own province, the Higher Education Quality Council of Ontario conducts extensive and valuable research on the role of work-integrated learning in post-secondary education. Its publications have been used as a primary resource by the Ontario Liberal provincial government to assert that internships be introduced at all levels of university study (Drummond 2012). Although student advocates, some conscientious college programs (CBC 2013; The Current 2013; Schwartz 2013), and even the HECQO itself (Sattler and Peters 2013) have cautioned against the exploitation of unpaid students in placements on or off campus, many universities, including my own, have investments in promoting work-integrated learning in various forms. With additional pressure from Ontario's Differentiation Policy Framework (2013), undergraduate-focused universities like my own in Northern Ontario are especially keen to take up any tactic that will allow us to survive the possible redundancy of our offerings when compared to other undergraduate and research-intensive universities and colleges. This may be especially so for undergraduate liberal arts and science-focused universities (Weingarten et al. 2013; Jonker and Hicks 2016). The differentiation strategy will directly compare programs across the province and identify duplications. At the extreme, for instance, a college nursing program in a particular region might be deemed better than that in a university, and the latter could be defunded. Or the number of programs within a field (e.g., WGS) might be considered too numerous, given student demand. The differentiation strategy, as proposed, is almost indifferent to place, not recognizing the real geographical and financial barriers to students studying away from home communities, even though HECQO's analysis clearly reveals that smaller undergraduate versus large research-intensive institutions invite equitable access to much higher numbers of first-generation, Aboriginal, francophone, persons with disabilities, and part-time learners (2016, 18). Unfortunately, as presented in the current literature, work-integrated learning has been under-theorized except as a way of repositioning graduates as workplace-ready in the Canadian—and indeed global—neoliberal economies.[2] It is in this context that academic programs examine what they may need to do to respond to this policy shift "from above" for the liberal arts.

The notion of territoriality is profoundly authoritarian in humanist terms and usually biologically determinist in scientific terms, and is thus not one I wish to deliberately claim here. "Territoriality" suggests the claiming of space for some people to the deliberate exclusion of others, sometimes with the objective of bringing like-minded groups together for their collective betterment. But one might also stake claim to a territory using the rhetoric of ownership (private property), a symbolic regime (nationalism), or brute force (the violent occupation of land such as through a practice of colonization). To *be* territorial is to suggest that a group consistently establishes and reinforces boundaries, and shares an internal compulsion to mark out a pathway or trajectory around a space, defining it as their own. The spectre of territoriality crept up on me as I explored whether and how students might access community placements via my own WGS program. Our courses have existed since 1979 at Laurentian University, and the program has functioned on campus and by distance education for over two decades. The program is somewhat sheltered from cuts within a federated university system, and yet we are among the two-thirds of WGS programs in Canada without an organized praxis component (Johnson and Luhmann 2016). So while we have a great deal of experience as a program, we are small. As one of two full-time faculty members in the program, I found the possibility of establishing a practicum was very slim. This is not because my colleagues and I are fundamentally opposed to a semi-guided activist experience for the sake of learning, but because many of the places we immediately assumed students could go for placements had already been claimed by other programs.

In our region there are many university and college programs seeking to place students in a limited number of organizations, mainly clustered within what are often called the "helping" professions, non-profit sectors, and volunteer-led organizations. At my own university, there are easily four large programs competing for placements with the same organizations, not to mention similar programs in three local colleges. It is significant that some of these programs are highly focused on graduating Indigenous and/or francophone learners, and seek to place them with Indigenous- and francophone-led organizations, seeing an organic connection to these groups. Within any of our programs there could be students for whom it would be very meaningful to have a linguistic, ethnic, or culturally-relevant placement experience, meaning that one program might inadvertently reduce opportunities for someone else's students in these organizations. It is possible, then, that multiple fields of territoriality over these placements exist simultaneously. Just as there could be a territoriality of sectors (social work, healthcare), another layer of territoriality in placements might be connected to identity, or an impetus to meaningfully connect students with home communities through language and identity, as many programs attempt to de-colonize and challenge linguistic marginalization in the curriculum.

It was in a workshop on establishing placements for students that I found myself making a list of organizations we might turn to for our program. Reading over the shoulder of a few colleagues, I realized we had all made similar lists. Where, I wondered, does that leave women's and gender studies? What assumptions had we made about the willingness of non-profit and women's organizations to accept our students as unpaid learners? Why is WGS in competition with many social work and healthcare-related programs for these placements? What might students learn if they did *not* spend time in these types of placements or joined with totally different organizations? With the ethical impetus to create long-term relationships with integrity, and to offer placements that do not require students to "pay to work" alongside the impulse to engage in self-reflexivity in our pedagogical practice, how can we and should we be developing practicums?

After the workshop, I went over what I thought I knew about my program. My program—and thus my students' educational pathways—are located within what is considered a small university with a population of just 9,000 students in a relatively small regional city of 158,000 in northern Ontario. In addition, we serve a linguistically and culturally mixed population of anglophone, francophone, and Indigenous students seeking courses that are culturally relevant to their experience and offered in either French or English. A minority of anglophone and francophone students are students of colour from northeastern Ontario, as well as Toronto, Ottawa, Montreal, and an even smaller minority from overseas. Most of our students are first-generation university learners, and the majority come from working-class and lower-middle-class backgrounds.

In the process of exploring how and why we might establish a praxis component, I became sensitive to the polyvocality of interest in student placements, and how narrowly defined they are in practical terms. From students during their first academic advising sessions I heard, "I want to help women, I'd like to work in a shelter one day…"; I have heard similar things from experts called in to help programs develop work-integrated learning: "Your students could work in a shelter, for example…" and of course, the internal voice that most of us have seeking learning opportunities and connections is noisy too: "The local sexual assault centre has an event coming up, they need people to take on the social media…." Regardless of our failure to develop a practicum in a form most would recognize, an active and vocal minority of students over the course of their studies consistently become involved in community work, activism, and many types of voluntarism. They ended up volunteering and even working at women's shelters, at centres organizing against domestic violence and sexual assault, mother and baby programs for teens and supports for women at friendship centres, and at queer organizations on campus. A larger group of students are exposed, many for the first time, to various types of feminism in our university and the wider community through their coursework and extracurricular activities. Some students even carry out supervised research for their final major research papers in conjunction with one of these organizations, and many are very curious about what it would be like to do a work placement there. Others still, who were active before, bring a lens to their paid or volunteer work as a result of having been in WGS; for example, they bring feminism, anti-racism, and a critical consciousness of nationalism. In other words, whether faculty help to organize it or not, students tend to make these opportunities for themselves based on their own interests and needs, only partly as a result of a class visit from a guest speaker, an assignment, or by learning about an event when the department assists in promoting or sponsoring one in the community. Despite these successes, we do not currently offer, nor do we seek to offer a practicum in WGS. This risks sounding as though our faculty do not want to put in the work to establish one, but the reality is that it would be too resource-intensive to pursue the types of practicums that are so carefully planned at many other institutions. Our challenge is that none of these other forms of learning are currently recognizable or counted as a practicum and only loosely understood as "work-integrated learning."

The logistics involved in offering a program to students dispersed throughout northeastern Ontario and who travel to our university to study—along with those permanently located elsewhere in Canada—are challenging when it comes to the prospect of university practicums. Like students at so many other universities, our students work part-time, full-time, or multiple jobs alongside their studies. This has been the case for the majority of students coming to our program since 1979, and as a result, our particular program has obligations to on-campus students as well as an equal number of students taking the Bachelor of Arts by distance education. Our program offerings online and in class must be equivalent in terms of quality and consistency as students move between them or only ever attend online. The practicum conceived as a traditional sort of "placement" arrangement is unrealistic in this setting, as it would draw too heavily on local organizations. It would also set up students in much smaller communities to work without direct support from a faculty member, and in the case of a small minority of learners studying from within penitentiaries, a practicum traditionally conceived is nearly impossible. Although much is accomplished through online platforms, the idea that WGS will have enough deeply established relationships in multiple communities to run practicums is unrealistic. Many on-campus students already commute regionally, so adding a placement component means that the financial stakes are higher; now in addition to tuition, students might need a private vehicle, and the costs associated become prohibitive for some.

Understanding WGS praxis components as something that happen in place and space is a useful intervention in a discussion where forces external to WGS departments—such as government policy about post-secondary education and popular views of the value of liberal arts—may hold sway over a program's existence. In their extensive study of Canadian women's studies programs, Alma Estable, Mechthild Meyer, and Roxanna Ng (2000) found that approximately half of the then forty institutions offering WGS programs in Canada had some type of praxis component. This important early study provided a practical guide for designing praxis components and a literature review. It also offered a qualitative overview of student, faculty, and organization experiences of the practicums but not a lot of analysis in relation to the literature of the time. In our much later survey of women's and gender studies programs and courses in eighty-one institutions across Canada in 2013, Susanne Luhmann and I made a similar observation to Estable et al. (2000): WGS programs tend to prefer certain types of placements for students, but unless required to do so, only 10 percent of students elect to take courses that involve unpaid placements. If we further recognize the responsibilities of unpaid work, child care, and other paid work, that narrow 10 percent who engage with a praxis component voluntarily makes more sense. When well organized, the praxis component brings course content into conversation with one's own genealogies and experience, demonstrating why students find these courses (for credit) to be so impactful (Taylor and de Laat 2013) but we also should question student hesitancy to take them in larger numbers.

In these cumulative results, it is evident that WGS programs tend to seek placement relationships (perhaps predictably, and with very little variation), at women's shelters, women's centres, sexual-assault crisis centres, and similar organizations more often than any other kind of organizational setting. This is no doubt a result of many factors, such as wanting to support local and marginalized voices of groups working to challenge the existence of violence directed at women and girls, for example, and to then help students combine their research skills in ways that might produce solutions deeply informed and in step with the groups they engage with. What first surprised us was how infrequently students might be sent to other types of non-profit organizations, such as labour union offices, social work settings and service organizations for immigrant communities, people doing sex work, HIV/AIDS or basic healthcare outreach, services for mothers and youth, and so on. How have praxis components come to rely so heavily on learning from largely not-for-profit organizations? Second, what has happened to feminist intervention at the daycare, the housing co-operative, and the landlord/tenants act office? What about the police station, the detox centre, the doctor's office, or the local public health unit? Not to mention the band council office, the mayor, and the local MPP or MP's office? What has happened to feminist interventions in private-sector spaces such as retail and industrial or trades workplaces? And, dare we ask, in our homes, including at the kitchen table and in the bedroom? Is it not important to find feminism in these places as well? Or is the pull of learning at the women's shelter based on some promise of a transformative politics that should be privileged above others? Whether by default or design, WGS programs drift in one direction and not others, and it is in this sense that I seek to de-territorialize the "places of learning" most frequently associated with them.

The more I considered the places students *do not* go, the longer my list became, and I forced myself to reconsider what we assume about the daily trajectories of learning; in other words, I began to examine the pathways people say they travel on a daily basis to arrive at the university and what they do to get back the following week. Through my course, Gender, Work and Families, I was able to examine these issues with more purpose.

Placing Work and Feminist Praxis

The two narratives I share with permission from students consist of discussions about the detailed time use diaries they kept during their paid work, unpaid work, leisure, and self-care time in an undergraduate course called Gender, Work and Families.[3] The narratives from Tracy and Jane (pseudonyms) are excellent examples of how the conscious documentation of one's movements through time and place is potentially transformative when intentionally subjected to a feminist analytic lens. Their classes received training on how to keep time for research purposes, and we read examples of time use studies in addition to the core material in the course, which has to do with the ways paid and unpaid work operate through relations of power such as gender, racialization, and heteronormativity. We studied the development and effects of occupational segregation by race and gender and examined historical moments where these relations of power intersect in Western (post-)industrial economies. Throughout, we also examined what happens to people's family-making practices, whether in the case of the white heteronuclear family, the chosen family of single men immigrating to Canada for work, or the impact of forming queer family on gender roles and domestic labour in large urban areas. Leading up to a final paper, students were asked to document how they use their time, day and night, for one week. I asked them to begin with the standard time use categories provided by Statistics Canada for time spent at paid work, formal education, domestic labour, elder care and child care, and "other" time. Feminist researchers have deliberately taken up studies of time use for a wide variety of groups to discover spatial and occupational patterns in daily activities that might otherwise go unnoticed, such as unpaid domestic labour (Waring 1999). The data generated from large-scale studies of thousands of people forms the basis of major policy development (Cranford, Vosko, and Zukewich 2003), while the study of marginalized groups can be used to explore qualitatively what is otherwise hidden by quantitative studies that do not include variables relating to peoples' daily lives. Time use studies often extend to include geographical methodologies that reveal what marginalized groups see from different perspectives (MacNabb 2002). At the level of the individual, the analytic possibilities are much more limited but still revealing. The method allows for my classes to study a much wider range of occupations in relation to one another than I could ever cover in the course material, and lets students compare their time use to one another and to the other statistical and qualitative literature. They can study biases about what types of work are considered valuable and how value is demonstrated through social rewards and policy limitations. Some focus on how policy, current labour law, direct protest to an employer, and other resources can be used to change the situations they find themselves working in as a result of the assignment. For example, a typical finding of students working in food and beverage service is that their emotional labour is stretched across time and place from the home to the paid workplace. Emotional labour is often layered onto tasks in a workplace without remuneration, or at times tied to forms of remuneration that actually rely on this labour, such as when tips go up if extra "care," or sexualized labour, is offered to a customer. Students already working as bartenders and food servers know this, but may not have realized how their industry calculates profit based on their ability to do this additional work. Surprisingly, students working in industries less associated with caring roles also discover they do a great deal of care work. The conversations emanating from these exchanges are lively, challenging, and critical, and on some occasions lay a foundation for challenging egregious workplace practices or even mundane but harmful ones that have come to be taken for granted. I offer two examples here.

Tracy is a young Indigenous woman, and is the first in her family to attend university. She has a partner in southern Ontario and is determined to have a career that allows flexibility in her place of work so that she can travel. She offered the following narrative to explain her time use in a twenty-four-hour period:

I know where I work, at a local boys' group home, the men get paid more than the women. I am not sure why because I feel I do more for the boys than he does. The duties I perform include cooking for 6 boys between the ages of 14 to 17, cleaning a three-floor home which has 6 bedrooms and three bathrooms, and providing emotional care and support. My routine consists of the following schedule: I start supper, then go into all the boys' rooms to grab their laundry and used dishes while asking them how they are doing, and if they need anything and simply just giving them attention. Once I have finished all of these things, I have to sweep, mop, do supper dishes, continue the laundry and spend more time with them to ensure they are on a good page for the night and also for the next day. I make sure I talk to them about making good choices, going to school, treating people with respect and teaching them how to do things around the house, like cooking, new vocabulary and how to care for themselves. By the end of the night I need to make snacks, do the dishes again and put the boys to bed, some like to be tucked in and others just need more attention by being spoken to. Putting 6 boys to bed who are all friends and have ADHD can be somewhat of a challenge; at this point this is typically where my co-worker steps in to assist me. For most of the night, I care for the boys emotionally and physically while my co-worker does not. Not to say he does nothing in the house but for the most part, I do everything. When the boys are misbehaving he steps in because he is seen as the father figure and is more intimidating than me, also mother figures tend to be seen as naggy and annoying, so some nights I am ineffective. This is precisely why men in my field get paid more to do their job because they are in demand for a father figure as most men are not social workers or child and youth workers.

This narrative is remarkable in that it clearly reflects the labour norms for many female students with child/youth or early childhood educator college degrees. Students with this background seek a transition from college to university employment streams, hoping that they can be better remunerated for what they now know is intensive domestic labour. But Tracy's experience is also at the more extreme end of how many students take up additional hours of feminized (read: part-time, casual, precarious) occupations to pay for school. When Tracy shared her story with classmates working in industries where men predominantly work, they were not shocked, as many had become aware of pay discrepancies between men and women and between white and Indigenous employees. Female-identified students in particular and many men in the class noted concrete evidence from their daily work experiences that gender and racial inequality exist in their work lives, and that women's ability to do care work is assumed and exploited. They also noted that while both men and women tended to work from contract to contract, women frequently felt they were without recourse to challenge pay discrepancies.

Tracy already had these "nagging" insights at the back of her mind and this assignment marked a moment where things changed for her. While initially willing to put in the long hours at the home for boys because she was *not yet* on placement for her social work program, even she gave pause when she counted up the hours worked for her *second* job where she experienced a lowered "female wage." She wrote, "At my part-time job at the daycare, I work with children three and under. At times there are over 25 kids with me and one other person to care for them all. It is very physically and emotionally demanding to give them attention…but to receive $12 an hour with a college diploma while men in trades receive almost double my wage with the same amount of time in school is disappointing." The complexity of this student's daily movements between class, two workplaces, unpaid care, and domestic labour in her own home and that of her partner's and back to school again, is staggering. The class provided a dedicated moment in time for her to map her time use, and ultimately she cut back some of her work hours for the daycare (which was clearly in violation of provincial standards for caregiver-to-toddler ratios). She also elected to move to a social work program with a focus on Indigenous perspectives, feeling that this offered a better opportunity to meet the needs of people in her community.

In the case of Jane, another first-generation university student who came from a semi-rural background, the class allowed her to make connections between time use and emotional labour across place. As a young white woman meeting a racially diverse university population for the first time, Jane struggled and challenged herself to learn about racism in her own community, and she seemed engaged with the course through those conversations in particular. But when it came to this assignment, she provided me with an oddly brief essay analysis that suggested little effort had been put into it, alongside extensively detailed timesheets suggesting the opposite. I queried why she had written so little while having documented so much about her week. What emerged from this discussion and in her later presentation to the class was a person completely overwhelmed by unpaid carework in her own life. Between the amount of overlap in the time and place of this work and school, she immediately realized why she had repeatedly failed some courses, as they coincided with caring for her infant niece (for free while the parents worked) and for her elderly grandfather after a surgery, spending her time working in three different households. It was not the intention of the exercise to elicit such emotions, but she expressed tremendous grief publicly as a result of seeing on paper how her time was divided and claimed by other people in spaces that did not reward her efforts at school. Because the numbers were so staggering for her, and also because she literally had no time, the mystery of the short paper was solved, but the problem itself was not. In another discussion she raised the possibility of government support for dependent care work and we discussed how to find this resource for her, but ultimately this student withdrew from school. What was especially important about her analysis is the value she placed on providing quality care to her niece and grandfather, and how proud she was to do so. I do not see this student's experience as a "failure" to make change by quitting university and choosing unpaid care work, but rather a more conscious valuation of the work she felt she had to do that might allow her to reconnect with the university in the future.

In addition to the time use diary, students in my course must produce a visual representation of their time use (collage, video, poster, sculpture, etc.). One very poignant display came in the form of a garment the student wore, with her data transcribed over different parts of her body to show how her efforts were divided and valued by others. A group of three students who worked at a Hooters Restaurant stole their uniforms and the employee instruction manual and analyzed them in a similar way, admittedly with much less room to record their data. Over the years, students completing this assignment have documented everything from paid and unpaid child care, domestic labour, paid work in retail, food service, sexual labour, paid sex work, bartending, operating the "cage" (elevator) in a mine, driving a forklift in a warehouse, swim coaching, ballet and dance instruction, and so many more occupations I have completely lost count. The sheer range of paid and unpaid work activities covers far more life experience than one could hope to pack into a ten-week student placement, and collective discussion of these frequently results in students attempting to change something about their work situation.

These contributions of place-making, place-changing, and so on are, I think, useful for understanding how classroom work that draws upon existing work trajectories beyond these walls may be able to inspire praxis outside of formal work placements. While the contributions of feminist and educational geography suggest movement outside the traditional classroom, they never relinquish the importance of critical analysis of power relations in place, a key aspect of feminist praxis. This is nothing less than a de-territorialization of knowledge production for knowledge's sake as belonging only in the university, and practical experience as belonging to the world of work. In other words, we have the existing pedagogical practice to bring together work experience and translate it for credit in ways that retain the integrity of WGS as a politically transformative field.

Feminist Praxis in Place

At the heart of the impetus to create "work-ready" graduates is the assumption that places of formal education and the paid workplace constitute two impermeable centres of activity that are dichotomously organized around theory/practice, or university/"real world." Most of us could not disagree more with the assertion that university is not part of a "real world" full of risks, consequences, and responsibilities, and argue that clinging to this dichotomy impoverishes our ability to develop curriculum that both advances the field of WGS and responds to the interests and needs of students and faculty. This dichotomy also perpetuates the notion that students either become productive citizens or liabilities for the state. It diminishes students who decide to become homemakers, who engage in other forms of unpaid care or volunteer work, or who choose non-standard work arrangements for any variety of reasons.

Feminist and critical geographers propose that disrupting the normative order of learning in post-secondary education is a spatial practice, and that our "physical situatedness" continues to be highly relevant to the conception of learning forwarded by an institution (Thomas 2010). I suggest it is through a sense of place that student bodies are given particular meaning, and that their efforts are valued differently when they have paid tuition in exchange for knowledge, as frequently is the case when they occupy formal sites of learning such as the university classroom or practicum placement. These places of learning normally exclude paid work done in the student's private time, and completely ignore the influence and learning that takes place during unpaid work done by students as parents, elders, caregivers, and so on. It may be that by giving credit for activities outside the classroom—work-integrated learning, experiential learning, practicums, and placements—obscures what WGS already knows: that embodied learning/teaching in place is part of what makes feminist or transformative knowledges applicable/possible in the paid workplace.

The spatial organization of post-secondary intellectual achievement and education has traditionally, in Western societies, been accomplished through exclusive forms of place-making. In other words, formal education at the post-secondary level occurs in sites imbued with meaning by the actions of a limited and elite number of people who enjoy the luxury of intellectual freedoms as well as certain social privileges.[4] Unfortunately it is just when this community is opening up to its intellectual and social Others (women, people of colour, people with disabilities, queer and trans people, and/or the children of more working-class families) more than ever before that, all of a sudden, the university is declared a less valuable place because it is constructed as hampering one's employment prospects in the neoliberal economy. It may be of interest, then, to note that students who predominantly seek college programs with placement or experiential learning components tend to be older women returning to school, while those who seek similar things in university programs tend to be from the families of new immigrants (Sattler and Peters 2013, 12), and that increasingly students of all backgrounds move between college and university or vocational education (Sattler and Peters 2013). Students are effectively, though not easily, making a place for themselves within and between family, sites of paid work, and formal education in a very difficult labour market.

The intellectual exclusivity of academic places has, not surprisingly, followed and/or perhaps led the material organization of its halls of learning to mirror these practices of exclusion/accessibility.[5] The university is not spatially organized to accommodate those social or intellectual Others, nor is it required to rigorously acknowledge forms of knowledge production in the "community" (including knowledge produced in the college system). While it is true that the universities of the 1950s and 1960s were meant to be different from the fortress-like quadrangle of the nineteenth century and earlier, thus welcoming a more diverse groups of learners—including women, for example—many of these universities were allotted land at the perimeters of cities, making it difficult for anyone to simply stumble across them. The "land fence," or expanse of industrial urban space kept/keeps undesirables out, and is a spatial metaphor that pretends students and faculty live in a separate and privileged world.

These rough spatial designations of belonging expert and external visitor/layperson are reflected again in the classroom, which is imagined as being composed of a hierarchy of knowers (teacher/student) and as being disconnected from the "real" world. The spatial organization of learning inside classrooms has been challenged by feminist teachers who displace the idea of the professor as an expert roaming free at the front of a classroom, lecturing to students fixed in rows of desks.[6] In fact, extensive literature in transformative pedagogy demonstrates that moving about in all sorts of ways actually helps us to learn. Many have experimented with place-making by necessitating spatial displacement and reconfiguration of learning environments in the curricula. First, Baeten, Dochy and Struyven (2013) advance the idea that learning environments, not bounded classrooms, are key to student engagement; this assertion recognizes that the social relations students bring with them, the location of the educational institution, the paid and unpaid work students do after class, and even the technology used are all interconnected parts of learning and teaching. Crook and Mitchell (2012) examine the importance of opportunities for sociality in informal spaces of learning, describing them as a way to enhance classroom learning, while Harrop and Turpin (2013) further explore students' ability to make place through informal learning spaces on campus. Hunter (2006), Thomas (2010), Wasko (2013), and many others comment extensively on student negotiation of eSpaces for learning as yet another dimension of movements that constitute disruptions to the fixity of classroom learning. Wasko (2013) also notes the value of "place-changing" to effective learning, where certain technologies allow students to engage continuously with a group of other students while on placement outside the classroom. Furthermore, scholars have also examined the paths taken by students themselves to eschew barriers between institutions of learning by combining vocational, college, and university streams of learning over their careers (Smith and Blake 2009), a practice that I have noted more frequently in the last few years at my own university.

Feminist geographers agree that teaching and learning are embodied practices (Grellier 2013; Moss 2009; Oberhauser 2008; Taylor and deLaat 2013). Grellier looks at the experiences of full- and part-time students' ability to make place, and concludes that a lack of student engagement in their learning is a direct result of the fragmentation of time spent in class, on the road to and from school, or perhaps even to a work placement. The student with a family, on a limited budget, rarely has the chance to "be" on campus, let alone to feel entitled to produce knowledge there, and the individual who can afford to study only part time is further disadvantaged. Rachel Fendler (2013) argues for a spatial understanding of teaching/learning practices that relies on Deleuze and Guattari's (1987/2004) social cartography of learning. Deleuze and Guattari are, of course, known for their exploration of the rhizome as a metaphor of learning, where networks of eventful places are marked when participants make meaning within them. Fendler (2013, 790) accomplishes this by having students map their educational experience in arts-based class-rooms and argues that "a mapping exercise can de-authorize the modernist narrative about the function of a school (teaching-based learning) and offer a vision of the learning-based processes of each student. This serves as a strat-egy for bringing together contradictory knowledges and generating heteroge-neous spheres of understanding." Grellier (2013, 89) further argues that such an approach constitutes a "deterritorialization of knowledge," again following Deleuze and Guattari.

For these reasons I would not like to see every WGS program host praxis components at all costs, even though there is pressure to do so. What we could be doing more consistently is signaling the analytic role of our programs in making these offerings—that is, developing community relationships, guid-ing students through a practical experience that involves a strong analytical component, and possibly going a step further to help make this experience intelligible for the purpose of their resumés. This potential glossing over, or diminishment, of analytic capacity in our praxis components is what concerns program directors the most, when dedicated full- and part-time faculty risk burnout from the intensity of offering a praxis component. Within the liberal arts, WGS is one of the fields that has had the impetus to follow academic and political goals related to organizations outside of the university. I argue that this finding speaks to the diverse applicability of feminist pedagogy and praxis, and the ongoing task of challenging the false dichotomy between uni-versity/paid work in one's field of interest.

Conclusion

In this chapter I make an argument for understanding praxis components in WGS programs as a spatialized process of learning that should transcend what is assumed to be the familiar "territory" of women's organizations in favour of all work spaces. The notion that WGS and a number of other fields may have territorialized our connections to certain types of community while excluding others is polyvocal, and should be carefully addressed. Some of these voices speak with an institutional or policy-driven goal of preparing work-ready graduates to meet provincial quality standards, and by doing so do not question problematic notions of entitlement to work in certain spaces and industries, while others reflect the genuine interest and productive anxiety of students that spurs people to learn new things. This chapter may sound like a rejection of formal student placements, and that it is even discouraging students to take up activism outside of the classroom in favour of examining the beaten paths they travel daily, but I am arguing instead for a validation of the diverse forms of experiential learning that WGS students are already engaged in. As others in this volume illustrate, placements present WGS students and our partner organizations with opportunities, while also placing political constraints on what they say and do because of the quasi-work relationship that develops. Additionally, these placements often commit faculty to extensive amounts of administrative and emotional labour.

It is the case that, for a long time, women's and gender studies has been preparing our students for work, activism, and careers in diverse areas of paid and unpaid work. But the range of possibilities after graduation may not be well articulated, or they may have changed since the inception of our programs. Case in point, a recent graduate who wrote a prize-worthy thesis on gender in the Canadian auto industry asked me for references to apply for jobs at women's shelters/rape-crisis centres. I wished at that moment that I could have met that student at the beginning of her studies to dispel the invisible lines that appear to have been drawn around the expectations for employment coming out of our field.

I suggest that the movement of student bodies through time and place, within and outside of the university, is in itself an important form of praxis in Canadian WGS programs, though perhaps it is taken for granted. In practice then, developing a spatial awareness in feminist praxis can be very effective when students are provided with an opportunity to reflect critically on their experiences in relation to the existing literature on the topic they seek to intervene in and learn from. My hope is that by investing in pedagogical practices that move students out of the classroom, or that draw upon existing community/university relationships, the analytic and spatial distinctions between formal education, paid work, and private relationships might be breached.

Notes

1   In fact, in one early 2000 study by Estable and Ng and in my own work with Susanne Luhmann (2016), the features of courses and placements they noted as "practicums" very closely and consistently resembled the interdisciplinary and broad notions of work-integrated learning argued for by HECQO. WGS tends toward the third strand of WIL, which is based on institutional partnerships and includes applied research projects and service-learning at the undergraduate level. WGS also tends to forward a range of practicums at

the undergrad and graduate levels under "structured work experience." But there is no reason that a WGS program could not develop some type of WIL in almost any field.

2   The focus in this literature is primarily on quantifying a connection between having completed a co-op or practicum and later paid employment as well as employer satisfaction with the quality of students and service provided by the university or college (Sattler, Wiggers, and Arnold 2011). Extensive quantitative research has also been done on student satisfaction as a measure of practicum placements associated with an institution (Sattler and Peters, 2013).

3   For the development of these assignments I would like to thank my collaborator Dr. Krista Johnston. Between 2007 and 2016 we actively shared and refined assignments for courses having to do with gender, work, and global economies.

4   At the periphery is society writ large, which is expected to consult and be consulted from time to time about what goes on within the walls of the university. Further in are the students, who are permitted selective entry to knowledge production. Further still we meet junior faculty, whose progress is marked by the number of publications and quality of their scholarship as measured by their peers. At the very centre are the scholars or experts who have achieved recognition within their fields of work. The scholar is sheltered by the notion of "academic freedom"; freedom from the demands and obligations that religion, the free market, and to a certain extent, government, might impose on their choices and expression.

5   We might for example, consider the construction of faculty offices and halls around the quadrangle of the nineteenth-century imperial era university, modelled upon its even earlier predecessor—the medieval fortress, as in the case of some British universities, Oxbridge and the like. The quad is a space exclusive to scholars, and to reach it visitors almost always pass through some type of secured point—an iron fence, a front office, or admissions area—so it might be thought of as the spatial expression of who belongs, and who does not. Those admitted, such as students, junior faculty, and visitors are required to merit their presence through intellect, scholarship, and of course, privilege.

6   Feminist pedagogies are notable for making visible the relations of power in post-secondary education (Briskin, etc.) while at the same time proposing teaching strategies that are resistant or disruptive to these things (Taylor and de Laat 2013).

FEELING ELSEWHERE

CATHERINE M. ORR

To begin this ending, let me pull back a bit. I write from what seems to have become a different place—unfamiliar, unprecedented—each day. As a US-based scholar who has been thinking about the location of feminism in the academy and women's and gender studies (WGS) as a disciplinary project for more than twenty years, the daily exercise of astonishment in the wake of a certain 2016 election produces a sort of disconnection between values and actions, my own sense of "elsewhere," even as it provides me endless opportunities to embrace the use-value of my pedagogy. This contradiction—reflected in the various modes, metaphors, and articulations of "elsewhere" in this volume—feels so suddenly practical. And why shouldn't it? The critical gift of WGS has always been that the key terms and generative questions our discipline organizes itself around have produced ever-expanding claims of relevance in an institutional context that too often resists what is relevant in the name of embracing the rarefied. And, yes, even while this same institution also lately seems compelled to speak about job readiness, transferrable skills, and neoliberal logics of the twenty-first century as the practicalities that must be embraced, this does not detract—at least for me—from the urgency of our disciplinary calling to interrogate what is before us now.

My own sense of disconnection is acute in those moments that blithe racist nationalism, anti-intellectualism, culturally sanctioned gender violence, and brazen crony capitalism are reported out each news cycle as "the will of the people." But if I am honest, I have to admit that the feeling of living in an unprecedented moment is really a comfortable fiction; these are what the stakes have been all along, at least for some of us. I know that because WGS taught me how see that. Given the colonialism, racism, gendered violence, ableism, and capitalist exploitations that constitute our respective national histories, any inklings of astonishment I or others might feel is that which demands interrogation. Thus, the sensation of "elsewhere," that felt abjection from the present that seemed to be right here just a minute ago, is a useful metaphor for understanding the engaged and relevant pedagogies of WGS, whether or not we ever ask our students to leave the classroom to learn.

The point is not that my particular elsewheres are new, unfamiliar, or unprecedented, and in all likelihood, neither are yours. And I have been gratified by the authors who preceded me in this text for reminding me of that. I fully endorse outrage and the rededication to justice that this moment fuels. But I also want to be careful as I try to reconnect value and action in the context of my pedagogical pursuits. As a member of the voting demographic that pushed our current president across the threshold to victory, I suddenly feel the need to rethink my place of belonging—and the elsewheres that make it possible—along with what laid the groundwork for my (and so many others') subsequent astonishment.[1] As you are no doubt gathering, I am "all up in my feelings" as one of my colleagues put it, and those affective dimensions of my here and now have functioned as data in theorizing how "elsewhere" does or should function for WGS.

Here is one bit of relevant data: three days after that 2016 election, I sat in a Montreal ballroom at a WGS conference listening to a plenary on "Decolonizing Institutions" (a title that one of the speakers assured the audience with a laugh was "an impossibility"). Native Studies scholar Kim Tallbear was one of those panellists. She started by thanking those of us in the audience for the work that we do, and then reminded us of the human costs of producing the elsewheres of our then newly horrifying imaginaries: "This week I do not grieve freshly. As a Dakota, we have struggled post-apocalyptically for a century and half. Genocidal US governance is the foundational condition of that country.... Many people have already seen that coming of horror. It almost wiped my people from the planet. Past is present. America is that horror. If you thought different, I am truly, truly sorry for what you must feel now." I appreciated Tallbear's generosity and felt deeply grateful for the reminder of the violence that produced the very contexts which I and others were fretting about. This is the affective context through which this volume has helped me rededicate myself to interrogating the effects of how we continuously—and in spite of our best efforts to do otherwise—produce the elsewheres of our current disciplinary imaginaries. It is the work before us. It is the work that has always been before us.

My struggle with community-based learning—like the struggle of the other authors in this volume—has always been about negotiating the tensions produced by contradictions embedded in the very history and culture of the academy: town and gown, theory and practice, service and justice, victims and agents, Indigenous and settler, activism and professionalism, and on and on. The frustration—and the delight—of my work is resisting the temporary purity of the "either/or" to embrace the protracted messiness of the "both/ and." And of course, it never feels like I am doing it quite "right."

In the final few pages of this volume, I would like to dwell on the frustration and delight of learning elsewhere by examining how our discipline is poised in this place and in this moment to embrace its use-value to our students, to our communities, and most of all, to ourselves. First, I offer an appreciation for what the preceding analysis on the literal and figurative locations of elsewhere means for my own pedagogy. Then, I seek to expose some identity issues embedded not just in the operations of community-based learning but in WGS as a disciplinary knowledge project writ large. Finally, I make a case for a radical embrace of ambivalence.

Placing Elsewhere

What I appreciate most from the preceding authors is the interrogation of how the spaces we move (or do not move) through in our everyday lives are actually *produced* as locations of learning, even as the lessons may be complicated, unintentional, or highly problematic. I feel like we cannot rehearse this denaturalizing gesture enough. These chapters creatively reframe the either/or logics of "university"/"community," divisions that too often lock down the meanings of service-learning for me and my students. I appreciate in particular the careful parsing of the "presumed homogeneity of 'the University'" that produces the equally homogenized "otherness" marked as "the community" (Dean, 29). Idealized in its passivity and receptiveness to our expert knowledges, such logics create "the community" we ask our students to engage with as an object lesson for identifying "social problems" that maintain the distance necessary to protect—in most cases—our privilege (Hurst, 119). At the same time, the community becomes a fraught and contradictory space; it is simultaneously the site of social justice activism (Muzak) and therefore the seemingly "proper place" of feminist praxis (Johnson, 148) but also the scary no-go zone of unexamined structural violence (Parkins, 102) with the potential to corrupt the supposed "purity" of our methodically constructed academic spaces of critique (Taylor).

For me, naming these practices of privileged distancing, and narrating the processes of their production in our classrooms *is* the work of WGS. As I have indicated elsewhere (Orr 2011, 2012; Dolgon 2017), anxieties about our disciplinary deficiencies are offered some solace by making this claim in community engagement contexts.[2] WGS does have a unique and valuable perspective to offer, even if we are not always confident in those perspectives. One reason for this lack of confidence, which a number of authors in this volume point out, is what I would call an inevitable loss of pedagogical control. Of course, this loss of control could and does happen in lots of courses; but in my experience the extra moving parts of a community-based learning context means that critical insights about the structural impediments that others experience go out the window more often and in ways that reproduce, rather than question, the community as "other" (see in particular Gotell's, Parkins', and Hurst's chapters, this volume). Returning to a familiar WGS frame that cautions all of us to account for our positionality as deeply implicated in our judgments seems so basic. But it is one of the most practical and distinctive teaching tools we have at our disposal. It allows us to take a meta-perspective at any given moment that gets beyond the grasp of our sense of control; it's a WGS lesson that gives us the gift of vulnerability to ask, what just happened here? Who is served (or not) by it? And how might we be complicit (or not) in its effects? More importantly though, the naming and narrating of privileged distancing is central because our classrooms are not spaces beyond these gestures of privileged differences, nor are they "safe spaces" free of the power relations we observe "out there." Either way, it is not easy work, and our students do not always appreciate its value.

With those reminders in hand, the authors in this volume provide carefully curated paths that I now want to follow to help me name and narrate the production of elsewhere in academic spaces. For example, Francis' "storying up" dispenses a committed example of naming and narrating the production of elsewhere, in that it invites students to both unpack their positionality and demonstrate the historical, cultural, and highly personalized practices embedded in their most intimate knowledges of self. The creative disruption of the classroom/community, theory/practice, and even self/other dualisms in her curation of readings and framing of the kinship history assignment is my pedagogical dream. Likewise, I see so much good WGS work that can come of Johnson's articulation of "place-making" assignments. Through them, she offers her students value—as in academic *currency*—for the hidden emotional labour that the most precariously situated students must engage in to simply show up regularly in our classrooms. In doing so, the borders that divide students' "public" educational practices from their "private" struggles—borders that higher education institutions are deeply invested in maintaining—is exposed and legitimated as an object of analysis. Similarly, Gotell's version of "social mapping"—seeing the ways in which multi-faceted social problems like sexual assault are framed and managed by various non-profit institutions— operates on a similar register, where the "situatedness of power relations" can be exposed, theoretically framed, and subsequently analyzed by students.

My attraction to these pedagogical projects, like my attraction to the field of WGS itself, is the way in which foregrounding justice can be articulated as a foundational condition for the discipline, *at the same time that any notion of our ability to actually achieve it must be constantly and forcefully interrogated.* Again, justice for whom? To what ends? And with what effects? More than teaching our students how to solve the social problems out there, I want to help them develop the intellectual habits that enable them to ask how they are positioned in the relations of power they seek, or are somehow forced, to enter. Raising critical questions about the very idea of community and the felt need for engagement with it—whether or not we actually send them here or there to do it—is the most important work I do. I emphasize it here mostly because in higher education's rush to engage the community, I do not see it going on anywhere else.

Disciplinary Identity Investments

So why do I feel the need to remind myself (or you) about the basic ideas of positionality in WGS? After all, anyone who picks up a book like this, by defi- nition, has been disciplined into this insight. I would like to posit, following both Dean and Parkins' use of Avery Gordon, that the present identity assump- tions implicit within WGS—about students, about ourselves, about the commu- nity—remain haunted by anti-intersectional understandings of our discipline's "subject" (in every sense of that word). The elsewheres of our intellectual, peda- gogical, and administrative labour have been produced and remain inhabited by particular kinds of bodies; that fact of discipline's identity politics is not neutral, and it has effects. For example, WGS has a long and highly theorized notion of community engagement as gendered; service is always already feminized (and to some extent classed), given the historical expansion of some women's politi- cal engagements in public spaces and in higher education over the twentieth century (see, e.g., Walker 2000; Berger and Radeloff 2011, and Musil 1992 for analyses of the intersection of "service" and gender). And I think that there is still much to say about gendering of community engagement both within our own discipline and across other disciplines. But I would say, following many of the essays here, the stakes of engaging "elsewhere" is tantamount to engaging with WGS's investment in its own white subjectivity.

Just to put it out there: historically and culturally, most of our WGS haunts tend to be white spaces—both our classrooms and locations of student place- ments have been founded on the values implicit in the production of white femininity and investments in white women's citizenship (see Brandzel 2011; Carillo Rowe 2008). And obviously, it is whiteness that I read when Srivistava remarks on "the moralism and racial innocence" (58) built into the educational assumptions of community engagement, or when Parkins voices concern about the lack of relationality in student understandings of engagement to the extent that they merely reproduce "white supremacist dimensions of violence against women" (94). But it is also whiteness—and the colonizing logics that whiteness stands in for—that I read tucked into footnotes and anecdotes that speak to the implied and actual student-subjects of community-based learn- ing. For example, Hurst notes that "intriguingly, students who come from or have prior relationships with the communities being served do not select those organizations for their placements" (129). Likewise, Dean recounts a student who "relied upon many of the social services" to be covered in an orientation tour and "did not relish the thought of having to revisit these sites with a group of gawking, albeit sympathetic in the most benevolent sense, classmates" (29). Passing mentions like these make me wonder about the ways in which the assumptions built into our community engagement pedagogies may be too often aligned with the very identities that we seek to decentre.

Here, I want to argue that the bodies that are in (and not in) our classrooms—*including our own*—are relevant objects for historical and theoretical classroom engagement in the production of various WGS "elsewheres." I will admit it here: making that insight meaningful has meant years of working against my own WGS training, a transformative experience that I now understand as powerful because of—not in spite of—how my raced/classed/gendered/sexualized/national identity was at the centre, *even as I simultaneously learned that centre was the very problem the discipline was attempting to solve.* I admit that this may be my own paranoid reading of the field (notwithstanding Taylor's cautions about being "too quick to the draw"). I am always primed to pounce on any quest for purity—my own and others. And I have divested in gender and feminism as the primary axis of curricular and administrative focus of my program in favour of a more robust uptake on intersectionality. Thus, I admit that my disciplinary loyalties can be read as questionable.[3] Nevertheless, it is in the WGS spirit of thinking otherwise that I am calling on us to consider our disciplinary identity investments in this present moment.

In my own institutional context, for example, the urgency of decentring whiteness has become dire. The self-described alt-right students who plastered the campus with white-pride slogans under the shroud of darkness and published "Identity Europa" zines anonymously before the 2016 election are now comfortably out as the College Republican Club.[4] This event was swiftly followed by the provost's announcement of trustee funding for curricular development that sought to include "conservative perspectives" as part of our commitment to diversity at the college. This shift in what is normative in my campus discourse has subsequently shifted my perspective on what should be normative in my classroom. This is not because the critique of whiteness was not embedded in my institutional context all along. It was, and I have always claimed as much. But up until this point, my pedagogical approaches have not gone far enough to embody—and make my own body relevant to—that claim.

Looking at my past syllabi, I see how the critiques of whiteness have always been there, but only after its centrality has been assumed *and* assumed to be necessary. I am not so much "grieving freshly" in Tallbear's terms as I "discover" the "elsewheres" she and others have always known and even inhabited; rather, I am attempting to name and narrate the effects of my own training that simultaneously produced that which is normative, and by implication, that which belongs elsewhere in the discipline. This assumption of whiteness produces what Amy Brandzel (2011) calls the "whitenormative citizen-subject" of WGS. She argues that "citizenship is a powerful normative discursive formation that works to socialize and regulate the national body, with its most formidable disciplinary mechanism being the ongoing (and never completely fulfilled) promise of the 'other'" (518). Thus I do not think it is just my training that centred whiteness; rather, white-normativity is our inheritance, regardless of how it positions us.[5]

It is time—at least it is time for me—to shift. I am currently in the process of revamping my introductory syllabus (again), as this is the location where I have my biggest student audience, and I hope the most opportunity to expose my students to the intellectual habits of the discipline. And given what I know has been there all along as the work of WGS coupled with an increasing willingness to let go of some previous assumptions about what must be passed on in the name of the discipline, I am now in the position to ask some different questions. What would it mean, in the Combahee River Collective sense,[6] if the implied student-subject of community-based learning were, say, Black and/or Indigenous women *regardless of whether or not Black and/or Indigenous women are in the room*? How would assignments shift if whiteness were decentred in a classroom that is mostly full of white people (inclusive of the professor)? How can my willingness to implicate myself and my discipline in producing various elsewheres offer students some practical, intellectual habits as they negotiate disconnections between values and actions inside and outside of the university?

The "Elsewhere" Within

Something that the reader may conclude as a result of the above is a certain amount of skepticism on my part for the entire endeavour of community-based learning. This is not wrong—at least not *all* wrong. By taking up "elsewhere" as a metaphor for my particular affective state, not to mention the mood in my national location, I have muddied the very waters that so much of community-engaged learning seeks to bridge. I guess that is because bridges imply divisions, and reproducing those divisions by enthusiastically joining the bridge-builders makes me deeply uncomfortable. Always has. What's more, I have written extensively about activism as a foundational concept of my discipline even as (because?) I feel deeply inadequate calling myself one. Relatedly, community-based learning (or "civic engagement") is another of my publishing subjects and, as mentioned before, I never feel like I am doing it right. My expertise is built on raising questions about the objects we claim to be expert on, and then questioning the very will of expertise. I delight in the interrogation.

Before I am dismissed as the nightmare produced by postmodernism (another term I am happy to interrogate), I would like to end with a plea for valuing the assets we bring to this endeavour whether or not we ever feel "right" about it. I guess I am arguing for the radical embrace of never quite feeling right. I have achieved a certain amount of success in this field, and I have never felt like I was doing it right. There are plenty of ways to support this claim. I will offer just one: I think that contemporary WGS—or maybe it's the humanities and the social sciences in North American higher education generally—is currently animated by a potent combination of critique and crisis. We are excellent at our paranoid readings, and especially astute at the vivisection of what is closest to us (doubly so when it gets us published). Likewise, I think there's a certain intellectual attraction to trouble. And no doubt trouble is a good way to describe many of our departmental budgets, tenure lines, and the desire for some simple acknowledgement for a job well done by the institutions that employ us.

Of course, there is plenty in front of us to critique, and crisis abounds. But sometimes, following Tallbear again, I think the critique and crisis that we rehearse in WGS is animated by telling ourselves a story of loss. And that story belies certain attachments that we may want to analyze more closely. I sometimes read this loss in laments about the newness of neoliberalism, workforce readiness, job skills, and, well, general resumé-building that our students are, to be fair, astutely demanding from us. Clare Hemmings (2011) has warned us about such attachments in the stories we tell, as we end up reproducing all kinds of exclusions in the name of recuperating our own identities as true feminists. In this case, I fear the effects of critique and crisis, because the stories of loss they foment means that we too easily cede the value of the liberal arts. Sure, let's give time to critique and crisis, but at the same time, let's speak to how the liberal arts is also providing the best job training any given student could have given the neoliberal contexts they are necessarily entering. We've got something important to offer in this moment. It's both/and.

Conclusion

In working my way through these chapters, I experienced the full range of enchantments and anxieties that bubble up when WGS seeks to take "elsewhere" seriously in a both/and kind of way. Each author commanded my focus as they turned the very idea of elsewhere on a different axis to consider what questions were not being asked, what assumptions were going uninterrogated, and, on a positive note, which assets were not accounted for in our rush to judgment about whether or not we are actually "making a difference" or "doing it right." As our WGS training mandates, going deep on one aspect of this work must be followed up by cautions about flattening out something else. To account for all the moving pieces in order to make a meaningful intervention illustrates the inevitability of our partial perspectives. While an outsider to our discipline might dismiss this endless both/and practice as a futile, self-absorbed, intellectual game of whack-a-mole, my hope is that we know (at least in our optimistic moments) differently. The investments we make in our students, our departments, and our curricula make this intellectual, pedagogical, and administrative struggle meaningful—not every minute, not for all time, and certainly not without deeply felt ambivalence—but meaningful in a way that can sustain most of us over the long haul of our careers. The gift of WGS is that, despite the feelings that we are buckling under bureaucratic minutiae or experiencing the isolation of this or that neoliberal moment, the reasons we get up every day to do this are compelling: Knowledge for what? Justice for whom? The questions are not just interesting, but are life-and-death in their nature. And of course, regardless of whatever fresh horror faces us, the stakes are now what they have been all along; the foundational condition has always been with us. It is my hope that these brief reframings of what has already been covered offers some inspiration to continuously rethink our respective elsewheres.

Notes

1 For a breakdown of the 2016 US presidential election demographics, see Fivethirtyeight.com. https://fivethirtyeight.com/features/clinton-couldnt -win-over-white-women/.

2 In "Women's Studies as Civic Engagement" (2011) as well as "Activism" (2012), WGS's uniqueness as it relates to civic engagement/service learning/activism is taken up from different angles for slightly different audiences.

3 For various takes on what could be called the disciplinary project of "letting go," see Ann Braithwaite and Catherine M. Orr's "Feminism's Attachments," *Feminist Studies* 39, no. 2 (2013): 512–16; Dana Olwan, AnaLouise Keating, Catherine M. Orr, and Beverly Guy-Sheftall's "Make/shift Pedagogies: Suggestions, Provocations, and Challenges for Teaching Introductory Gender and Women's Studies Courses," *Atlantis* 37, no. 2 (2016): 8–21; and Braithwaite and Orr's "Note to Instructors, or Is This the New Textbook for Your Intro Course?" in *Everyday Women's and Gender Studies* (New York: Routledge, 2017), xiii–xxiv.

4 See https://wagingnonviolence.org/feature/alt-right-safe-space-racism-college -campuses/ for background on the infrastructure of this nationally manufactured movement on US campuses.

5 Neither I nor Brandzel are seeking to push aside identity categories such as transness, dis/ability, class, and so on by way of landing on the whiteness of WGS, since we know that those other categories can be read through white normativity as well. That is the gift of intersectionality, and both of us are seeking to take it seriously in the context of theorizing how the discipline

passes on the centrality of whiteness in theorizing, historicizing, and teaching the subject (in every sense of that word) of WGS.

6 "A Black Feminist Statement" posits: "If Black women were free, it would mean that everyone else would have to be free since our freedom would necessitate the destruction of all the systems of oppression."

REFERENCES

Ahmed, Sara. *The Promise of Happiness*. Durham, NC: Duke University Press, 2010.
———. *Strange Encounters: Embodied Others in Post-Coloniality*. New York: Routledge, 2000.
———. "Intimate Touches: Proximity and Distance in International Feminist Dialogues." *Oxford Literary Review* 19, no. 1–2 (1997): 19–46.
Amadahy, Zainab, and Bonita Lawrence. "Indigenous People and Black People in Canada: Settlers or Allies?" In *Breaching the Colonial Contract: Anti-Colonialism in the US and Canada*, edited by A. Kempf, 105–36. Dordrecht, The Netherlands: Springer, 2009.
Baeten, Marlies, Filip Dochy, and Katrien Struyven. "The Effects of Different Learning Environments on Students' Motivation for Learning and Their Achievement." *British Journal of Educational Psychology* 83, no. 3 (2013): 484–501.
Baines, Donna. "Neoliberal Restructuring, Activism/Participation, and Social Unionism in the Nonprofit Social Services." *Nonprofit and Voluntary Sector Quarterly* 39, no. 1 (2010): 10–28.
Baker Collins, Stephanie, Marge Reitsma-Street, Elaine Porter, and Sheila Neysmith. "Women's Community Work Challenges Market Citizenship," *Community Development* 42, no. 3 (2011): 297–313.
Barber, Benjamin R. "Can We Teach Civic Education and Service-learning in a World of Privatization, Inequality, and Interdependence?" *Journal of College and Character* 13, no. 1 (2012): 1–10.
Battiste, Marie, and James [Sákéj] Youngblood Henderson. *Protecting Indigenous Knowledge and Heritage: A Global Challenge*. Saskatoon, SK: Purich, 2000.
Beeby, Dean. "Canada Revenue Agency's Political-Activity Audits of Charities." *CBC News*, August 5, 2014, http://www.cbc.ca/news/politics/canada-revenue -agency-s-political-activity-audits-of-charities-1.2728023.
Beres, Melanie, Barbara Crow, and Lise Gotell, "The Perils of Institutionalization in Neoliberal Times: Results of a National Survey of Sexual Assault Centres." *Canadian Journal of Sociology* 34, no. 1 (2009): 135–63.
Berger, Michelle Tracy, and Cheryl Radeloff. *Transforming Scholarship: Why Women's and Gender Studies Students Are Changing Themselves and the World*. New York: Routledge, 2011.

Bernal, Victoria, and Interpal Grewal, eds. *Theorizing NGOs: States, Feminisms and Neoliberalism.* Durham, NC: Duke University Press, 2014.

Bhabha, Homi. *The Location of Culture.* New York: Routledge, 1994.

Bickford, Donna M., and Nedra Reynolds. "Activism and Service-Learning: Reframing Volunteerism as Acts of Dissent." *Pedagogy: Critical Approaches to Teaching Literature, Language, Composition, and Culture* 2, no. 2 (2002): 229–52.

Bojar, Karen, and Nancy A. Naples. "Introduction: Teaching Feminist Activism Experientially." In Bojar and Naples, *Teaching Feminist Activism,* 1–6.

———, eds. *Teaching Feminist Activism: Strategies from the Field.* New York: Routledge, 2002.

Bonilla-Silva, Eduardo. *Racism without Racists: Color-blind Racism and the Persistence of Racial Inequality in the United States.* Maryland: Rowan and Littlefield, 2006.

Bourdieu, Pierre. *Outline of a Theory of Practice.* Cambridge: Cambridge University Press, 1977.

Boyd, Nan Alamilla, and Jillian Sandell. "Unpaid and Critically Engaged: Feminist Interns in the Non-profit Industrial Complex." *Feminist Teacher* 22, no. 3 (2012): 251–65.

Braithwaite, Ann. "The Personal, the Political, Third-wave and Postfeminisms." *Feminist Theory* 3 (December 2002): 335–44.

Braithwaite, Ann, and Catherine M. Orr. "Feminism's Attachments." *Feminist Studies* 39, no. 2 (2013): 512–16.

———. "Note to Instructors, or Is This the New Textbook for Your Intro Course?" In *Everyday Women's and Gender Studies,* xiii–xxiv. New York: Routledge, 2017.

Brandzel, Amy. "Haunted by Citizenship: Whitenormative Citizen-Subjects and the Uses of History in Women's Studies." *Feminist Studies* 37, no. 3 (2011): 503–33.

Broadbent Institute. "Right-Leaning Charities Reporting Zero 'Political' Activity Raises New Questions about CRA's Auditing Program." *The Broadbent Blog,* October 20, 2014, http://www.broadbentinstitute.ca/right_leaning_charities_reporting_zero_political_activity_raises_new_questions_about_cra_s_auditing_program.

Brodhead, Tim. "On Not Letting a Crisis Go to Waste." *The Philanthropist* 23, no. 1 (2010): 3–26.

Brodie, Janine, "We Are All Equal Now: Contemporary Gender Politics in Canada." *Feminism Theory* 9, no. 2 (2008): 145–64.

Brown, Wendy. *Edgework: Critical Essays on Knowledge and Politics.* Princeton, NJ: Princeton University Press, 2005.

Brulé, Elizabeth. "Going to Market: New-liberalism and the Social Construction of the University Student as an Autonomous Consumer." In *Inside Corporate U: Women in the Academy Speak Out,* edited by Marilee Reimer, 247–64. Toronto: Sumach Press, 2004.

Bubriski, Anne, and Ingrid Semaan. "Activist Learning vs. Service Learning in a Women's Studies Classroom." *Human Architecture: Journal of the Sociology of Self-knowledge* 7, no. 3 (2009): 91–98.

Bumiller, Kristin. *In an Abusive State: How Neoliberalism Appropriated the Feminist Movement Against Sexual Violence.* Durham, NC: Duke University Press, 2008.

Bunch, Charlotte. *Passionate Politics: Essays 1968–1986.* New York: St. Martin's Press, 1987.

Butin, Dan. "Disciplining Service-Learning: Institutionalization and the Case for Community Studies." *International Journal of Teaching and Learning in Higher Education* 18, no. 1 (2006a): 57–64.

———. "The Limits of Service-learning in Higher Education." *Review of Higher Education* 29, no. 4 (2006b): 473–98.

———. "Focusing Our Aim: Strengthening Faculty Commitment to Community Engagement." *Change* (Nov./Dec. 2007): 34–37.

Butler, Judith. *Bodies That Matter: On the Discursive Limits of Sex.* New York: Routledge, 1993.

Canada. Status of Women Canada. *Women's Program Evaluation Report and Management Response.* Ottawa, ON: Government of Canada, 2006.

Canada. "Government Response to the Eighteenth Report of the Standing Committee on the Status of Women: The Impacts of Funding and Changes at Status of Women Canada." Ottawa, ON: Parliament of Canada. N. date. http://www.parl.gc.ca/HousePublications/Publication.aspx?DocId=3077423&Language=E&Mode=1&Parl=39&Ses=1.

Canadian Association of University Teachers (CAUT). "Government Funding and Tuition as Share of University Operating Revenue, Canada." Ottawa, ON: CAUT / ACPPU, 2012a. http://www.caut.ca/ pages.asp?page=517.

———. "Average Annual Cost of University Tuition in Canada, 2010." Ottawa, ON: CAUT / ACPPU, 2012b. http://www.caut.ca/pages.asp?page=517.

———. "CAUT Almanac of Postsecondary Education in Canada." Ottawa, ON: CAUT / ACPPU, 2013–14. https://www.caut.ca/docs/default-source/almanac/almanac_2013-2014_print_finalE20A5E5CA0EA6529968D1CAF.pdf?sfvrsn=2.

Canadian Broadcasting Corporation. "Help Wanted: Panel Debates Value of Post-Secondary School." *CBC News*, May 21, 2013, http://www.cbc.ca/news/canada/windsor/help-wanted-panel-debates-value-of-post-secondary-school-1.1392182.

Canadian Federation of University Women (CFUW). "Major Federal Government Cuts Impacting Women in Canada since 2006." *CFUW Advocacy Blog*, May 25, 2012, https://cfuwadvocacy.wordpress.com/2012/05/25/.major-federal-government-cuts-impacting-women-in-canada-since-2006/.

Canadian Press. "Tories to Cut Off Funding for Women's Lobby Groups." *CBC News*, October 6, 2006, http://www.cbc.ca/news/canada/tories-to-cut-off-funding-for-women-s-lobby-groups-1.594392.

Canadian Research Institute for the Advancement of Women (CRIAW). "New Federal Policies Affecting Women's Equality: Reality Check," *CRIAW Fact Sheets,* November 8, 2006.

Canadian Women's Health Network (CWHN). "CWHN Announces Suspension of Activities Due to Lack of Funds." Press release. November 21, 2014. http://www.cwhn.ca/en/node/46597.

Cannon, Martin J. "Bill C-31 – *An Act to Amend the Indian Act:* Notes Toward a Qualitative Analysis of Legislated Injustice." *Canadian Journal of Native Studies* 25, no. 1 (2005): 153–67.

Carrick, Tracy Hamler, Margaret Himley, and Tori Jacobi. "Ruptura: Acknowledging the Lost Subjects of the Service Learning Story." *Language and Learning across the Disciplines* 4, no. 3 (2000): 56–75.

Carrillo Rowe, Aimee. "Be longing: Toward a Feminist Politics of Relation." *NWSA Journal* 17, no. 2 (2005): 15–46.

———. *Power Lines: On the Subject of Feminist Alliances.* Durham, NC: Duke University Press, 2008.

———. "Institutionalization." In Orr, Braithwaite, and Lichtenstein, *Rethinking Women's and Gender Studies,* 293–309.

Clark, Ian D., Greg Moran, Michael Skolnik, and David Trick. *Academic Transformation: The Forces Reshaping Higher Education in Ontario.* Montreal: McGill-Queen's University Press, 2009.

Cranford, Cynthia J., Leah F. Vosko, and Nancy Zukewich. "Precarious Employment in the Canadian Labour Market: A Statistical Portrait." *Just Labour* 3 (2003).

Crook, Charles, and Gemma Mitchell. "Ambience in Social Learning: Student Engagement with New Designs for Learning Spaces." *Cambridge Journal of Education* 42, no. 2 (2012): 121–39.

The Current. "Unpaid Internships Come Under Scrutiny," *CBC,* April 10, 2013. http://www.cbc.ca/airplay/episodes/2013/04/10/unpaid-internships-come-under-scrutiny/.

Davis, Angela. *Women, Race and Class.* New York: Random House, 1981.

Dean, Amber. "Colonialism, Neoliberalism, and University-Community Engagement: What Sorts of Encounters with Difference Are Our Institutions Prioritizing?" In *Unravelling Encounters: Ethics, Knowledge, and Resistance under Neoliberalism,* edited by Caitlin Janzen, Donna Jeffery, and Kristin Smith, 175–94. Waterloo, ON: Wilfrid Laurier University Press, 2015.

———. "Representing and Remembering Murdered Women: Thoughts on the Ethics of Critique," *English Studies in Canada* 34, no. 2–3 (2008): 229–41.

———. "Teaching Feminist Activism: Reflections on an Activism Assignment in Introductory Women's Studies." *Review of Education/Pedagogy/Cultural Studies* 29, no. 4 (2007): 351–69.

Deane, Patrick. "Forward with Integrity: A Letter to the McMaster Community." 2011. http://dailynews.mcmaster.ca/images/forwardwithintegrity.pdf.

Deleuze, Gilles, and Félix Guattari. *A Thousand Plateaus: Capitalism and Schizo-phrenia*. Translated and foreword by Brian Massumi. London: Continuum, 1987/2004.

DeMuth, Danielle. "Doing Feminist and Activist Learning Outcomes: What Should Students Be Able to Do as a Result of this Women's and Gender Stud-ies Project/Course/Curriculum?" *Atlantis: Critical Studies in Gender, Culture & Social Justice* 35, no. 2 (2012): 86–95.

Derrida, Jacques. *Specters of Marx: The State of the Debt, the Work of Mourning, and the New International*. Translated by Peggy Kamuf. New York: Rout-ledge, 1994.

Detore-Nakamura, Joanne. "When Our Feminist Is Not Feminist Enough." In *Fractured Feminisms: Rhetoric, Context, and Contestation*, edited by Laura Gray-Rosendale and Gil Harootunian, 45–64. New York: SUNY Press, 2012.

DeVries, Laura. *Conflict in Caledonia: Aboriginal Land Rights and the Rule of Law*. Vancouver: UBC Press, 2012.

Dippo, Don. "Redefining Community–Urban University Relations: A Project for Education Faculties?" *Teaching Education* 16, no. 2 (June 2005): 89–101.

Dolgon, Corey. "Women's Studies and Community-Based Pedagogy and Schol-arship: An Interview with Catherine Orr." In *The Cambridge Handbook of Service Learning and Community Engagement*, edited by Corey Dolgon, Tania Mitchell, and Timothy Eatman, 283–93. New York: Cambridge University Press, 2017.

Donald, Dwayne. "Indigenous Metissage: A Decolonizing Research Sensibility." *International Journal of Qualitative Studies in Education* 25, no. 2 (2012): 533–55.

Drevland, Randi. "Women's Activism and the Marketing of the Nonprofit Com-munity." In *Remapping Gender in the New Global Order*, edited by Marjorie Griffen Cohen and Janine Brodie, 151–65. New York: Routledge, 2007.

Drummond, Don. "Chapter 7: 'Postsecondary Education.'" *Public Services for Ontarians: A Path to Sustainability and Excellence*. Commission on the Reform of Ontario's Public Services, Ontario Ministry of Finance, April 5, 2012, http://www.fin.gov.on.ca/en/reformcommission/chapters/ch7.html#ch7-d.

Dugger, Karen. *Handbook on Service Learning in Women's Studies and the Disci-plines*. Towson, MD: Institute for Teaching and Research on Women, 2008.

Endres, Danielle, and Mary Gould. "'I Am Also in the Position to Use My White-ness to Help Them Out': The Communication of Whiteness in Service Learn-ing." *Western Journal of Communication* 73, no. 4 (2009): 418–36.

Enloe, Cynthia. *Curious Feminist: Searching for Women in A New Age of Empire*. Berkeley, CA: University of California Press, 2004.

Epp, Roger. *We Are All Treaty People: Prairie Essays*. Edmonton, AB: University of Alberta Press, 2008.

Estable, Alma, Mechthild Meyer, and Roxanna Ng. *A Resource Guide for Women's Studies Practica: Students Linking Academe and Community*. Ottawa, ON: Canadian Research Institute for the Advancement of Women, 2000.

Evans, Stephanie Y., Jennifer Ozer, and Havrede Hill. "Major Service: Combining Academic Disciplines and Service-learning in Women's Studies." *Feminist Teacher* 17, no. 1 (2006): 1–14.

Fendler, Rachel. "Becoming-learner Coordinates for Mapping the Space and Subject of Nomadic Pedagogy." *Qualitative Inquiry* 19, no. 10 (2013): 786–93.

Forbes, Katheryn, Linda Garber, Loretta Kensinger, and Janet Trapp Slagter. "Punishing Pedagogy: The Failings of Forced Volunteerism." *Women's Studies Quarterly* 27, no. 3/4 (1999): 158–68.

Francis, Margot. *Creative Subversions: Whiteness, Indigeneity, and the National Imaginary.* Vancouver: UBC Press, 2011.

Freeman, Victoria. "'Toronto Has No History!' Indigeneity, Settler Colonialism and Historical Memory in Canada's Largest City." Unpublished Ph.D. thesis, University of Toronto, 2010.

Freire, Paolo. *Pedagogy of the Oppressed.* Translated by Myra Bergman. New York: Continuum, 1970/2000.

Frueh, Joanna. *Swooning Beauty: A Memoir of Pleasure.* Reno, NV: University of Nevada Press, 2006.

Fyfe, Nicholas, and Christine Milligan. "Out of the Shadows: Exploring Contemporary Geographies of Voluntarism." *Progress in Human Geography* 27, no. 4 (2003): 397–413.

Garrow, Eve E., and Yeheskel Hasenfeld. "Social Enterprises as an Embodiment of a Neoliberal Welfare Logic." *American Behavioral Scientist* 58, no. 11 (2014): 1475–493.

Gergin, Maria. "Silencing Dissent: The Conservative Record." Canadian Centre for Policy Alternatives, April 6, 2011. https://www.policyalternatives.ca/publications/commentary/silencing-dissent-conservative-record.

Gilmore, Ruth Wilson. "In the Shadow of the Shadow State." In INCITE! Women of Color Against Violence, *The Revolution Will Not Be Funded*, 41–52.

Ginsburg, Benjamin. "Tenure and Academic Freedom: The Beginning of the End." *Academic Matters*, May 2012, https://academicmatters.ca/2012/05/tenure-and-academic-freedom-the-beginning-of-the-end/.

Gordon, Avery. *Ghostly Matters: Haunting and the Sociological Imagination.* Minneapolis, MN: University of Minnesota Press, 1997.

———. *Ghostly Matters: Haunting and the Sociological Imagination.* 2nd edition. Minneapolis, MN: University of Minnesota Press, 2008.

Gotell, Lise. "The Discursive Disappearance of Sexualized Violence: Feminist Law Reform, Judicial Resistance and Neo-liberal Sexual Citizenship." In *Reaction and Resistance: Feminism, Law, and Social change,* edited by Dorothy Chunn, Susan B. Boyd, and Hester Lessard, 127–63. Vancouver: University of British Columbia Press, 2007.

———. "Rethinking Affirmative Consent in Canadian Law: Neoliberal Sexual Subjects and Risky Women." *Akron Law Review* 41 (2008): 865–98.

———. "Complicating the Agent/Victim Dichotomy: Service-learning Pedagogy and Sexual Violence." Unpublished conference paper presented at the Canadian Women's Studies Association Conference, Ottawa ON, May 2009.

Green, Ann E. "Difficult Stories: Service-learning, Class and Whiteness." *College Composition and Communication* 55, no. 2 (2003): 276–301.

Grellier, Jane. "Rhizomatic Mapping: Spaces for Learning in Higher Education." *Higher Education Research & Development* 32, no. 1 (2013): 83–95.

Gunew, Sneja. "Feminist Cultural Literacy, Translating Differences, Cannibal Options." In *Women's Studies on Its Own: A Next Wave Reader in Institutional Change,* edited by Robyn Wiegman, 47–65. Durham, NC: Duke University Press, 2002.

Guy-Sheftall, Beverly, and Evelynn M. Hammonds. "Whither Black Women's Studies: An Interview." In *Women's Studies on the Edge,* edited by Joan W. Scott, 155–68. Durham, NC: Duke University Press, 2002.

Hall, Rachel. "It Can Happen to You: Rape Prevention in an Age of Risk Management." *Hypatia* 19, no. 3 (2004): 1–19.

Halley, Janet. *Split Decisions: How and Why to Take a Break from Feminism.* Princeton, NJ: Princeton University Press, 2006.

Harder, Lois. *State of Struggle: Feminism and Politics in Alberta.* Edmonton, AB: University of Alberta Press, 2003.

Harney, Robert F. *From the Shores of Hardship: Italians in Canada, Essays by Robert F. Harney.* Edited by Nicholas Harney. Welland, ON: Soleil Publishing, 1993.

Harrop, Deborah, and Bea Turpin. "A Study Exploring Learners' Informal Learning Space Behaviors, Attitudes, and Preferences." *New Review of Academic Librarianship* 19, no. 1 (2013): 58–77.

Heberle, Renée. "Deconstructive Strategies and the Movement Against Sexual Violence." *Hypatia* 11, no. 4 (1996): 63–76.

Hemmings, Clare. *Why Stories Matter: The Political Grammar of Feminist Theory.* Durham, NC: Duke University Press, 2011.

Heron, Barbara. *Desire for Development: Whiteness, Gender and the Helping Imperative.* Waterloo, ON: Wilfrid Laurier University Press, 2007.

Hill, Susan M. "Conducting Haudenosaunee Historical Research from Home: In the Shadow of the Six Nations-Caledonia Reclamation." *American Indian Quarterly* 33, no. 4 (2009): 479–98.

Himley, Margaret. "Facing (Up To) 'The Stranger' in Community Service Learning." *College Composition and Communication* 55, no. 3 (2004): 416–38.

hooks, bell. *Ain't I a Woman? Black Women and Feminism.* Boston, MA: South End Press, 1981.

———. *Feminist Theory: From Margin to Center.* Boston, MA: South End Press, 1984.

HR Council for the Nonprofit Sector. "Trends and Issues: Gender Mix in the Nonprofit Sector." 2008. http://hrcouncil.ca/documents/LMI_gender_mix.pdf.

Hughes, Sheila Hassal. "Making Service Learning in Women's Studies from Scratch: Notes from the Test Kitchen of a New Major." In *Handbook on Service Learning in Women's Studies and the Disciplines,* edited by Karen Dugger, 37–40. Towson, MD: Institute for Teaching and Research on Women, 2008.

Hui, S. Mei-Yen. "Difficult Dialogues about Service Learning: Embrace the Messiness." *About Campus* 14, no. 5 (2009): 22–26.

Hunter, Bob. "The E-spaces Study: Designing, Developing and Managing Learning Spaces for Effective Learning." *New Review of Academic Librarianship* 12, no. 2 (2006): 61–81.

Hurst, Rachel Alpha Johnston. "How to 'Do' Feminist Theory Through Digital Video: Embodying Praxis in the Undergraduate Feminist Theory Classroom." *Ada: A Journal of Gender, New Media, and Technology* 5 (2014a). http://adanewmedia.org/blog/2014/07/07/issue5-hurst/.

———. "A 'Journey in Feminist Theory Together': The *Doing Feminist Theory Through Digital Video* Project." *Arts & Humanities in Higher Education* 13, no. 4 (2014b): 333–47.

———. "Doing feminist theory through digital video." 2014c. http://www.doingfeministtheory.ca/.

Imagining America. "Specifying the Scholarship of Engagement: Skills for Community-based Projects in the Arts, Humanities, and Design." *Imagining America: Artists and Scholars in Public Life*. N. date. http://artofregional change.ucdavis.edu/files/2010/03/SpecifyingScholarship.pdf.

INCITE! Women of Color Against Violence, eds. *The Revolution Will Not Be Funded: Beyond the Non-profit Industrial Complex*. Boston: South End Press, 2009.

Jafri, Beenash. "Privilege vs. Complicity: People of Colour and Settler Colonialism." *Equity Issues Portfolio's Series on Indigenizing the Academy and Indigenous Education*, 2012. http://blog.fedcan.ca/tag/Indigenous-education/.

Jefferess, David. "Benevolence, Global Citizenship, and Post-racial Politics." *Topia* 25 (2011): 77–95.

———. "The 'Me to We' Social Enterprise: Global Education as Lifestyle Brand." *Critical Literacy: Theories and Practices* 6, no. 1 (2012): 18–30.

Johnson, Holly. "Limits of a Criminal Justice Response: Trends in Police and Court Processing of Sexual Assault." In *Sexual Assault in Canada: Law, Legal Practice, and Women's Activism*, edited by Elizabeth Sheehy, 613–34. Ottawa, ON: University of Ottawa Press, 2012.

Johnson, Jennifer L., and Susanne Luhmann. "Social Justice for (University) Credit? The Women's and Gender Studies Practicum in the Neoliberal University." *Resources for Feminist Research* 34, no. 3/4 (2016): 40–59.

Jonker, L., and Hicks, M. "The Differentiation of the Ontario University System: Where Are We Now and Where Should We Go?" Toronto, ON: Higher Education Quality Council of Ontario, July 12, 2016.

King, Samantha. "Pink Ribbons Inc.: Breast Cancer Activism and the Politics of Philanthropy." *International Journal of Qualitative Studies in Education* 17, no. 4 (2004): 473–92.

Kirkby, Gareth. "An Uncharitable Chill: A Critical Exploration of How Changes in Federal Policy and Political Climate Are Affecting Advocacy-Oriented Charities." M.A. thesis, Royal Roads University, Victoria, BC. 2014a. http://garethkirkby.ca/thesis/posting-final-version/.

———. "Why Is CRA Reinterpreting Rules to Shut Down Charities It Doesn't Agree With?" *Huffington Post*, December 22, 2014b. http://www.huffingtonpost.ca/gareth-kirkby/cra-charities_b_6364572.html.

Laforest, Rachel. "Rerouting Political Representation: Is Canada's Social Infra-structure in Crisis?" *British Journal of Canadian Studies* 25, no. 2 (2012): 187–91.

Lawrence, Bonita. "Rewriting Histories of the Land: Colonization and Indig-enous Resistance in Eastern Canada." In *Race, Space and the Law: Unmap-ping a White Settler Society,* edited by Sherene Razack, 21–46. Toronto, ON: Between the Lines Press, 2002.

Lawrence, Bonita, and Enakshi Dua. "Decolonizing Anti-racism." *Social Justice* 32, no. 4 (2005): 120–43.

Lewis, Tammy. "Service Learning for Social Change? Lessons from a Liberal Arts College." *Teaching Sociology* 32, no. 1 (2004): 94–108.

Lorde, Audre. *Sister Outsider: Essays and Speeches.* Berkeley, CA: Crossing Press, 1984.

Mahmood, Saba. "Feminism, Democracy, and Empire." In *Women's Studies on the Edge,* edited by Joan W. Scott, 81–114. Durham, NC: Duke University Press, 2008.

Mailloux, Louise, Heather Horak, and Colette Godin. *Motivations at the Mar-gins: Gender Issues in the Canadian Voluntary Sector.* Voluntary Sector Ini-tiative, 2002. http://www.vsi-isbc.org/eng/knowledge/motivation_margins/index.cfm.

Mananzala, Rickke, and Dean Spade. "The Nonprofit Industrial Complex and Trans Resistance." *Sexuality Research & Social Policy* 5, no. 1 (2008): 53–71.

Maparyan, Layli. "Feminism." In *Rethinking Women's and Gender Studies,* edited by Catherine M. Orr, Ann Braithwaite, and Diane Lichtenstein, 17–33. New York: Routledge, 2012.

Maracle, Lee. "Oratory on Oratory." In *Trans.Can.Lit.: Resituating the Study of Canadian Literature,* edited by Smaro Kamboureli and Roy Miki, 55–70. Waterloo, ON: Wilfrid Laurier University Press, 2007.

Marcus, Sharon. "Fighting Bodies, Fighting Words." In *Feminists Theorize the Political,* edited by Judith Butler and Joan Scott, 385–403. New York: Rout-ledge, 1992.

Mardorossian, Carine. "Towards a New Feminist Theory of Rape." *Signs: Journal of Women in Culture and Society* 38, no. 3 (2002): 743–75.

Marshall, Andrew Gavin. "The Québec Student Strike: From 'Maple Spring' to Summer Rebellion?" *The People's Book Project, The Beginning of Some-thing New.* April 30, 2012. http://thepeoplesbookproject.com/2012/04/30/the-quebec-student-strike-from- maple-spring-to-summer-rebellion.

Marullo, Sam, and Bob Edwards. "From Charity to Justice: The Potential of Uni-versity–Community Collaboration for Social Change." *American Behavioral Scientist* 43, no. 5 (2000): 895–912.

Matthews, Nancy. *Confronting Rape: The Feminist Anti-rape Movement and the State.* London: Routledge, 1994.

McMaster University. *Forward with Integrity.* Community Engagement Task Force Position Paper. 2012. http://www.mcmaster.ca/presidentsoffice/documents/PP_CE_final.pdf.

McNabb, David. *Circles of Time: Aboriginal Land Rights and Resistance in Ontario.* Waterloo, ON: Wilfrid Laurier University Press, 1999.

McNabb, Paul. "There Must Be a Catch: Participatory GIS in a Newfoundland Fishing Community." *Community Participation and Geographic Information Systems* (2002): 173–91.

Messer-Davidow, Ellen. *Disciplining Feminism: From Social Activism to Academic Discipline.* Durham, NC: Duke University Press, 2002.

Meisel, Joseph. "The Ethics of Observing: Confronting the Harm of Experiential Learning." *Teaching Sociology* 36 (2008): 196–210.

Miller, Brian. "Skills for Sale: What Is Being Commodified in Higher Education?" *Journal of Further & Higher Education* 34, no. 2 (May 2010): 199–206.

Million, Dian. "There Is a River in Me: Theory from Life." In *Theorizing Native Studies*, edited by Audra Simpson and Andrea Smith, 31–42. Durham, NC: Duke University Press, 2014.

Ministry of Training, Colleges and Universities. "Ontario's Differentiation Policy Framework for Postsecondary Education." November 2013. http://www.tcu.gov.on.ca/pepg/publications/PolicyFramework_PostSec.pdf.

Mohanty, Chandra Talpade. *Feminism without Borders: Decolonizing Theory, Practicing Solidarity.* Durham, NC: Duke University Press, 2003.

Molaski, Holly. "*Acts of Resistance*: A Theatre Project." *Equity Talk*, Newsletter of the Equity Committee, Department of Sociology, Queen's University, Winter 2016.

Moraga, Cherrie, and Gloria Anzaldúa, eds. *This Bridge Called My Back: Writings by Radical Women of Color.* New York: Kitchen Table Press, 1981.

Morales, Aurora Levin. "Radical Pleasure: Sex and the End of Victimhood." In *Women's lives: Multicultural Perspectives*, edited by Gwyn Kirk and Margo Ozakawa-Rey. Boston: McGraw-Hill, 2007.

Moreton-Robinson, Aileen. *Talkin' Up to the White Woman: Aboriginal Women and Feminism.* Queensland, AU: University of Queensland Press, 2000.

Morton, Keith. "The Irony of Service: Charity, Project, and Social Change in Service-learning." *Michigan Journal of Community Service Learning* 2, no. 1 (Fall 1995): 19–32.

Moss, Pamela. "Positioning a Feminist Supervisor in Graduate Supervision," *Journal of Geography in Higher Education* 33, no. 1 (2009): 67–80.

Musil, Caryn McTighe, ed. *The Courage to Question: Women's Studies and Student Learning.* Association of American Colleges and National Women's Studies Association, 1992.

Muzak, Joanne. "Women's Studies, Community Service-Learning, and the Dynamics of Privilege." *Atlantis: Critical Studies in Gender, Culture & Social Justice* 35, no. 2 (2012): 96–106.

Najmabadi, Afsaneh. "Teaching and Research in Unavailable Intersections." In *Women's Studies on the Edge*, 69–80.

Naples, Nancy A. "The Dynamics of Critical Pedagogy, Experiential Learning, and Feminist Praxis in Women's Studies." In Bojar and Naples, *Teaching Feminist Activism*, 9–21. 2002a.

———. "Teaching Community Action in the Introductory Women's Studies Classroom." In Bojar and Naples, *Teaching Feminist Activism*, 71–94. 2002b.

———. "Negotiating the Politics of Experiential Learning in Women's Studies: Lessons from the Community Action Project." In *Women's Studies on Its Own: A Next Wave Reader in Institutional Change*, edited by Robyn Wiegman, 383–415. Durham, NC: Duke University Press, 2002c.

Newson, Janice, and Claire Polster, eds. *Academic Callings: The University We Have Had, Now Have, and Could Have*. Toronto, ON: Canadian Scholars' Press, 2010.

Novek, Eleanor M. "Service-learning Is a Feminist Issue: Transforming Communication Pedagogy." *Women's Studies in Communication* 22, no. 2 (1999): 230–40.

Nussbaum, Martha. *Cultivating Humanity: A Classical Defense of Reform in Liberal Education*. Cambridge, MA: Harvard University Press, 1998.

Oberhauser, A. "Feminist Pedagogy: Diversity and Praxis in a University Context." In *Feminisms in Geography: Rethinking Space, Place, and Knowledges*, edited by Pamela Moss and Karen Falconer Al-Hindi, 215–20. Lanham, MD: Rowman & Littlefield, 2008.

O'Grady, Kathleen. "Status of Women Canada Cuts a Loss for Healthy Democracy: Grassroots Organizations Play an Instrumental Role in Government Accountability and Contribute to Healthy Public Policies." *Canadian Women's Health Network* 9, no. 1/2 (2006/07). http://www.cwhn.ca/en/node/39454.

Olwan, Dana, AnaLouise Keating, Catherine M. Orr, and Beverly Guy-Sheftall. "Make/shift Pedagogies: Suggestions, Provocations, and Challenges for Teaching Introductory Gender and Women's Studies Courses." *Atlantis: Critical Studies in Gender, Culture, and Social Justice* 37, no. 2 (2016): 8–21.

Ong, Aiwa. *Neoliberalism as Exception: Mutations in Citizenship and Sovereignty*. Durham, NC: Duke University Press, 2006.

Ontario Progressive Conservatives. "On Education Doug Ford Will Respect Parents and Get Back to Basics." *Ontario Progressive Conservative Platform*. 8 May, 2018 https://www.ontariopc.ca/on_education_doug_ford_will_respect_parents_and_get_back_to_basics.

Orr, Catherine M. "Activism." In *Rethinking Women's and Gender Studies*, edited by Catherine M. Orr, Ann Braithwaite, and Diane Lichtenstein, 85–101. New York: Routledge, 2012.

———. "Women's Studies as Civic Engagement: Research and Recommendations." A Teagle Foundation White Paper prepared for the Teagle Working Group on Women's Studies and Civic Engagement and the National Women's Studies Association, 2011. http://www.teaglefoundation.org/Library-Resources/Fresh-Thinking/Women's-Studies-as-Civic-Engagement-Research-and.

Orr, Catherine M., Ann Braithwaite, and Diane Lichtenstein, eds. *Rethinking Women's and Gender Studies*. New York: Routledge, 2012.

Paglia, Camille. *Sexual Personae: Art and Decadence from Nefertiti to Emily Dickinson*. New York: Vintage, 1991.

Parker, Jan. "Reconceptualising the Curriculum: From Commodification to Transformation." *Teaching in Higher Education* 8, no. 4 (October 2003): 529–43.

Parkins, Ilya. "'Nineteen Funerals': Ethics of Remembering Murdered Women in a Service Learning Classroom." *Review of Education, Pedagogy, and Cultural Studies* 36, no. 2 (2014): 127–43.

Patel, Shaista. "Defining Muslim Feminist Politics through Indigenous Solidarity Activism." *Feminist Wire,* August 1, 2012. http://thefeministwire.com/2012/08/defining-muslim-feminist-politics-through-Indigenous-solidarity-activism/.

Pedwell, Carolyn. "Weaving Relational Webs: Theorizing Cultural Difference and Embodied Practice." *Feminist Theory* 9, no. 1 (2008): 87–107.

Penhorwood, Claire. "Canada's Youth Face Job Crunch." *CBC News*, March 26, 2012, http://www.cbc.ca/news/canada/canada-s-youth-face-job-crunch-1.1163846.

Pérez, Amara H. "Between Radical Theory and Community Praxis: Reflections on Organizing and the Non-profit Industrial Complex." In INCITE! Women of Color Against Violence, *The Revolution Will Not Be Funded,* 91–99.

Pollack, Shoshana. "Building Bridges: Experiential and Integrative Learning in a Canadian Women's Prison." *Journal of Teaching in Social Work* 36, no. 5 (2016): 503–18.

Polster, Claire, and Janice Newson. "A Penny for Your Thoughts: How Corporatization Devalues Teaching, Research and Public Service in Canada's Universities." Ottawa, ON: Canadian Centre for Policy Alternatives, 2015.

Razack, Sherene. *Dark Threats and White Knights: The Somalia Affair, Peacekeeping, and the New Imperialism.* Toronto, ON: University of Toronto Press, 2004.

———. "Gendered Racial Violence and Spatialized Justice: The Murder of Pamela George." *Canadian Journal of Law and Society* 15, no. 2 (2000): 91–130.

Reaume, Amanda. "Conservatives Sneak 'Equality' Back into Status of Women Mandate…Or at Least Pretend to…" *Antigone Magazine* (blog), February 6, 2008. http://antigonemagazine.blogspot.ca/2008/02/conservatives-sneak-equality-back-into.html.

Reimer, Marilee, and Melanie Ste-Marie. "Denied Access: The Focus on Medicalized Support Services and 'Depressed' Women Students in the Corporate University." *Resources for Feminist Research/Documentation sur la recherche féministe* 33, no. 3/4 (2010): 137–59.

Ristock, Janice. "Taking off the Gender Lens in Women's Studies: Queering Violence against Women." *Canadian Woman Studies* 24, no. 2–3 (2005): 65–70.

Rizvi, Fazal, and Bob Lingard. *Analyzing Education Policy During Neoliberal Times: Globalizing Education Policy.* New York: Routledge, 2010.

Rocheleau, Jordy. "Theoretical Roots of Service-Learning: Progressive Education and the Development of Citizenship." *Service-Learning: History, Theory, and Issues,* edited by B. Speck and S. Hoppe, 3–21. London: Praeger, 2004.

Roiphe, Katie. *The Morning After: Sex, Fear, and Feminism on Campus.* Boston, MA: Little Brown, 1993.

Roman, Katrina. "Update: Liberals Circulate 'Interesting' Government Funding List." *CBC News*, May 5, 2010. http://www.cbc.ca/politics/insidepolitics/2010/05/liberals-circulate-interesting-government-funding-list.html.

Rosenberg, Sharon. "Neither Forgotten nor Fully Remembered: Tracing an Ambivalent Public Memory on the 10th Anniversary of the Montreal Massacre." *Feminist Theory* 4, no. 1 (2003): 5–27.

Rosenberger, Cynthia. "Beyond Empathy: Developing Critical Consciousness through Service Learning." In *Integrating Service Learning and Multiculturalism in Colleges and Universities,* edited by Carolyn R. O'Grady, 23–44. Malwah, NJ: Erlbaum, 2000.

Rutherford, Scott, and Bonita Lawrence. "Colonialism and the Indigenous Present: An Interview with Bonita Lawrence." *Race & Class* 52, no. 1 (2010): 9–18.

Sattler, Peggy, and J. Peters. *Work-integrated Learning in Ontario's Postsecondary Sector: The Experience of Ontario Graduates.* Toronto, ON: Higher Education Quality Council of Ontario, 2013.

Sattler, Peggy, Richard Wiggers, and Christine Helen Arnold. "Combining Workplace Training with Postsecondary Education: The Spectrum of Work-Integrated Learning (WIL) Opportunities from Apprenticeship to Experiential Learning." *Canadian Apprenticeship Journal* 5 (2011): 1–33.

Schaap, Andrew. "The Time of Reconciliation and the Space of Politics." In *Law and the Politics of Reconciliation*, edited by Scott Veitch, 9–31. Burlington, VT: Ashgate, 2007.

Schwartz, Zane. "Unpaid Internships Are Just Wrong." *Globe and Mail,* May 3, 2013, http://www.theglobeandmail.com/news/national/education/unpaid-internships-are-just-wrong.

Scott, Ellen. "Creating Partnerships for Change: Alliances and Betrayals in the Racial Politics of Two Feminist Organizations." *Gender & Society* 12 (1998): 400–23.

Scott, Joan W., ed. *Women's Studies on the Edge*. Durham, NC: Duke University Press, 2008.

Scudeler, June. "Gifts of Maskihkiy: Gregory Scofield's Cree Métis Stories of Self-acceptance." In *Queer Indigenous studies: Critical Interventions in Theory, Politics and Literature*, edited by Q. Driskill, 190–210. Tucson, AZ: University of Arizona Press, 2011.

Sedgwick, Eve Kosovsky. *Touching, Feeling: Affect, Pedagogy, Performativity.* Durham, NC: Duke University Press, 2003.

Sehdev, Robinder Kaur. "People of Colour in Treaty." In *Cultivating Canada: Reconciliation through the Lens of Cultural Diversity*, edited by Ashok Mathur, Jonathan Dewar, and Mike DeGagné, 263–74. Ottawa, ON: Aboriginal Healing Foundation, 2011.

Sharma, Nandita, and Cynthia Wright. "Decolonizing Resistance: Challenging Colonial States." *Social Justice* 35, no. 3 (2008/9): 120–38.

Shelden, Randall, and Daniel Mallair. *Juvenile Justice in America: Problems and Prospects.* Longrove: Waveland Press, 2008.

Simon, Roger, and Claudia Eppert. "Remembering Obligation: Pedagogy and the Witnessing of Historical Trauma." *Canadian Journal of Education* 22, no. 2 (1997): 175–91.

Simpson, Leanne, and Kiera L. Ladner, eds. *This Is an Honour Song: Twenty Years since the Blockades.* Winnipeg, MB: Arbeiter Ring Publishing, 2010.

Smith, Andrea. "Introduction: The Revolution Will Not Be Funded." In INCITE! Women of Color Against Violence, *The Revolution Will Not Be Funded,* 1–18.

———. "American Studies without America: Native Feminisms and the Nation-State." *American Quarterly* 60, no. 2 (2008): 241–49.

———. "Heteropatriarchy and the Three Pillars of White Supremacy: Rethinking Women of Color Organizing." In *Color of Violence: The INCITE! Anthology,* edited by INCITE! Women of Color Against Violence, 66–73. Durham, NC: Duke University Press, 2016.

Smith, Dorothy. *Writing the Social: Critique, Theory, and Investigations.* Toronto, ON: University of Toronto, 1999.

Smith, Linda Tuhiwai. *Decolonizing Methodologies: Research and Indigenous Peoples.* London: Zed Books, 1999.

Smith, Peter J., and Damian Blake. "The Influence of Learning Environment on Student Conceptions of Learning." *Journal of Vocational Education & Training* 61, no. 3 (2009): 231–46.

Sontag, Susan. *Regarding the Pain of Others.* New York: Farrar, Straus and Giroux, 2003.

Spencer, Jonathan, ed. *Sri Lanka: History and the Roots of Conflict.* London: Routledge, 2004.

Srivastava, Sarita. "Troubles with 'Anti-Racist Multiculturalism': The Challenges of Anti-Racist and Feminist Activism." In *Race and Racism in 21st Century Canada: Continuity, Complexity, and Change,* edited by Sean P. Hier and B. Singh Bolaria, 291–312. Toronto, ON: University of Toronto Press, 2007.

———. "Tears, Fears and Careers: Anti-racism, Emotion and Social Movement Organizations," *Canadian Journal of Sociology* 31, no. 1 (2006): 55–90.

———. "'You're Calling Me a Racist?': The Moral and Emotional Regulation of Anti-Racism and Feminism." *SIGNS: Journal of Women and Culture in Society* 31, no. 1 (2005): 29–62.

Srivastava, Sarita, and Margot Francis. "The Problem of 'Authentic Experience': Storytelling in Anti-Racist and Anti-Homophobic Education." *Critical Sociology* 32, no. 2/3 (2006): 275–307.

Standing Committee on the Status of Women. Tenth Report: Cuts to the Status of Women. 39th Parliament, 1st Session. Parliament of Canada, 2007. http://www.parl.gc.ca/HousePublications/Publication.aspx?DocId=2520144&Language=E&Mode=1&Parl=39&Ses=1.

Statistics Canada. "The Daily, Friday September 8, 2017," Labour Force Survey, August 2017. Component of Statistics Canada catalogue no. 11-001-X. http://www.statcan.gc.ca/daily-quotidien/170908/dq170908a-eng.pdf.

Status of Women Canada (SWC). Women's Program Evaluation Report and Management Response. Ottawa, ON: Government of Canada, 2006.

———. "Who We Are." http://www.swc-cfc.gc.ca/abu-ans/who-qui/index-eng.html.

———. Evaluation of Women's Program: Final Report, 2011–12 to 2015–16, ii. Ottawa, ON: Government of Canada, 2018. http://www.swc-cfc.gc.ca/trans/account-resp/pr/wpeval-evalpf/wpeval-evalpf-en.pdf.

Stoeker, Randy. *Liberating Service Learning and the rest of Higher Education Civic Engagement.* Philadelphia: Temple University Press, 2016.

Stringer, Rebecca. "Vulnerability after Wounding: Feminism, Rape Law, and the Differend." *SubStance* 43, no. 3 (2013): 148–68.

Stukas, Arthur A. Jr., E. Gil Clary, and Mark Snyder. "Service Learning: Who Benefits and Why." *Social Policy Report for the Society for Research in Child Development* 13, no. 4 (1999): 1–20.

Taylor, Judith, and Kim de Laat. "Feminist Internships and the Depression of Political Imagination: Implications for Women's Studies." *Feminist Formations* 25, no. 1 (2013): 84–110.

Thomas, Herbert. "Learning Spaces, Learning Environments and the dis'placement' of Learning." *British Journal of Educational Technology* 41, no. 3 (2010): 502–11.

Tomasevski, Katrina. 2006. "Globalizing What? Education as a Human Right or a Traded Service." *Indiana Journal of Global Legal Strategies* 12, no. 1 (2006): 1–78.

Trethewey, Anna. "Critical Organization Communication, Feminist Research Methods, and Service-learning: Practice as Pedagogy." In *Voices of Strong Democracy: Concepts and Models for Service Learning in Communication Studies*, edited by David Droge and Bren Ortega Murphy, 177–90. Sterling, VA: Stylus Publishing, 1999.

Trigg, Mary, and Barbara Balliet. "Learning across Boundaries: Women's Studies, Praxis, and Community Service." In *The Practice of Change: Concepts and Models for Service-Learning in Women's Studies*, edited by B. Balliet and K. Heffernan, 87–102. Washington: American Association for Higher Education, 2000.

Valentine, Gil. "Images of Danger: Women's Sources of Information about the Spatial Distribution of Male Violence." *Area* 24, no. 1 (1992): 22–36.

———. "The Geography of Women's Fear." *Area* 21, no. 4 (1989): 385–90.

Vickers, Jill. "Thinking about Violence." In *Gender, Race, and Nation: A Global Perspective*, edited by Vanaja Dhruvarajan and Jill Vickers, 222–72. Toronto, ON: University of Toronto Press, 2002.

Vizenor, Gerald. *Fugitive Poses: Native American Indian Scenes of Absence and Presence.* Lincoln: Nebraska University Press, 1998.

Voices-Voix. "Status of Women Canada: What Happened." *Voices-Voix* (blog), Sept. 27, 2012. http://voices-voix.ca/en/facts/profile/status-women-canada.

Walker, Tobi. "The Service/Politics Split: Rethinking Service to Teach Political Engagement." *PS: Political Science and Politics* 33, no. 3 (2000): 646–49.

Walters, David, and Kristyn Frank. *Exploring the Alignment between Postsecondary Education Programs and Labour Market Outcomes in Ontario.* Toronto, ON: Higher Education Quality Council of Ontario, 2010.

Ward, Jane. *Respectably Queer: Diversity Culture in LGBT Activist Organizations.* Nashville, TN: Vanderbilt University Press, 2008.

Waring, Marilyn. *Counting for Nothing: What Men Value and What Women Are Worth.* Toronto, ON: University of Toronto Press, 1999.

Warner, Michael. "Introduction." In *Fear of a Queer Planet: Queer Politics and Social Theory,* vii–xxxi. Minneapolis: University of Minnesota Press, 1993.

Washington, Patricia A. "From College Classroom to Community Action." *Feminist Teacher* 13, no. 1 (2000): 12–34.

Wasko, Christopher. "What Teachers Need to Know about Augmented Reality Enhanced Learning Environments." *TechTrends* 57, no. 4 (2013): 17–21.

Webb, Patricia, Kristi Cole, and Thomas Skeen. "Feminist Social Projects: Building Bridges between Communities and Universities." *College English* 69, no. 3 (2007): 238–59.

Wiegman, Robyn, ed. *Women's Studies on Its Own: A Next Wave Reader in Institutional Change.* Durham, NC: Duke University Press, 2002.

Weingarten, Harvey P., Martin Hicks, Linda Jonker, and Shuping Liu. "The Diversity of Ontario's Universities: A Data Set to Inform the Differentiation Discussion." Toronto, ON: Higher Education Quality Council of Ontario, July 23, 2013.

Welch, Mary Agnes. "Doors Close at Health Network: Federal Funding Cuts Crush Women's Research Centre." *Winnipeg Free Press,* November 22, 2014. http://www.winnipegfreepress.com/local/doors-close-at-health-network -283574091.html.

Wente, Margaret. "Quebec's University Students Are in for a Shock." *Globe and Mail,* May 1, 2012. http://www.theglobeandmail.com/commentary/ quebecs-university-students-are-in-for-a-shock/article4104304/.

Wexler, Ellen. "When Service Learning Doesn't Really Serve." *Inside Higher Education,* May 16, 2016.

Whittier, Nancy. *The Politics of Child Sexual Abuse: Emotions, Social Movements and the State.* Oxford: Oxford University Press, 2009.

Williams, Rhonda L., and Abby L. Ferber. "Facilitating Smart-girl: Feminist Pedagogy in Service Learning in Action." *Feminist Teacher* 19, no. 1 (2008): 47–52.

Williams, Tamara, and Erin McKenna. "Negotiating Subject Positions in a Service Learning Context: Toward a Feminist Critique of Experiential Learning." In *Twenty-first Century Feminist Classrooms: Pedagogies of Identity and Difference,* edited by Amie Macdonald and Susan Sanchez-Casal, 135–54. Houndmills, UK: Palgrave Macmillan, 2002.

Wolsh, Jennifer. "The Shadow State: Transformations in the Voluntary Sector." In *The Power of Geography: How Territory Shapes Social Life,* edited by Jennifer Wolsh and Michael Dear, 197–221. Boston: Unwin Hyman, 1989.

———. *The Shadow State: Government and Voluntary Sector in Transition.* New York: Foundation Centre, 1990.

Zimmerman, Bonnie. "The Past in Our Present: Theorizing the Activist Project of Women's Studies." In *Women's Studies on Its Own: A Next Wave Reader in Institutional Change,* edited by Robyn Wiegman, 183–90. Durham, NC: Duke University Press, 2002.

ABOUT THE AUTHORS

Amber Dean is Associate Professor of English and Cultural Studies, cross-appointed to the graduate program in Gender Studies and Feminist Research at McMaster University. Her research focuses on public mourning, violence, and cultural memory. She is the author of *Remembering Vancouver's Disappeared Women: Settler Colonialism and the Difficulty of Inheritance* (University of Toronto Press, 2015), which has won several awards, and was co-winner of the Women's and Gender Studies et Recherches Feministes' Outstanding Scholarship Prize. With Chandrima Chakraborty and Angela Failler, she has also co-edited *Remembering Air India: The Art of Public Mourning* (University of Alberta Press, 2017).

Margot Francis is Associate Professor of Women's and Gender Studies, cross-appointed to the Department of Sociology. She is the author of *Creative Subversions: Whiteness and Indigeneity in the National Imaginary* (University of British Columbia Press, 2011), and has published in journals such as *Native American and Indigenous Studies*, *Feral Feminisms*, and *Critical Sociology*. Her research interests include Indigenous and decolonializing perspectives on settler societies; community-based art projects for Indigenous resurgence; contemporary alliances between Indigenous and anti-racist movements in sexual violence activism; queer activism; and analysis of gender, sexuality and the body.

Lise Gotell is the Landrex Distinguished Professor in the Department of Women's and Gender Studies at the University of Alberta. She is an expert on gender and the law and has published widely on sexual-assault law. Lise is the National Chair of the Women's Legal Education and Action Fund, and is a member of Edmonton's Safe City Collaboration Committee.

Rachel Alpha Johnston Hurst is Associate Professor of Women's and Gender Studies at St. Francis Xavier University in Antigonish, Nova Scotia. She is author of *Surface Imaginations: Cosmetic Surgery, Photography, and Skin* (McGill-Queen's University Press, 2015), and a co-editor of *Skin, Culture, and Psy-*

choanalysis (with Sheila L. Cavanagh and Angela Failler, Palgrave, 2013). Her research is broadly concerned with the relationships between embodiment, (visual) culture, and power, from the perspectives of psychoanalysis and decolonial thought.

Jennifer L. Johnson is Associate Professor and Chair of the Department of Women's, Gender, and Sexuality Studies at Thorneloe University, federated with Laurentian University. Her research and teaching includes feminist geographical approaches to the study of social reproduction and global economies; gender, race, and racism; and feminist pedagogies. She is co-editor of *Feminist Issues: Gender, Race, and Class,* 6th edition, with Nancy Mandell (Pearson Education, 2016) and is a past editorial board member of *Atlantis: Critical Studies in Gender, Culture & Social Justice / Études critiques sur le genre, la culture, et la justice sociale.* With Krista Johnston she is also co-editor of a forthcoming collection entitled *Maternal Geographies: Mothering In and Out of Place.* Her current research explores how gender and race are socially constructed through the spatialization of work and, in particular, the nuclear family home.

Susanne Luhmann is Associate Professor and Chair of the Department of Women's and Gender Studies at the University of Alberta. Research interests include the institutionalization of Women's and Gender Studies, Prairie sexualities, unsettling queer and feminist pedagogies, and trauma and cultural memory studies. She is co-author with Ann Braithwaite, Susan Heald, and Sharon Rosenberg of *Troubling Women's Studies: Pasts, Presents, Possibilities* (Canadian Scholars' Press 2004), and her work has appeared in journals such as *Yearbook of Women in German, New German Critique, Topia,* and *Jahrbuch der Frauen-und Geschlechterforschung,* as well as in many book chapters. She is currently finishing a monograph tentatively entitled *Domesticating the Nazi Past: The Familial Turn in German Memory.*

Joanne Muzak has taught Women's and Gender Studies at the University of Alberta and Concordia University in Montreal. In 2008, she held Canada's first postdoctoral fellowship in CSL with the Community Service-Learning Program at the University of Alberta, developing core CSL courses, promoting CSL to faculties across campus, and routinely integrating CSL into her WGS courses. She's now a professional editor, specializing in academic editing and writing consultation.

Catherine M. Orr is Professor and Chair of Critical Identity Studies at Beloit College (Wisconsin). She is co-editor of *Rethinking Women's and Gender Studies* (Routledge 2012) and co-author of *Everyday Women's and Gender Studies:*

Introductory Concepts (Routledge 2017), both with Ann Braithwaite. Her work has appeared in *Souls, Feminist Studies, Women's Studies Quarterly, Hypatia,* and *NWSA Journal.* She lives in Madison, Wisconsin.

Ilya Parkins is Associate Professor of Gender and Women's Studies at the University of British Columbia, Okanagan Campus, where she teaches introductory and advanced core curriculum in feminist studies. She is the author of *Poiret, Schiaparelli, Dior: Fashion, Femininity and Modernity* (Berg, 2012) and the co-editor, with Elizabeth M. Sheehan, of *Cultures of Femininity in Modern Fashion* (University Press of New England, 2011). Her research on fashion, feminist theory, and mediations of femininities in modernist and contemporary contexts has appeared in periodicals including *Time & Society, Feminist Review, Australian Feminist Studies,* as well as various edited collections. Her current project examines a burgeoning feminist wedding culture, considering what it might tell us about new feminisms, femininities, and queer subjectivities.

Sarita Srivastava's research has focused on social movements, the sociology of gender and race, and the sociology of emotions. Her forthcoming book, *"You're Calling Me a Racist?" The Emotional Landscape of Racial Encounters,* will explore the historical debates, emotional responses, and pedagogical practices that arise when social movements such as feminism are faced with anti-racist challenges. A former environmental activist, she has also been active in community radio, Indigenous, labour, and feminist movements. She is Associate Professor in the Department of Sociology, the Department of Gender Studies and the Cultural Studies graduate program at Queen's University, Kingston, Ontario, where she has taught a Social Justice Practicum for many years, as well as seminars in graduate research methods, the sociology of the body, and the sociology of race.

Judith Taylor is Associate Professor of Sociology, jointly appointed to the Women and Gender Studies Institute, at the University of Toronto. She conducts research on feminist movements, community organizing, and friendship among women, publishing in journals such as *SIGNS, Feminist Formations,* and *Feminist Studies.* She is working on a project about organized feminism in Canada, drawing on interviews with grassroots activists across five provinces.

INDEX

victim/agent dichotomy, 77, 78
violence against women, 95, 141. *See also* sexual violence
Vizenor, Gerald, 143
volunteerism, 15, 57, 58, 66, 76

Ward, Jane, 66
Wasko, Christopher, 160
Webb, Patricia, 46
Wendat people, 141
Wexler, Ellen, 59
white femininity, 169
whiteness, 140, 169, 170, 171
whitenormative citizen-subject, 4, 171
Whittier, Nancy, 113
Wiegman, Robyn, 110
Williams, Tamara, 96
women: hyper-responsibilization of marginalized, 81–82; impact of fear on, 79; living in poverty, 25–26; at risk, 82
women-centred non-profit organizations: budget cuts, 12, 42–43; reduction of capacity of, 42, 52; resistance to neoliberalism, 45
Women's and Gender Studies course at the University of Toronto: assigned readings, 105–6; classroom discussions, 108; pedagogical goals, 106; students' assignments, 106; students' expectations from, 109; students' learning experience, 106, 107; volunteer work, 105, 106–7
Women's and Gender Studies (WGS) praxis component: analysis of, 17–18, 161–62; approaches to, 3, 4, 5; creation of partnerships, 14;

in graduate courses, 18; number of institutions with, 152–53; promotion of, 15–16; between service and activism, 9–13
Women's and Gender Studies (WGS) programs: in American vs. Canadian context, 9; attachment to activism, 10; community service component, 13; contemporary trends, 8, 162–63n1, 172; core value of, 1; curriculum component, 9; debates on "natural affinity" of, 53n6; disciplinary identity, 169–71; dual orientation of, 1–2; emergence of, 9–10; focus on community-based learning, 2–3, 9, 10, 115; identity assumptions within, 169; at Laurentian University, 150–52; online descriptions of, 4–5; practice of privileged distancing in, 167–68; scholarly studies of, 9, 152, 165; skill training, 16–17; student placements, 148, 162; surveys of, 1, 152–53; teaching partners, 18; as white spaces, 169
Women's Health Contribution Program, 40
Women's Studies on Its Own (Wiegman), 110
work-integrated learning (WIL), 147, 148–49
workplaces: as sites for feminist praxis, 147–48
Wright, Cynthia, 134, 135

Zimmerman, Bonnie, 13, 58, 76